AF394533

FURBEX

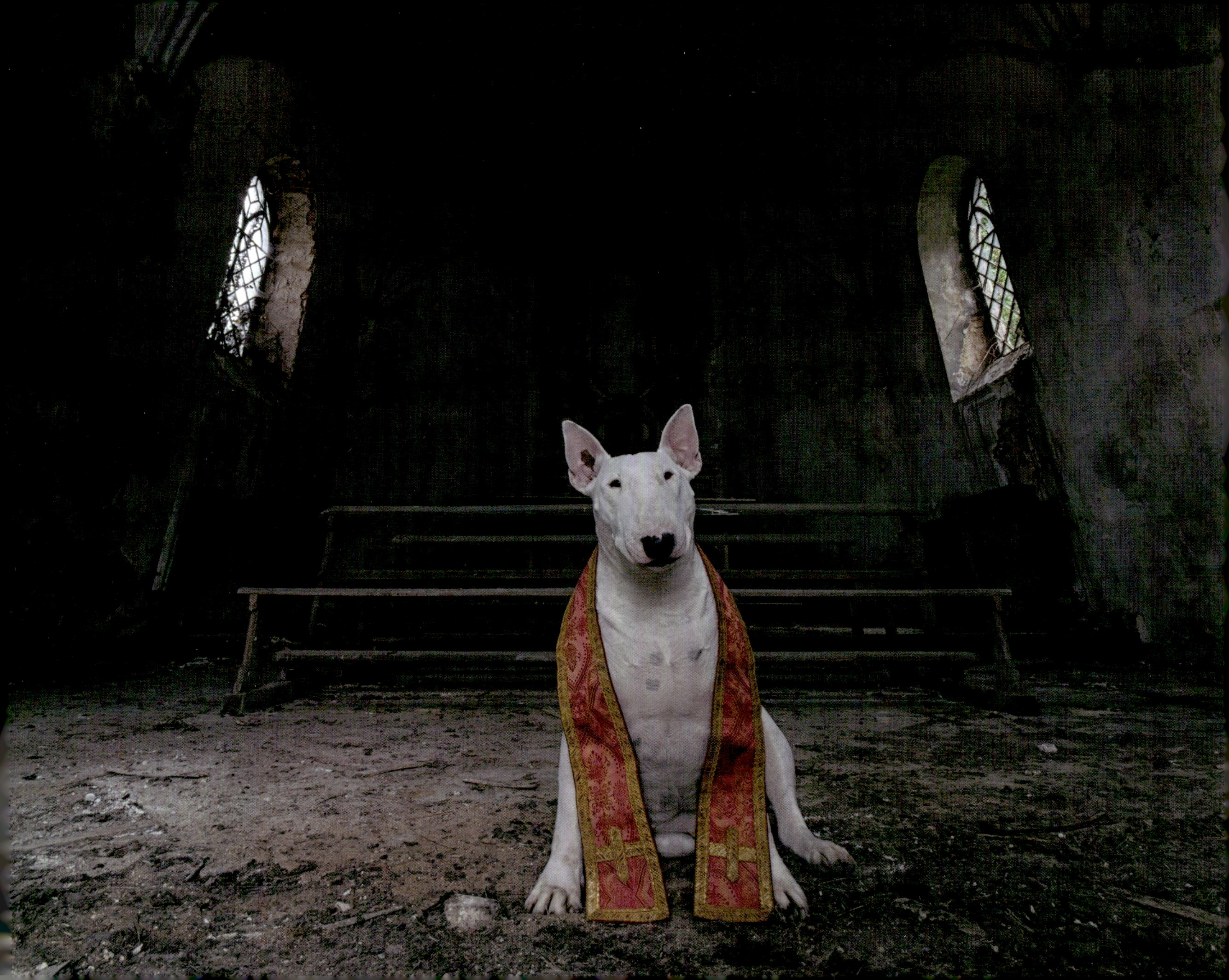

FURBEX

A dog's life of urban exploration

Alice van Kempen & Claire

Foreword by Rafael Mantesso & Jimmy

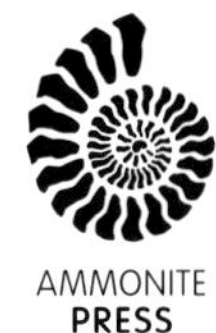

AMMONITE
PRESS

"I'd love that," David said.

Moira and David lost themselves in theories as to why, exactly, some dead souls remained tethered to the mortal plane, while reaching over each other for tarts and more sugar for coffee.

Rhys leaned back in his chair, and as he watched the two loves of his life, a pain so sweet sang through him that he felt as though his heart had been pierced by swords.

Maybe this time, he hoped, the good things would last. Maybe happiness didn't need to come hand-in-hand with heartache, at least not this time.

When Rhys McGowan was fifteen years old, he had gone looking for the sacred. His entire adult life had been one winding and crooked path towards anything that felt divine, whether in the darkness or in the light. He had mistaken many things for divinity along the way. The pursuit of power, the hardline structure of organized religion, the shadowy temptations of the occult. He had tried and failed many times to grasp for God.

But as Rhys sat there in his kitchen, watching Moira and David gossip over the food he had prepared for them, Moira's brown eyes alight with interest, David's mouth curving into a smile, Rhys felt that this might be a glimmer of the thing he had been ceaselessly searching for.

He felt, perhaps for the first time in his life, holy.

First published 2018 by
Ammonite Press
an imprint of Guild of Master Craftsman
Publications Ltd
Castle Place, 166 High Street, Lewes,
East Sussex, BN7 1XU,
United Kingdom

ISBN 978 1 78145 332 2

Publisher: Jason Hook
Designer: Robin Shields
Editor: Jamie Pumfrey

Colour reproduction by GMC Reprographics
Printed and bound in China

Foreword
Rafael Mantesso and Jimmy

I first saw photographs of Claire, a beautiful and very patient bull terrier (the same breed as my dog, Jimmy), on the internet and the main thought that went through my mind was "oh my god, this is fu@#ing awesome". I immediately searched for the author and found Alice and, of course, more photos of Claire. Wow, I was hypnotized by this amazing pair. From the very beginning, my eyes were drawn to Claire, but the second thing that impressed me was the extraordinary backgrounds.

This type of photography is exactly the opposite of my work. Jimmy is always shot against a white background, in a clean studio. People ask me how I get Jimmy to pose for my photographs, but really they should be asking Alice how she finds those incredible places. Claire and Alice visit the most stunning and beautiful settings in the world.

The conditions aren't always great and you never know what you might find, but she always manages to create something unique.

And finally, this is not a foreword just to list all the amazing things about Alice, but instead this is to thank her. To thank her for bringing inspiration, fun and love into our lives through pictures of Claire. And to thank her for shedding light on the most amazing breed in the world, the bull terrier, showing the world what amazing dogs they can be, and how beautiful and loyal they are.

In every one of her pictures I see Jimmy and I have no doubt that other dog owners will see their furry friends as well. Thank you to Alice for sharing her adventures and her stories with us. They fill our hearts with love.

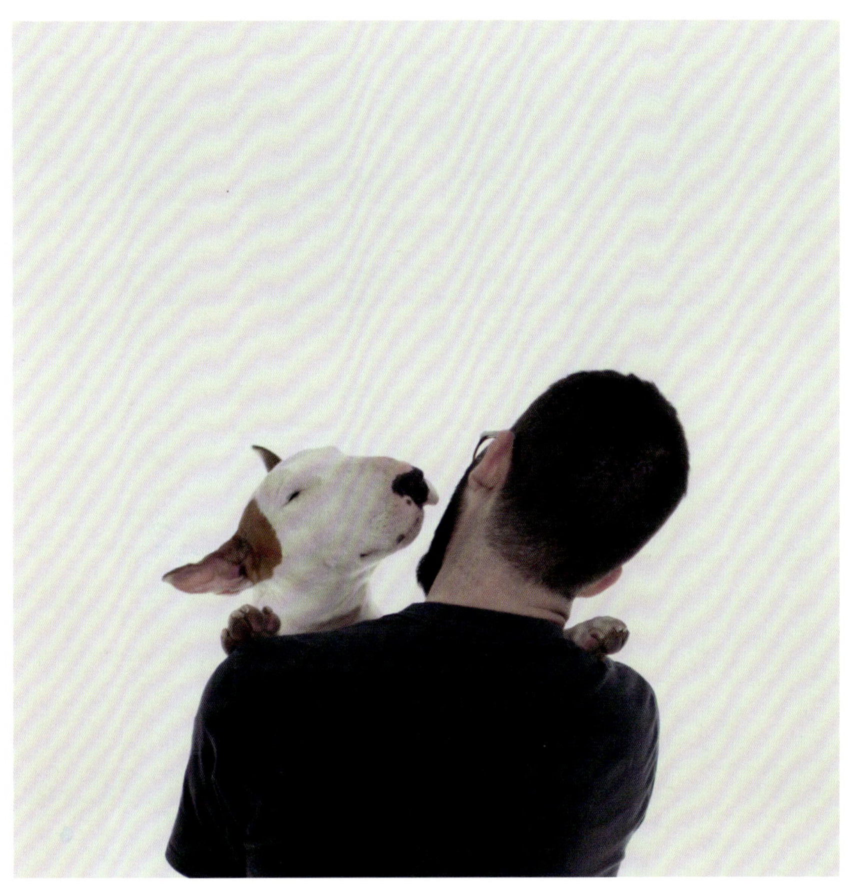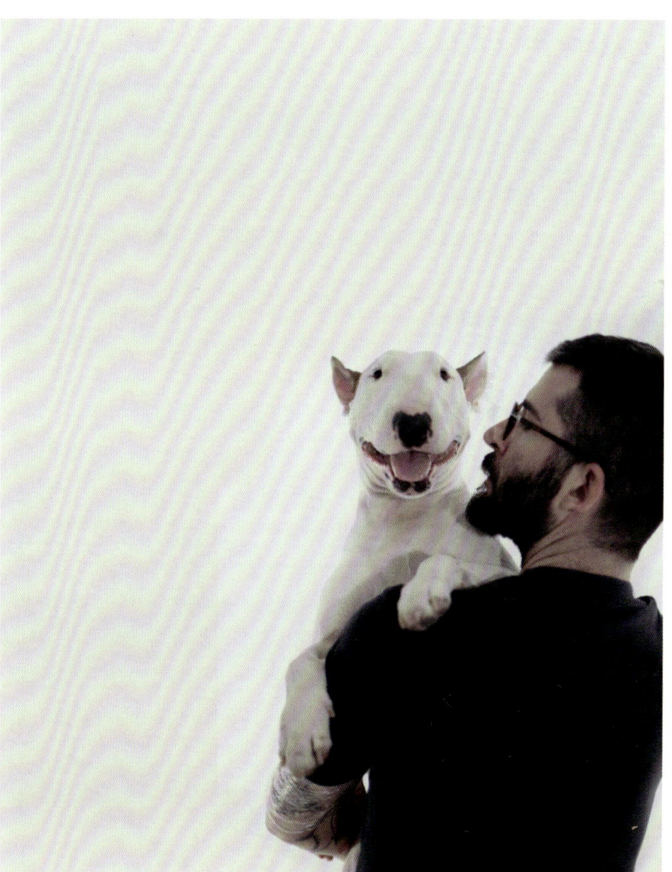

Introduction
Alice van Kempen

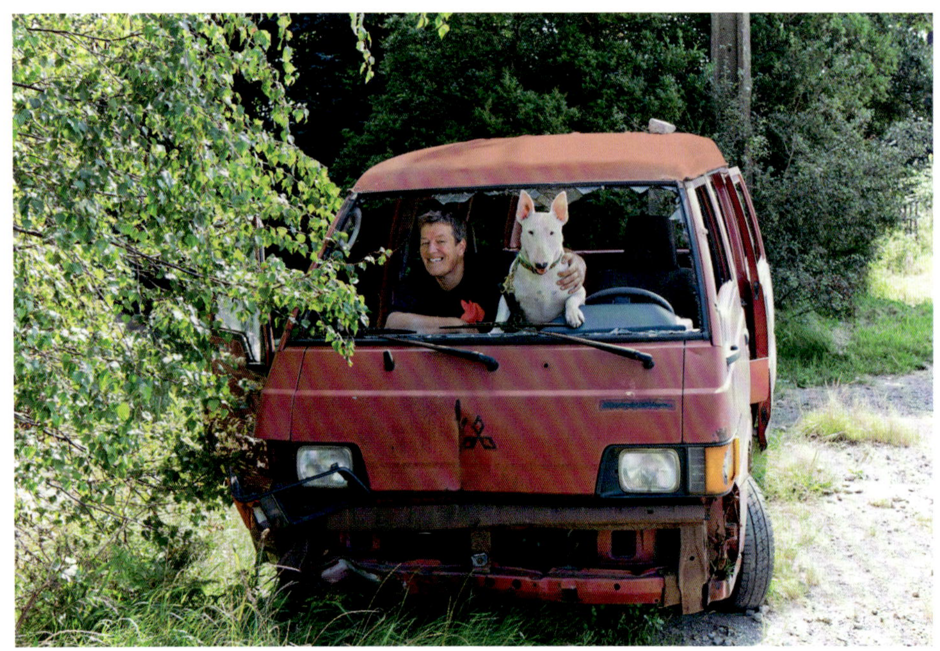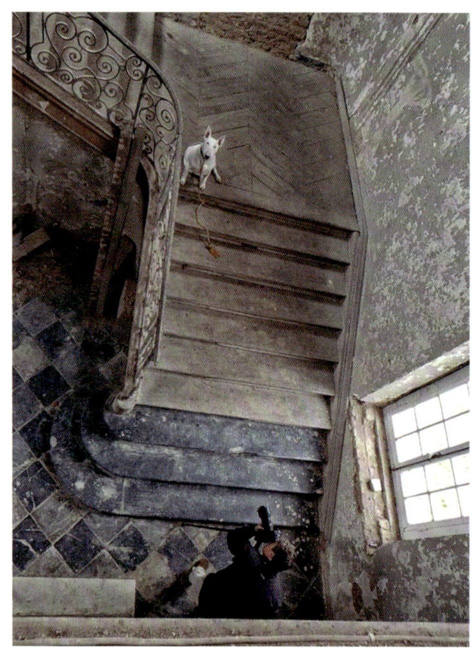

Urbex (Urban Exploring) is about the exploration of abandoned places: overgrown industrial complexes, neglected hospitals, disused churches, forgotten farms, deserted houses, crumbling palaces and empty prisons. It is about discovering the beauty in decay and piecing together the story through what's been left behind. Every step into these hidden spots gives you a feeling of excitement, an adrenaline rush. You are walking into the unknown, a mysterious dark world of deterioration, peeling paint and rotting wood.

Five days after the partial lunar eclipse on 4 June 2012, Claire was born. From day one it was clear that she was a very special puppy. With lots of love, patience and rewards, we taught her a lot and she was, and still is, a very enthusiastic companion. She is clever and she learned quickly. After four days of training, we brought home truffles from the forest, all thanks to Claire. When the winds aren't too strong, Claire joins us on our open catamaran, tackling the waves with ease.

When she was about a year old, a friend and I took Claire and her half-sister Pip to a ghost village in Belgium. After taking a few pictures, it was obvious that she loved posing in front of the camera. New ideas are constantly streaming through my head and I came up with a plan that on my next adventure I would let Claire pose as a model in an abandoned building. My intention was to create art rather than just 'simple' portraits. Art should be ambitious. It should have meaning and be original, and I wanted to apply a personal touch to my photographs of Claire. Urbex with my furry friend as my model – Furbex.

Light is so important to photography and, when shooting in derelict buildings, the light conditions are far from ideal. As we never know what to expect, or how long we'll have to shoot, I only make use of existing light. Luckily, Claire is an excellent model and has mastered sitting motionless at shutter speeds of one, two and sometimes even four seconds. Every location offers up a different challenge and added to this is a constant possibility of being caught for trespassing or bumping into dodgy characters. This type of photography feels like going back in time, to when photography was still considered a skill. It's in complete contrast to the point-and-shoot world we currently live in.

When exploring, we strictly follow urbex rules. Not all our visits have been legal; sometimes it's simply not possible to ask permission because the owners are deceased, or no-one, not even the nearest neighbours, knows who the owners are. We never break anything to enter a site, there must be an existing entrance otherwise it's a no-go. We're always respectful of every site we visit and we always leave the place untouched, following the Furbex motto: "Take only pictures, leave only paw-prints." Before each trip we do a lot of preparation to ensure we stay safe, but if a location doesn't feel right, even after travelling hundreds of kilometres, we don't go in.

For me Furbex photography is the ideal combination of all my interests: photography, travelling, working with animals, nature, history, geography and playing detective. And Claire seems to be as passionate about it as I am – she always enjoys discovering new spots and is eager to pose for the pictures.

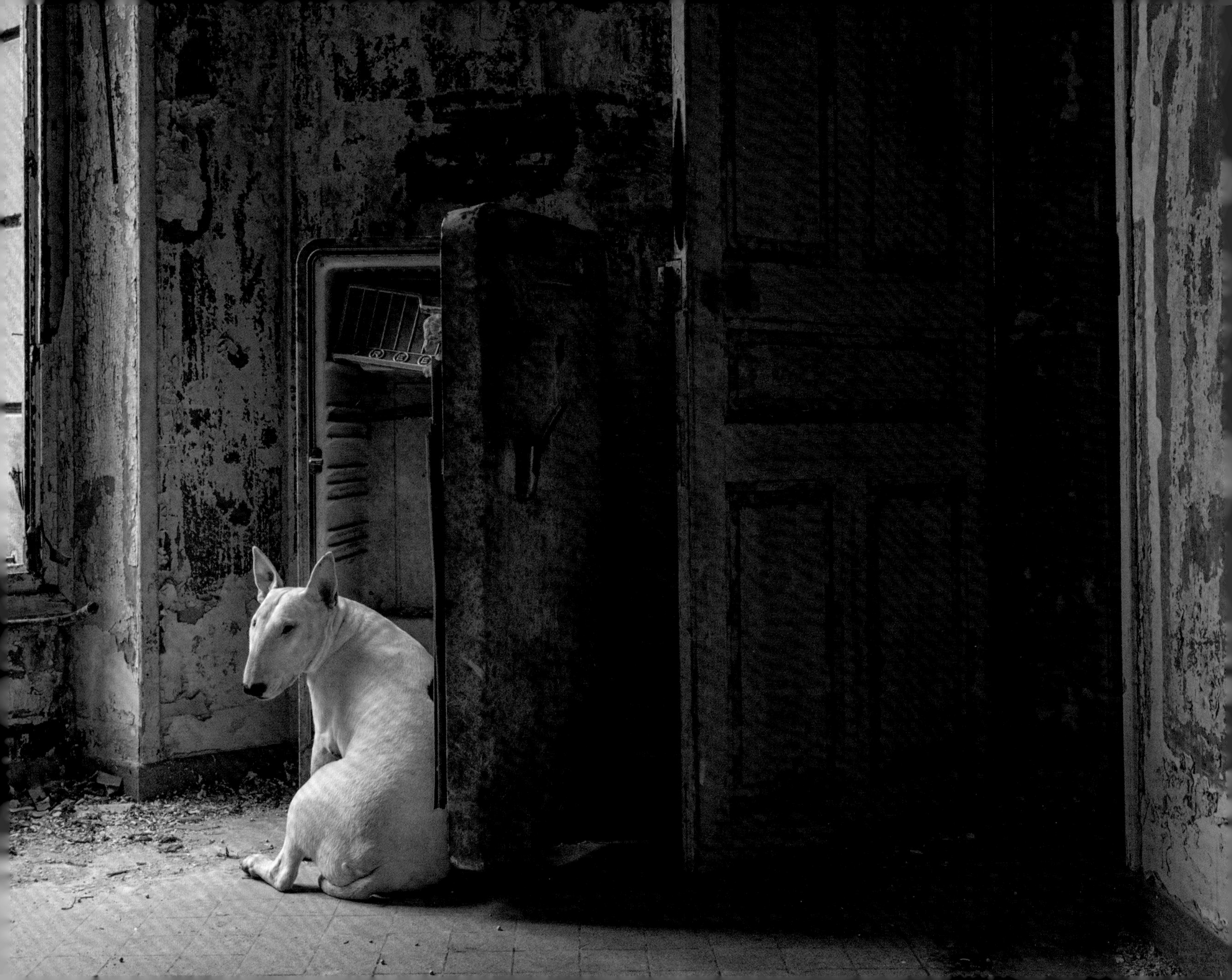

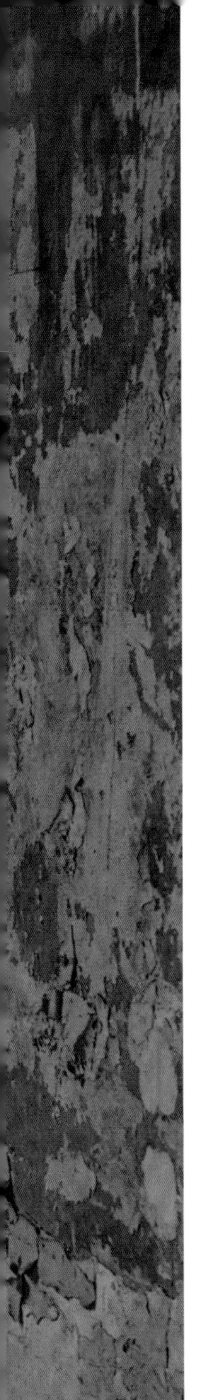

Sanatorium dans la Forêt

France

Every exploration I undertake starts at home; urbex is much more than the explore itself. As well as finding the location I'll always try to check a few other things as well, which is particularly important if I travel with Claire. For a start, I need to know whether a location is accessible for her or if it's too dangerous – I rarely visit industrial sites with my furry companion, as there is always the risk of chemicals or other dangerous substances.

I'll also use Google Earth to check the surroundings and see if there are neighbours – and how close they are – and if there is parking nearby (but not too close). Then I go "down to earth" and use Google Earth/Streetview to see what the neighbour's view of the property is like, whether there's a fence around the building, where best to park, what kind of neighbourhood it is, and whether I should visit early or during the day. I'll take a virtual "walk" around the neighbourhood several times to check anything that might be helpful. This generally works well, although some Google Earth satellite images are out of date, so what you see on screen may not match the "real world". The building we are about to explore was the first hospital in France to be used exclusively for the treatment of tuberculosis patients. When the hospital opened its doors, the known "cure" for the white plague was fresh air in a clean environment, good food, restful sleep and surgical intervention, which included the "pneumothorax technique" invented by the hospital's Chief Medical Officer.

At the start of the 20th century, one in six deaths in France were caused by tuberculosis and "Sanatorium dans la Forêt" (as the hospital is known in the urbex community) was a sanatorium for the middle and upper classes. The patients were provided with study rooms, games rooms, a library, a bookbinding club and a radio club, and given excellent care and constant medical attention; in contrast, the poor had to enter hospitals that resembled prisons. However, despite the benefits of this "perfect" treatment, around half of the patients who were admitted died within five years.

Before the First World War, the sanatorium was strictly for male patients, but after the Second World War the administration decided that one of the two pavilions would be open to women. It was

> "The building… was the first hospital in France to be used exclusively for the treatment of tuberculosis"

Right The Sanatorium dans la Forêt was a hospital for the middle and upper classes. It offered excellent care and constant medical attention.

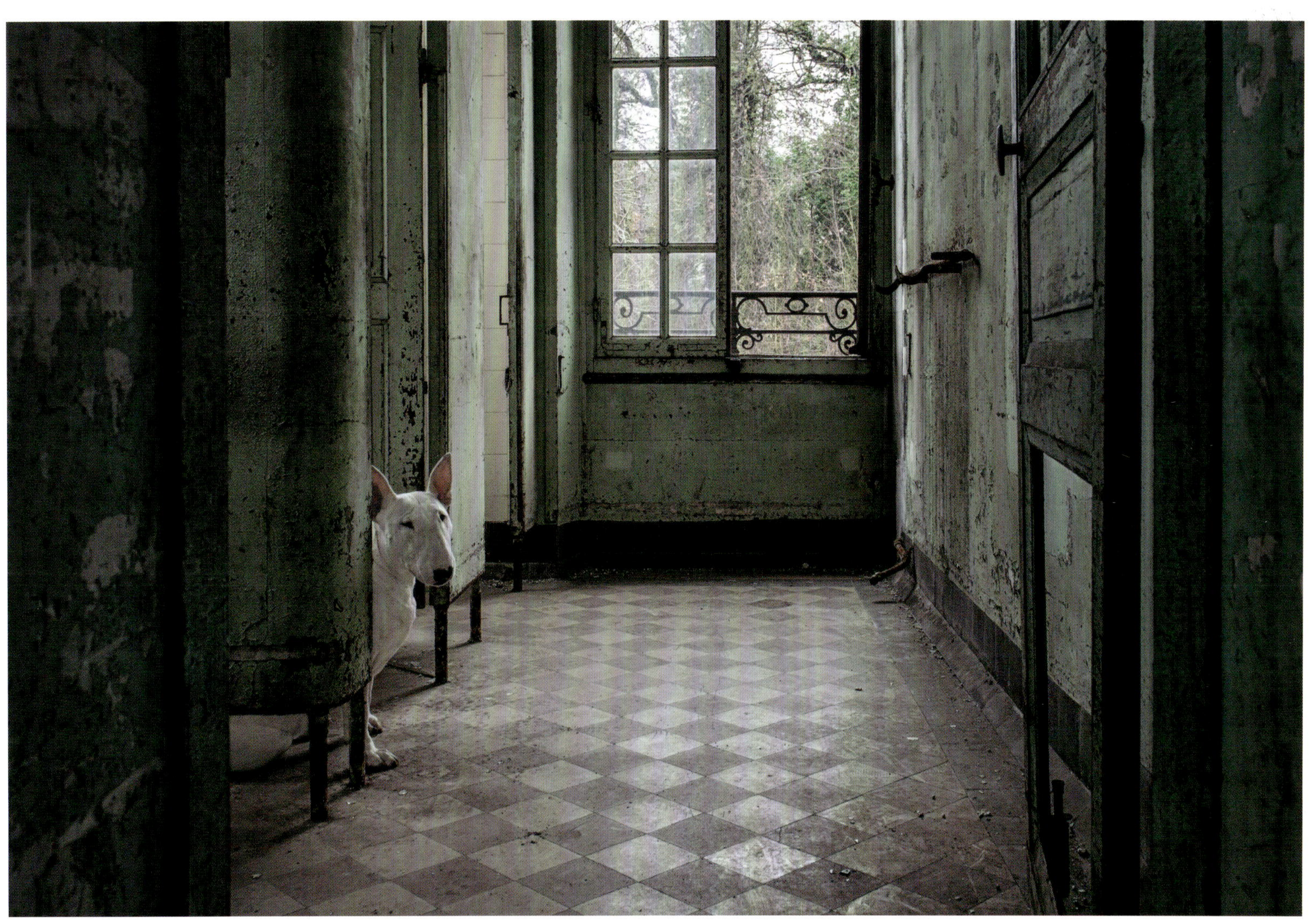

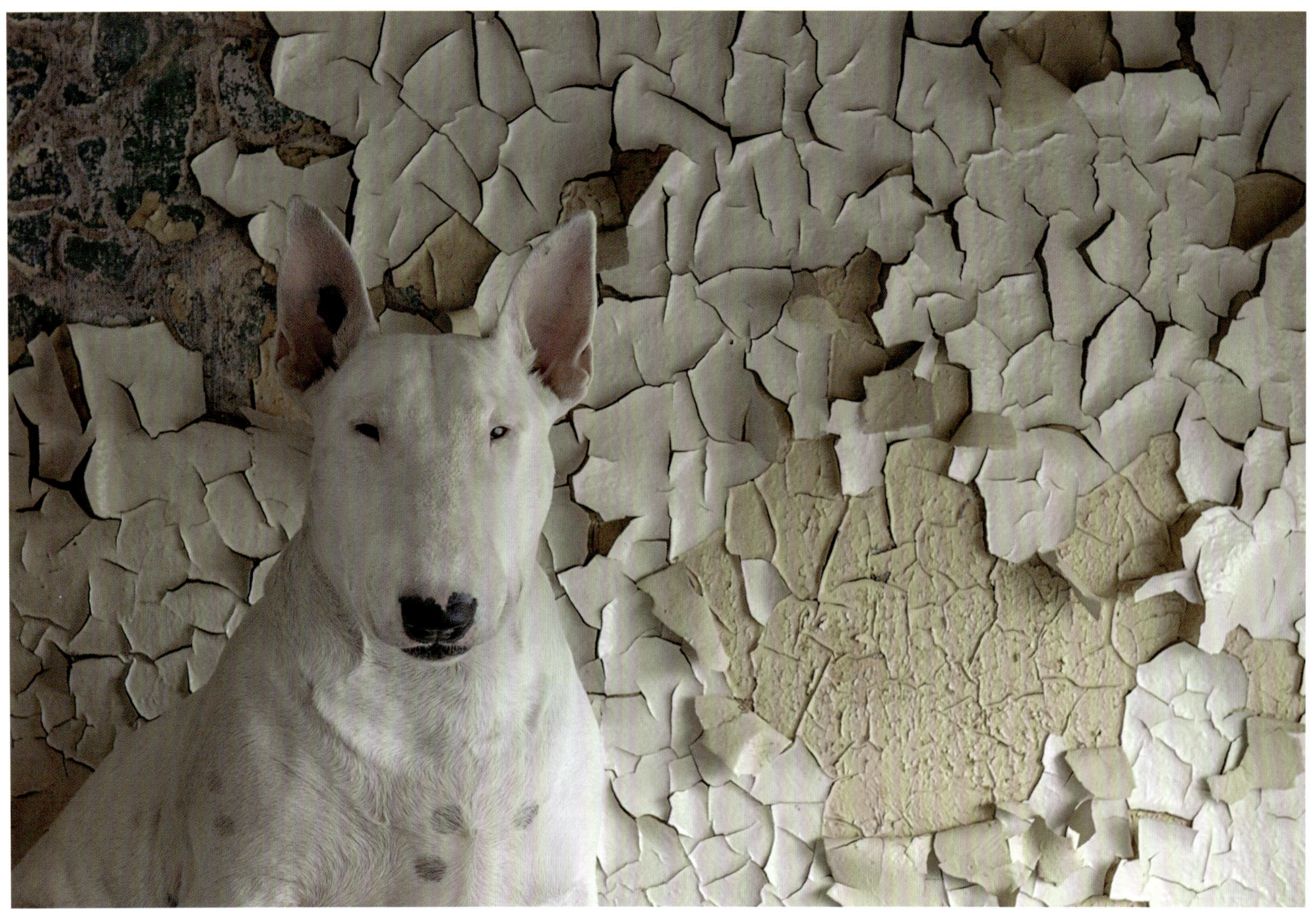

during this period that a major change in the control of tuberculosis took place, thanks to the discovery of antibiotics (which made it possible to cure tuberculosis patients) and the development of the BCG vaccine (which helped to protect the unaffected). The medical complex eventually closed down in 2000.

Today, the forest is dense and the trees are thick and old. Light streaks through the branches in beautiful golden beams – I love these hikes in the forest and so does Claire. The first building we enter is empty. The paint on the walls is diffuse and mottled; layers of paint applied over the years are now appearing again due to decay.

I am about to grab my camera bag to go and check out another building when I hear footsteps. Before I get a chance to hide, a female security guard steps out of the hallway, catching me in the act. Although I understand quite a bit of French, I sometimes prefer to pretend that I don't speak a language at all, so I call out to one of my friends who is fluent. The security guard explains that the buildings and surroundings are private property, and while we claim ignorance and tell her we didn't see any signs, I am pretty sure she has heard that excuse quite a few times before. Even so, she's very kind and advises us to leave the area as soon as possible, as a police unit is due to be training its dogs in the area in about an hour; if we get caught by them we will get a fine or be taken to the police station. We follow up on her advice, but not before she gives Claire a cuddle.

"I am about to grab my camera bag to go and check out another building when I hear footsteps…"

Hotel Atlantis
Germany

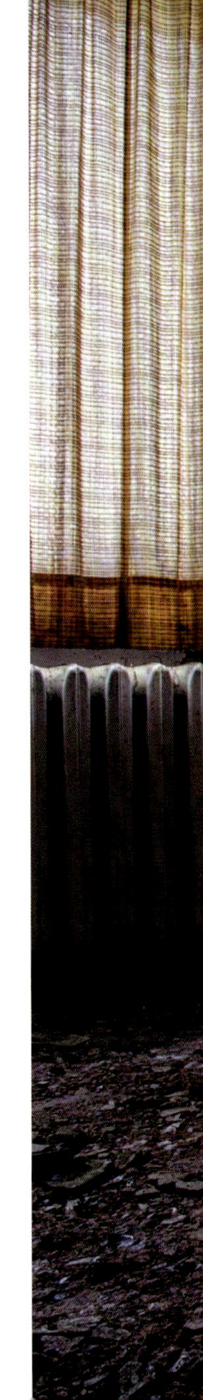

Right There are three parts to the hotel. The oldest building is over 100 years old. Water drips through holes in the ceiling and green mould covers the walls. What was once the height of luxury is now being reclaimed by nature.

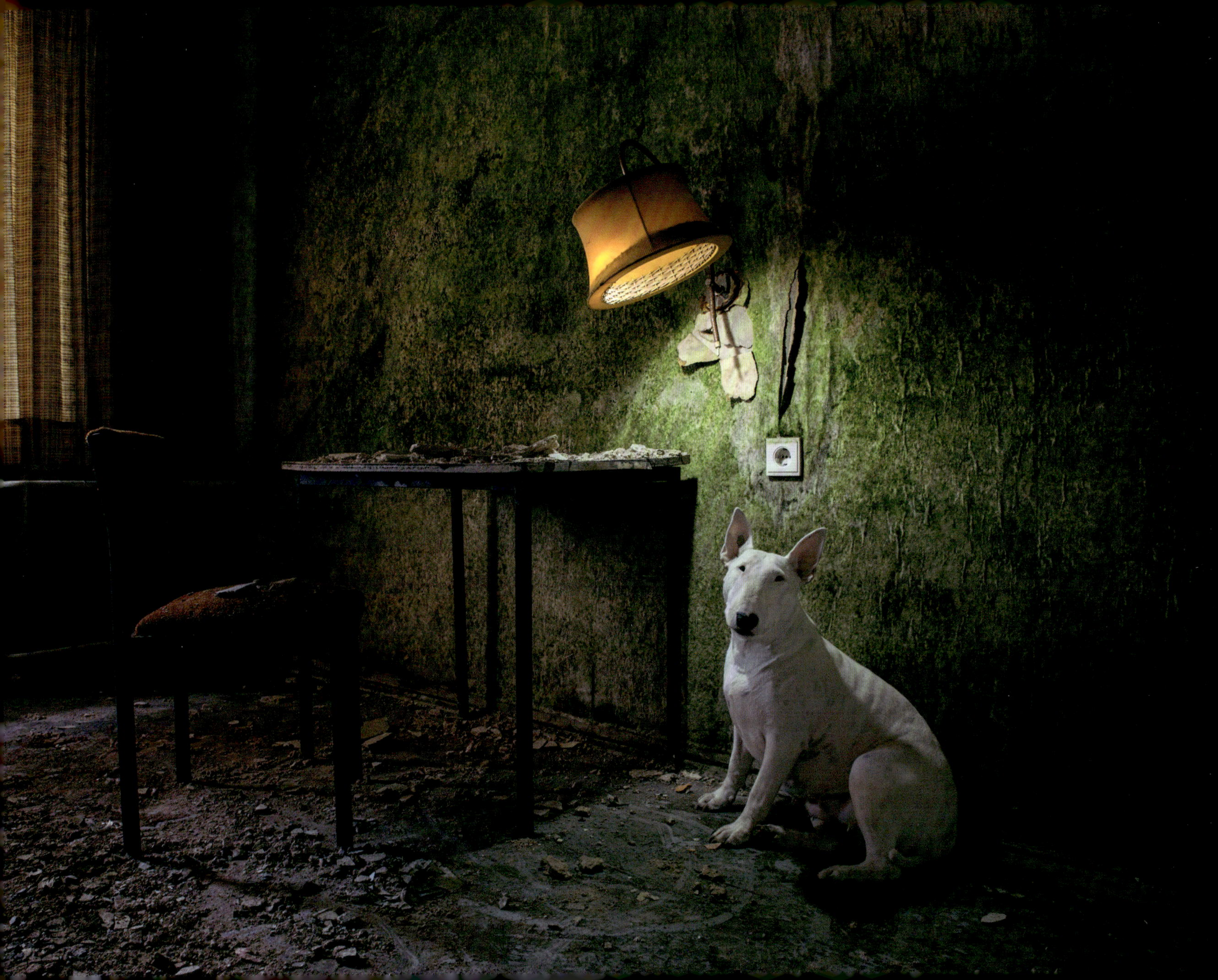

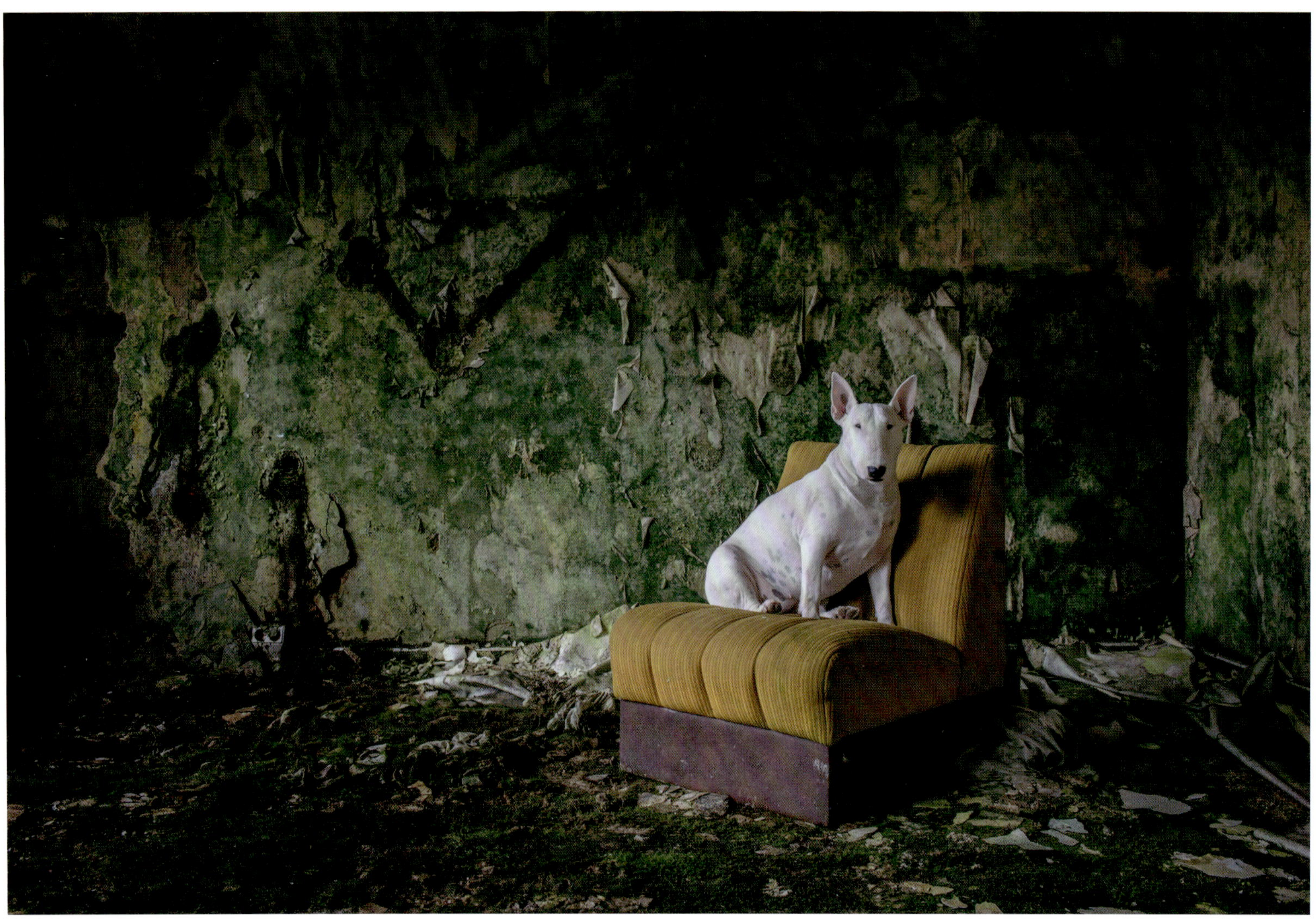

Shortly after the end of the Second World War, the Free German Trade Union Confederation (FDGB) founded its holiday service, which provided subsidized vacations for the residents of the German Democratic Republic (East Germany). As most people were not allowed to travel abroad, billions was spent on the country's domestic tourism industry, with colourful propaganda posters advertising vacations that were regulated down to the smallest detail.

Built in 1911 and located high up in the mountains, "Hotel Atlantis" (as it's now known) had been a popular winter sports destination. When it was constructed it was the most modern and luxurious hotel in the region, with electric lighting, central heating, a music hall, billiard room and chic restaurant. Unsurprisingly, it quickly became one of the FDGB's most popular "holiday homes" and for ordinary people in the GDR it was like winning the lottery if their application to stay at the hotel was approved.

However, after the reunification of Germany – and with an end to vacation restrictions – guests largely stayed away, although the hotel continued as a sports hotel until 1998. At that point, an inspection of the property concluded that it was in such a bad state that renovation would not be feasible, and it was simply left to decay. Twenty years later, the hotel's former luxury is still visible from the outside, but the bricked-up windows and doors, and metre-high weeds are a clear indicator that the last hotel's guests checked out a long time ago.

I am alone by the building with Claire, while my husband waits in our camper van; he loves the photos I make, but I can't get him to come with me. I walk around the building twice, but cannot find an entrance, so I decide to go online and ask someone who has been there recently for help. I am lucky and get an answer right away – it turns out that I overlooked a door in a courtyard.

The hotel's interior dates from the late 1970s or early '80s. Water seeps through the ceiling and out of the walls and I wonder if this is why the hotel was called Hotel Atlantis by the explorer who discovered it. It is so damp inside that large bracket fungi grow on the door posts and the walls are green with mould.

It is a large hotel and I decide to work systematically in order not to get lost. We start at the top and as we work our way down, floor by floor, I try to imagine what it must have been like to live in the GDR; to go on a well-organized vacation in a beautiful state-owned hotel controlled by the Stasi. The rooms were probably equipped with listening devices and hidden cameras, but if they were, they are now long gone. Every time I discover a nice spot in the hotel I stop and take pictures. There is still some lovely retro furniture that has been left behind, which matches beautifully with the mouldy green walls. This is the ultimate decay and I love it: fungi on the walls, moss on tables and ferns on the floor. It doesn't get much better than this.

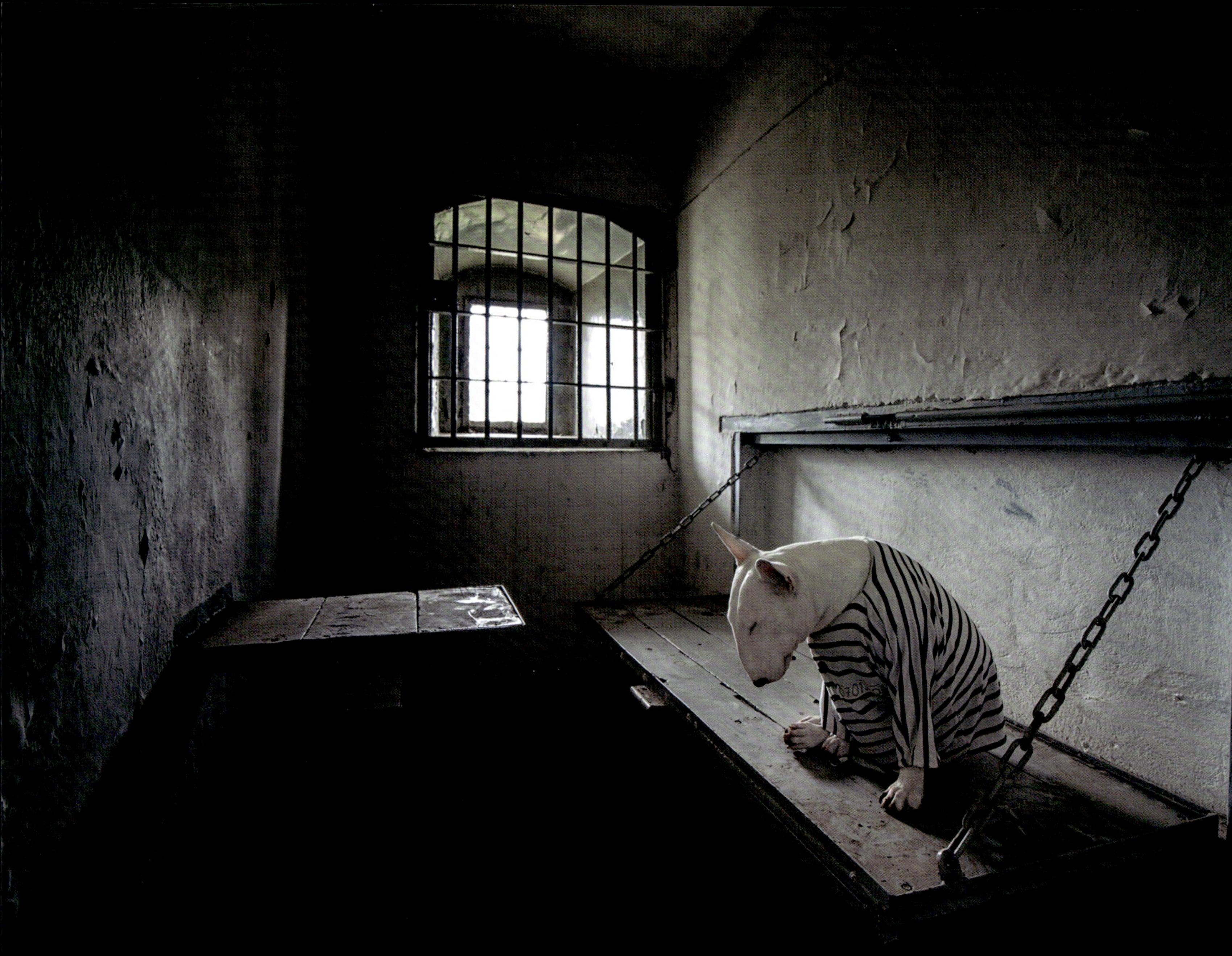

Prison 1555
Germany

Left Claire takes on the role of a juvenile prisoner. It is very dark in the cell, so to take this picture she has to sit still for four seconds. When I finish a series of photos I gently whisper her name. She looks up and blinks; it is as if she just woke up from another world.

The prison we are visiting is surrounded by a 20ft (6m) high wall, but you wouldn't necessarily know it from the street side, where the wall is a little over 3ft (1m) above ground level. A driver recently lost control of his car and drove at full speed right through the wall, which meant that people walking past could easily fall through the gap. To make it safe, the local authority deposited a large mound of sand behind the hole, into the prison yard below. They didn't have to worry about any prisoners escaping, as the former inmates were mainly political prisoners who had been released after the fall of the Berlin Wall.

Today, the mound of sand is the only way to get into the prison grounds and three of us slide gently down the hill to join Claire, who is waiting for us at the bottom. A friend has drawn us a map, so we know where to enter. Or at least we think we do – the door that was open when our friend visited is now barricaded with wooden planks. We look for another entrance and I find a hole in the wall and crawl through it, with Claire right behind me. It's a wasted effort, though, as it's a dead end. We continue walking around the building, checking every door, and can't believe our luck when we see an open window on the first floor with a ladder underneath it. One of my friends goes up first to help me get Claire in, and we're inside the building.

The prison used to be a castle, the oldest part of which was built in the 13th century, with the most recent addition coming in the second half of the 16th century. Two centuries later the castle was turned into a prison and as I walk in the dungeons I try to imagine what life would have been like for the prostitutes, female vagrants, beggars and criminals who were condemned to hard labour here – some for life, others for a shorter period. The prison started as a spinhaus, where female prisoners spun wool for the textile industry, but in later years this dungeon was turned into a small shoe factory. Although the machines are still here it is way too dark to photograph Claire.

The building is like a maze; I get lost several times and haven't seen my friends for over an hour. I am trying to find some small cells with medieval wooden beds that I've seen in other urbex photographs

"The building is like a maze; I get lost several times and haven't seen my friends for over an hour."

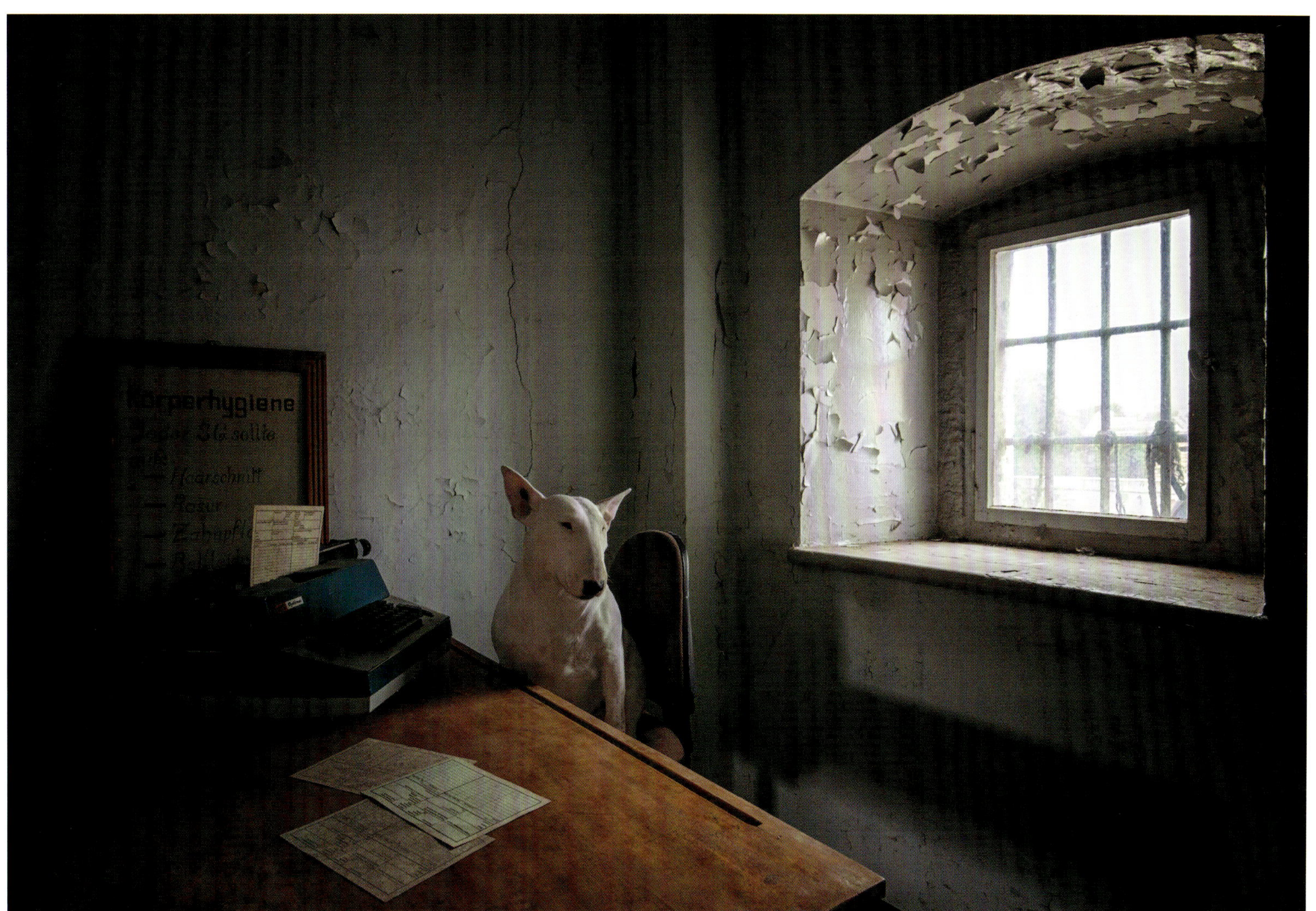

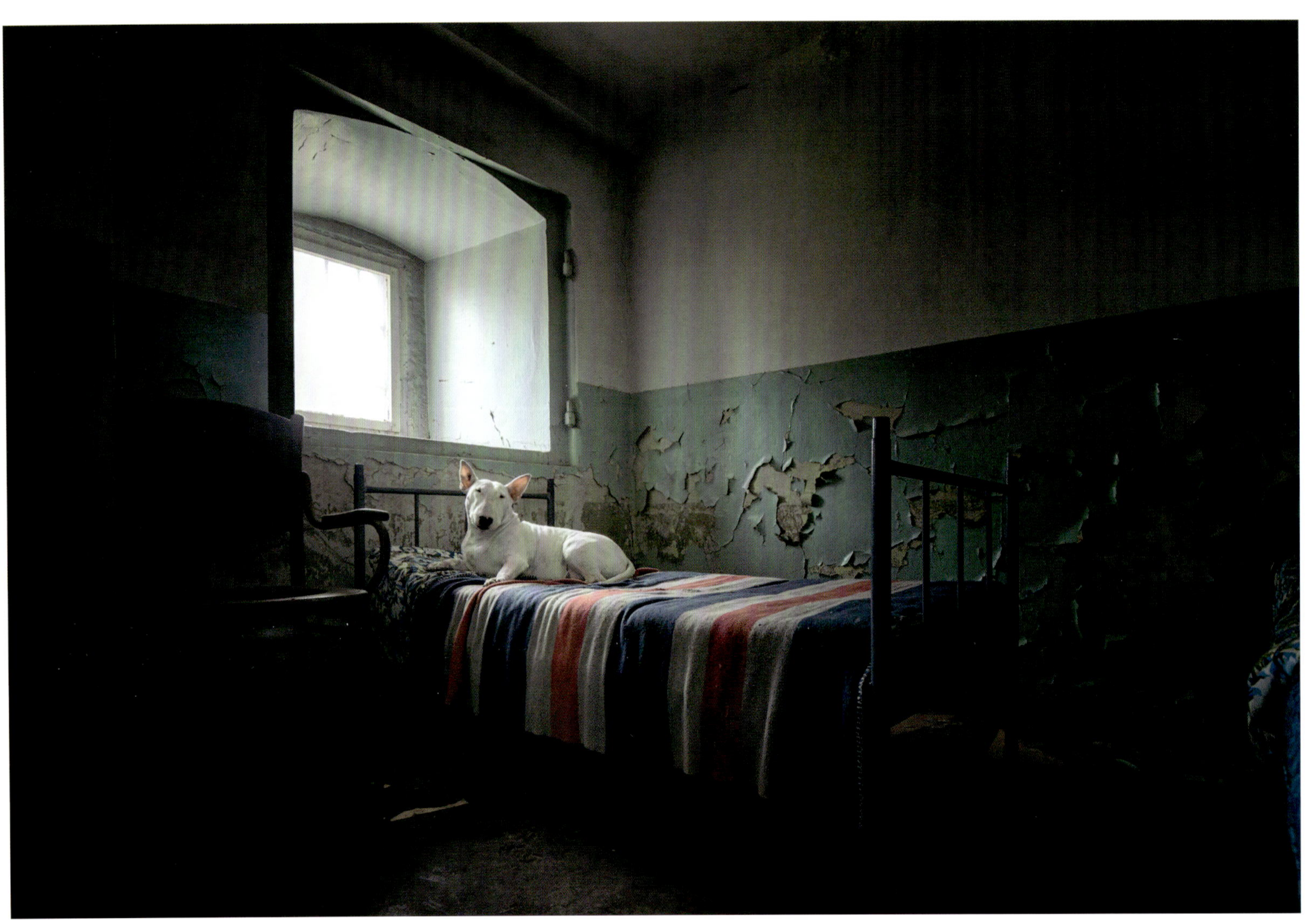

when I suddenly hear voices speaking German. A couple of people walk around the corner and pull up quickly when they see me. For a brief moment they think I'm a guard with a dangerous dog, but then they notice my camera. As we pass each other, one of them points at Claire and asks how I got inside with her; they can't believe it when I tell them I used the same ladder entrance as they had.

Eventually I find the row of small prison cells I was looking for. Claire jumps up on to one of the beds and I sit down next to her, allowing myself to taste the atmosphere as I think of all the prisoners who spent their time in this 10ft x 5ft (3m x 1.5m) cell. Everything is hard and cold; it's a concrete box with neither heating nor air conditioning, just a square, barred window that would be shut during winter and wide open in summer. With a toilet bucket in the cell and clothes washed only once every 14 days, there would have been no chance of escaping the unbearable smell of urine, excrement and sweat.

During the Cold War, the German Democratic Republic (GDR) had one of the most effective and repressive intelligence and secret police agencies that has ever existed. Prisons like this were overcrowded with political prisoners, as well as thieves, thugs and murderers, and children as young as 14. For burning a GDR flag you would serve a six-month sentence, while trying to escape to the free west could cost you years in prison. I am trying to imagine what it would be like for a 14-year-old child in this harsh environment, where both guards and fellow prisoners used differing methods to break the weaker inmates; a place where prisoners fought for a piece of bread or a stolen pin-up poster. Violence dominated: prisoners were beaten by guards with batons and bare fists and then placed in isolation cells until their injuries healed. There was nothing humane about this place.

"Prisons like this were overcrowded with political prisoners, as well as thieves, thugs and murderers, and children as young as 14."

Left This cell was relatively luxurious compared to the cells with the wooden beds, and Claire was more than willing to have a lie down.

Château Verdure
France

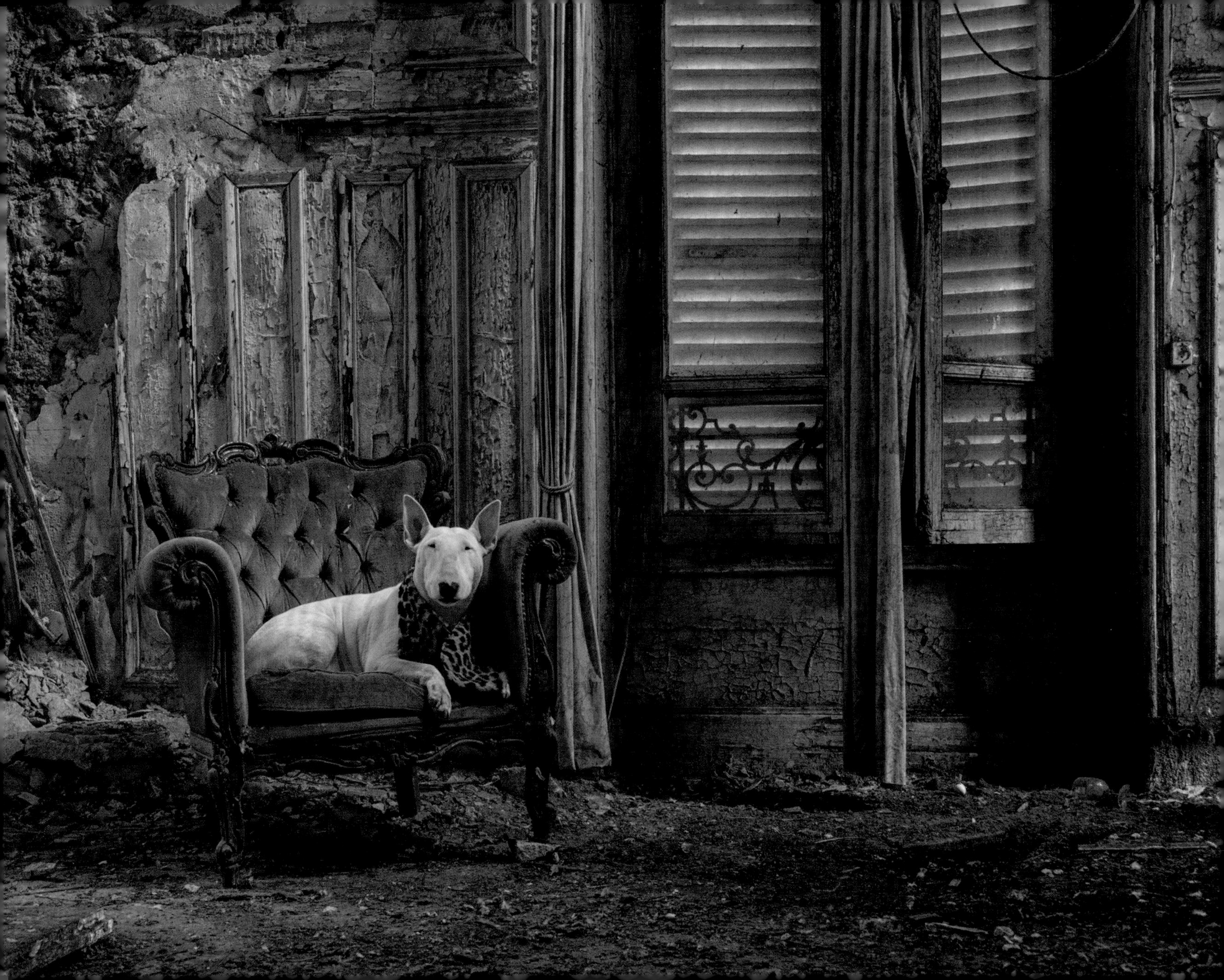

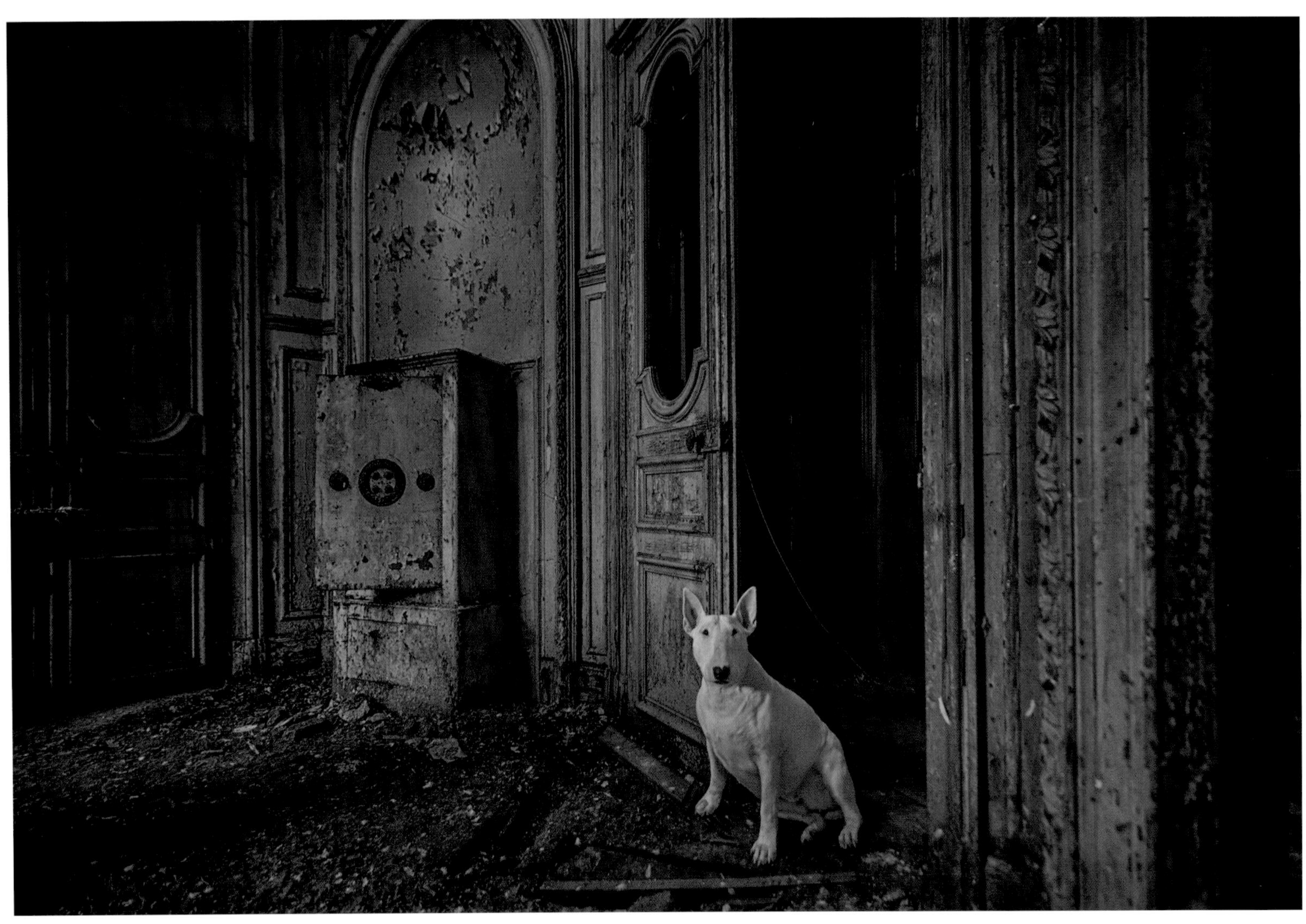

t is a freezing cold morning in December and we have just spent the night at an Airbnb in a suburb of Paris. The very kind grandmother and her granddaughter who it belongs to are still asleep when we leave; we want to get to our destination early to avoid detection. The small castle we are heading to is located in a very classy part of the city, just a couple of minutes away. It's still dark when we enter the neighbourhood, but we still park our car a few blocks away, as the local residents have been asked to warn the police as soon as they see suspicious people or vehicles. In this community, any car with a value less than €40,000 ($50,000) immediately stands out and our vehicle isn't even close to that figure.

Were it not for the large trees and shrubs that make it invisible from the road, the dilapidated building that dates back to 1863 would be really out of place among the luxury villas. Thankfully, it's much easier to enter the garden of the Louis XV-style castle than we first thought. According to our information we were expecting to have to climb a very high iron gate with sharp spikes at the top, so I had planned on leaving Claire in the car, but the night before we recced the site and discovered a hole in the fence, which meant Claire could come with us after all.

At the back of the building there's an open window, but it's quite high up. I lift Claire and put her on the wide windowsill where she sits and waits until I climb up next to her. Inside, the walls of the castle are crumbling and the ceilings have disappeared completely. In the living room are two velvet armchairs, where Monsieur le Claire, the château's first resident, probably sat next to the fireplace on cold December mornings like this. An old safe stands wide open, next to a billiard table whose green cloth has been replaced with a thick layer of pigeon droppings. Monsieur le Claire is long gone; the pigeons are the residents now.

Unlike the rest of the castle, the entrance hall is in immaculate condition. A magnificent marble staircase shelters a beautiful old piano, which looks as if it intentionally crawled beneath the indestructible stairs for protection. Unfortunately, this spot is way too dark to take pictures of Claire, so I decide to focus on the living room instead. While Claire poses, pigeons fly back and forth in the ridge of the roof. Sometimes one escapes to the outside world.

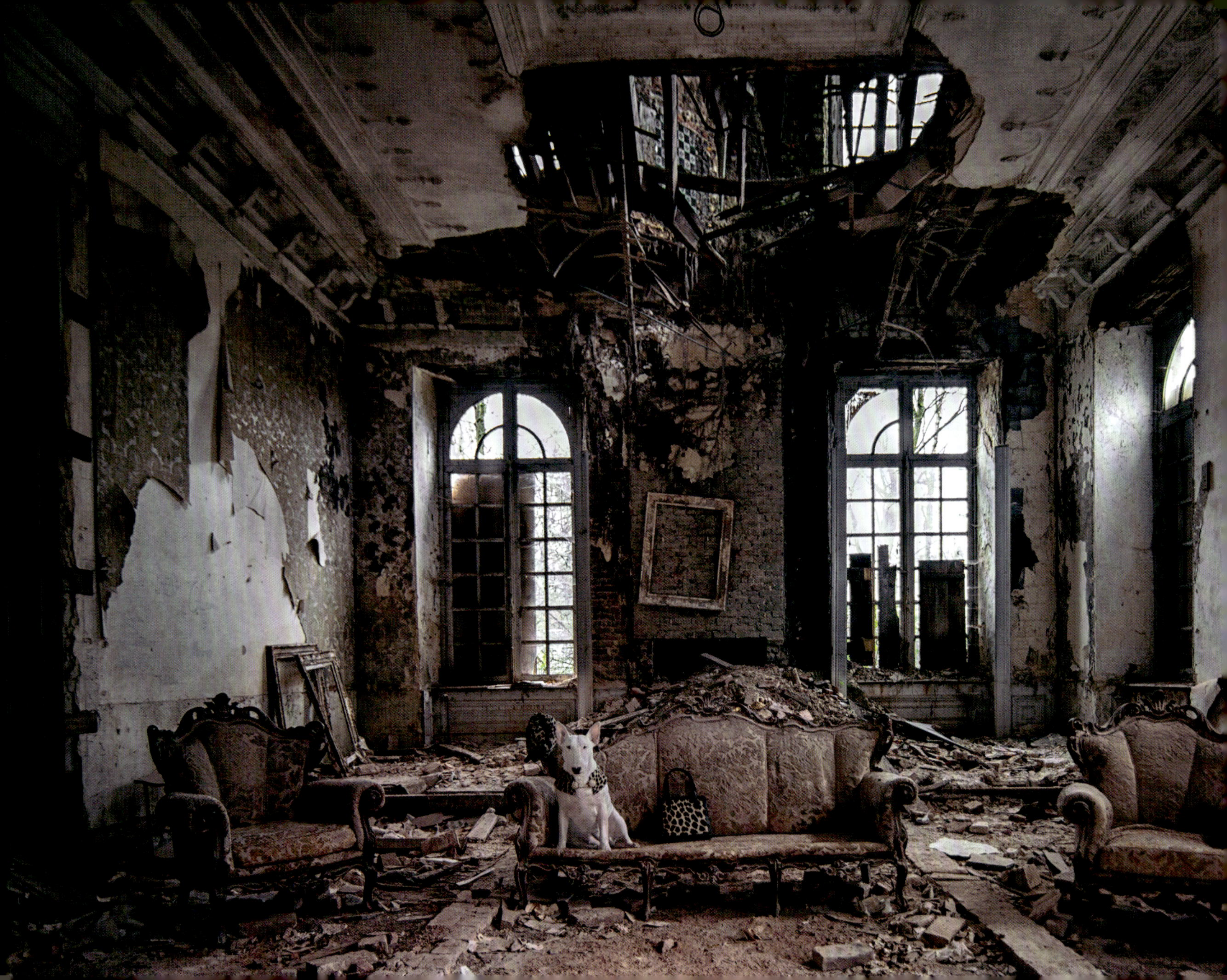

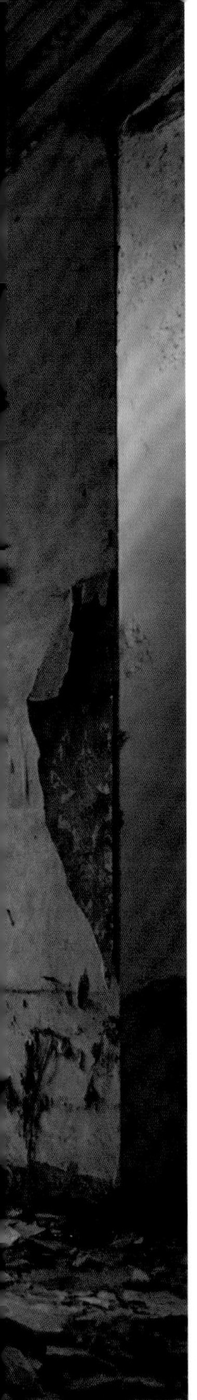

Château Congo
Belgium

Left The ceiling of the living room is beginning to collapse as the wooden joists rot away. Sunlight pours in through the decaying roof above, illuminating what's left of the remaining furniture, which sits covered in dust.

The professor is on his way to his favourite cafe, Café de la Paix in the Democratic Republic of the Congo, where he met his girlfriend, Ambiance, just a couple of months earlier. She immediately caught his eye that day; she was tall and slender with a pretty face, short curly hair and a beautiful smile. He invited her for drinks and after that they walked to his house. She never left.

Tonight he will meet her family for the first time. He has no idea what to expect, although Ambiance has told him about the local traditions in Congo. She is pregnant, so he is expected to ask her parents for their daughter's hand, but that is not all. He will also have to pay a dowry, and as he is much older than her – and a wealthy westerner – the family will probably ask for a number of cows. Many tribes across Africa measure wealth in cows, and a man cannot marry without paying a bovine dowry.

Life in Congo is difficult for the professor, especially when president Mobutu begins a campaign known as Authenticité (or "Zairianization") that sees foreign-owned companies nationalized and western investors forced out of the country. The professor decides to leave Congo before his baby is born. Ambiance will miss her family, but the life that's waiting for her in Belgium sounds like a fairytale: she is going to live with her prince in a castle.

The castle in question dates back to the early 19th century, but the professor does everything he can to make his wife feel at home. He paints the walls of the castle in vivid tones or covers them with brightly coloured wallpaper and uses an antique treadle sewing machine to make long drapes inspired by the vibrant fabrics of Congo. He attaches these colourful drapes to the ceiling and it is in this bright interior that his first child – a son – is born.

A second child is born – a girl – but despite being happy with the birth of his children, the professor misses Congo and decides to return. As he doesn't want to leave his wife all alone in the castle with their two young children, he asks his mother to move in with them.

> *"The life that's waiting for her in Belgium sounds like a fairytale: she is going to live with her prince in a castle."*

***Right** I photographed Claire sitting on a couch, wearing a leopard-print collar and matching handbag – a female Mobutu after the Congolese dictator who was well known for his leopard-fur hats and matching shirts.*

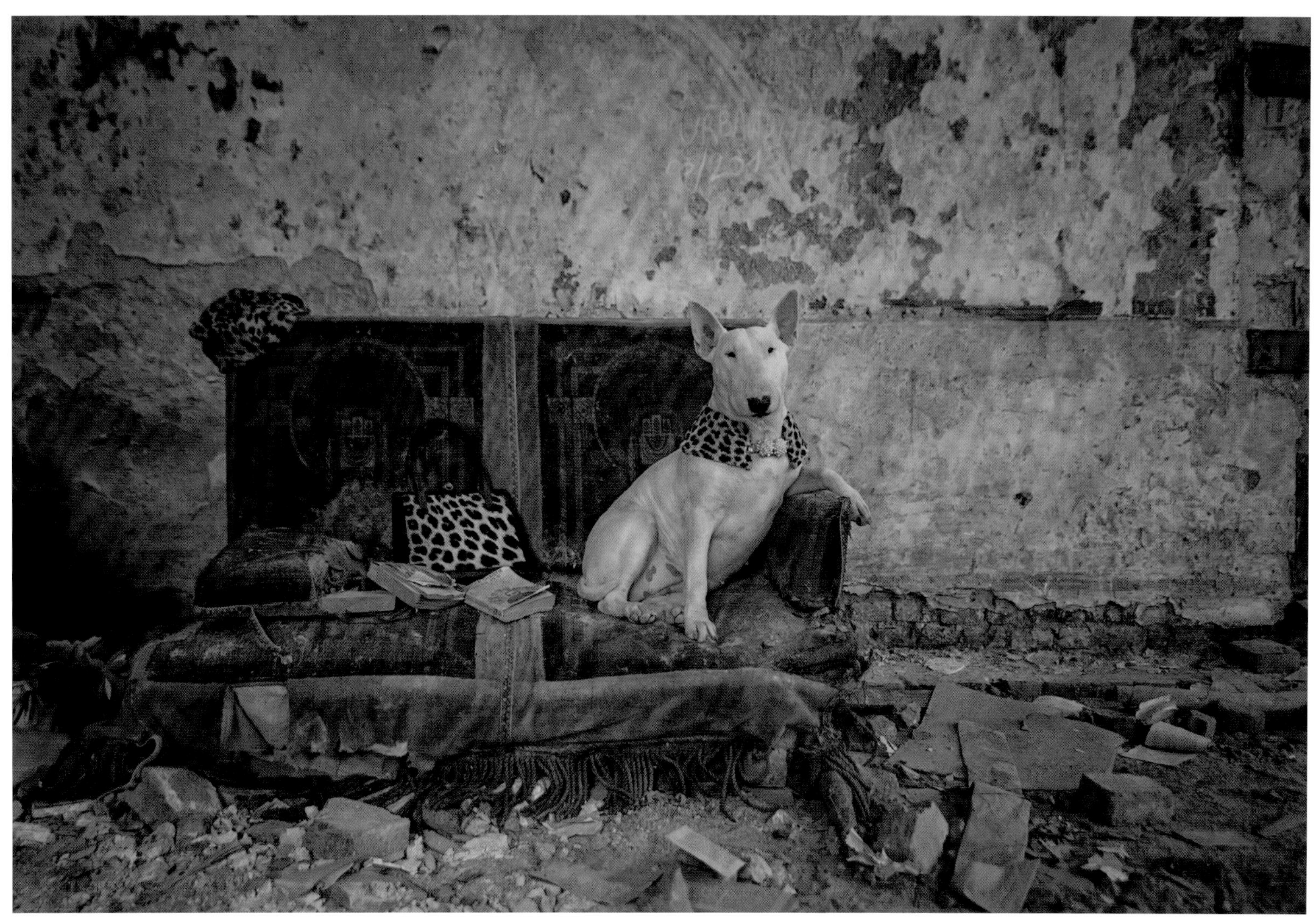

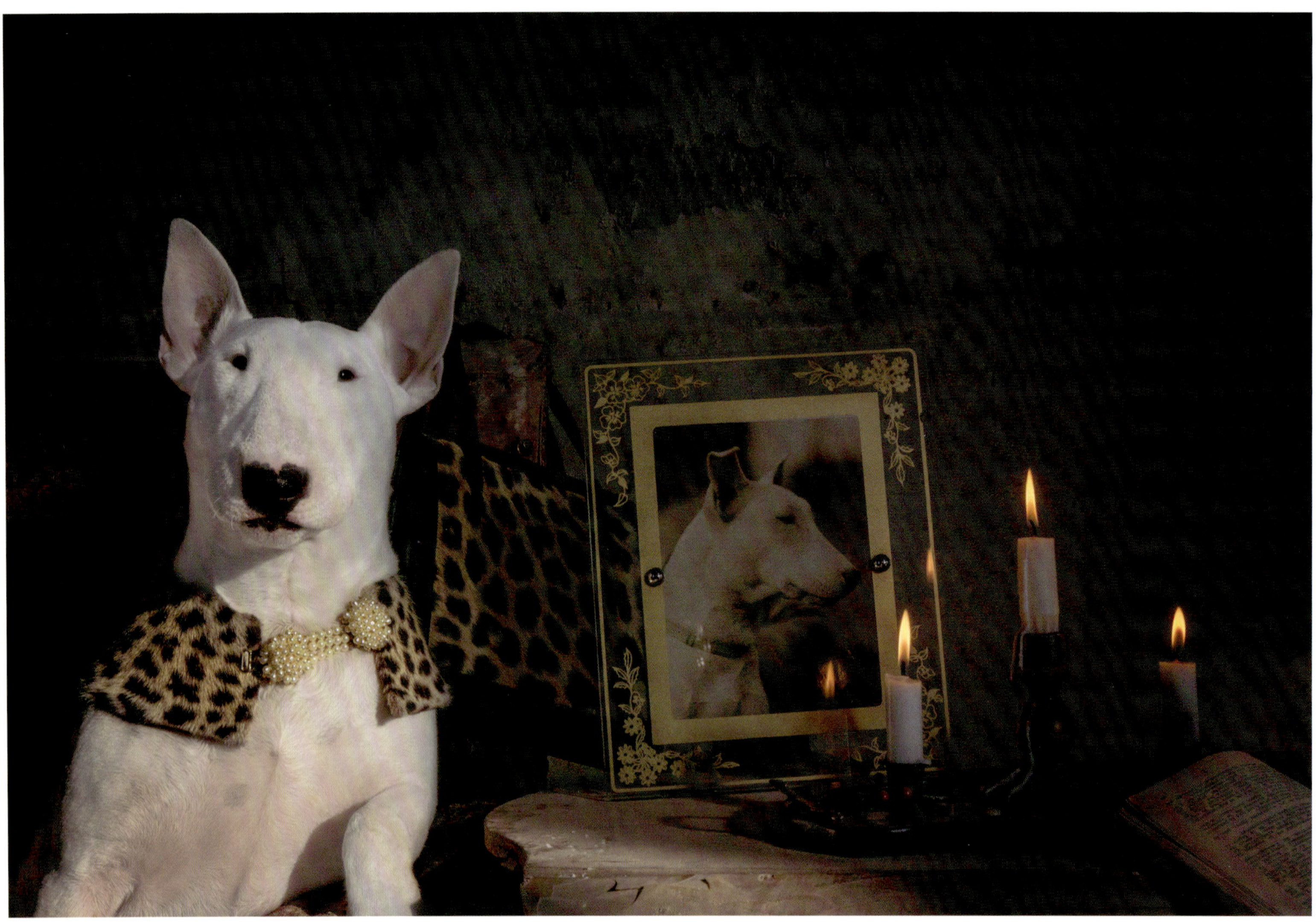

The professor's mother was raised in Congo's colonial era and treats her daughter-in-law as she would a servant. One day she cannot take any more and flees the castle for Brussels, leaving her two children and all of her belongings behind.

With their grandmother now looking after them, the children's upbringing is extremely harsh. Their father visits occasionally, but always goes back to his beloved Congo. Far too young, the children start their own lives, away from the castle and their evil grandmother.

Things take a turn for the worse in Congo, as Mobutu is overthrown as president, there are several coups, and rebels from different tribes fight each other for power. The professor decides to leave Africa and return to his castle. With his mother now dead, and his wife and children gone, he gathers animals around him to fight off loneliness: Afghan hounds, horses, ostriches and emus all join his menagerie, but it is clear he is not well. The son, his wife and three young children move in and look after the professor until his death.

I have visited Château Congo on four occasions, three of which were with Claire. There's something about this castle that calls to me – I can almost feel the longing for Africa when I'm here. The decay is overwhelming, though. The castle is completely stripped both inside and out, as if the son took revenge for his terrible childhood by deliberately plundering the castle. Although he lived in the castle for a couple of years after his father's death, the son had no money to maintain it. During winter it was very cold, so he started tearing up the hardwood floors to burn in the stoves and heat the rooms; when most of the flooring was gone, a wooden staircase went up in flames.

To get some income for his family, the heir started to sell all of the antique furniture and art, keeping just a few chairs and couches so they wouldn't have to sit on what remained of the wooden floors. Once the furnishings were sold, parts of the building itself were removed: antique shutters, iron ornaments, the tower chime, centuries-old stone ornaments, bluestone lintels from the façade and even parts of bearing walls – among other things – all disappeared from the castle.

When there was almost nothing left to sell and no more wood to keep them warm, the son and his family simply left. There are still reminders of their presence, though: children's shoes, dolls and a Michael Jackson poster. Even the son's bed in the long hallway survived, a silent witness to an awful childhood. The family also left behind a beautiful antique couch and two matching chairs, which have become urbex icons.

Left Château Congo was purchased by a local businessman in 2016 to prevent any further ruin and revive the desolate building. The renovations will restore the château to its former glory, albeit in the form of 12 luxury apartments.

Crystal Factory
Belgium

Right The crystal factory was founded in 1826 on the site of Val-Saint-Lambert Abbey. Its proximity to raw materials and good transport links made it the ideal location to establish the business.

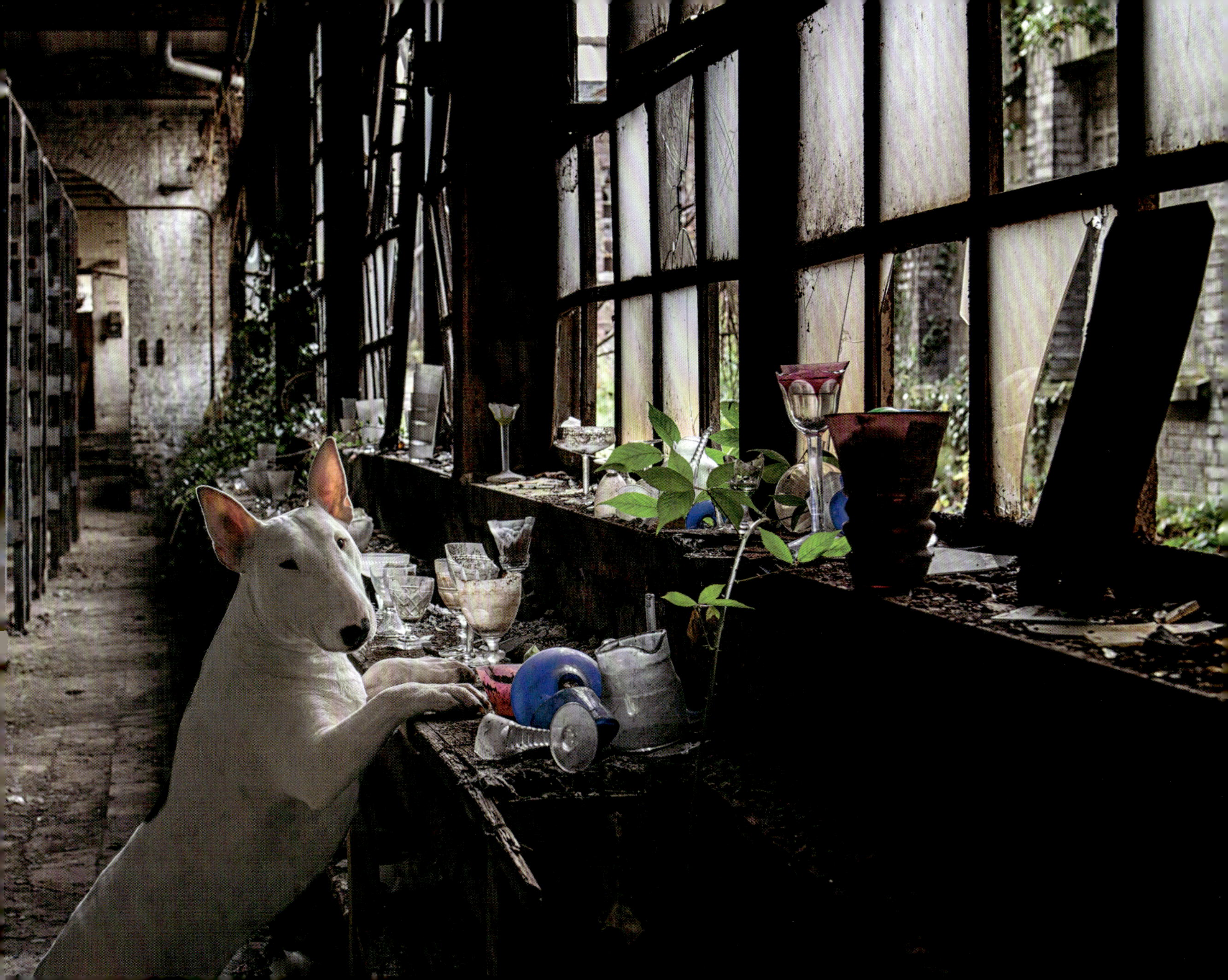

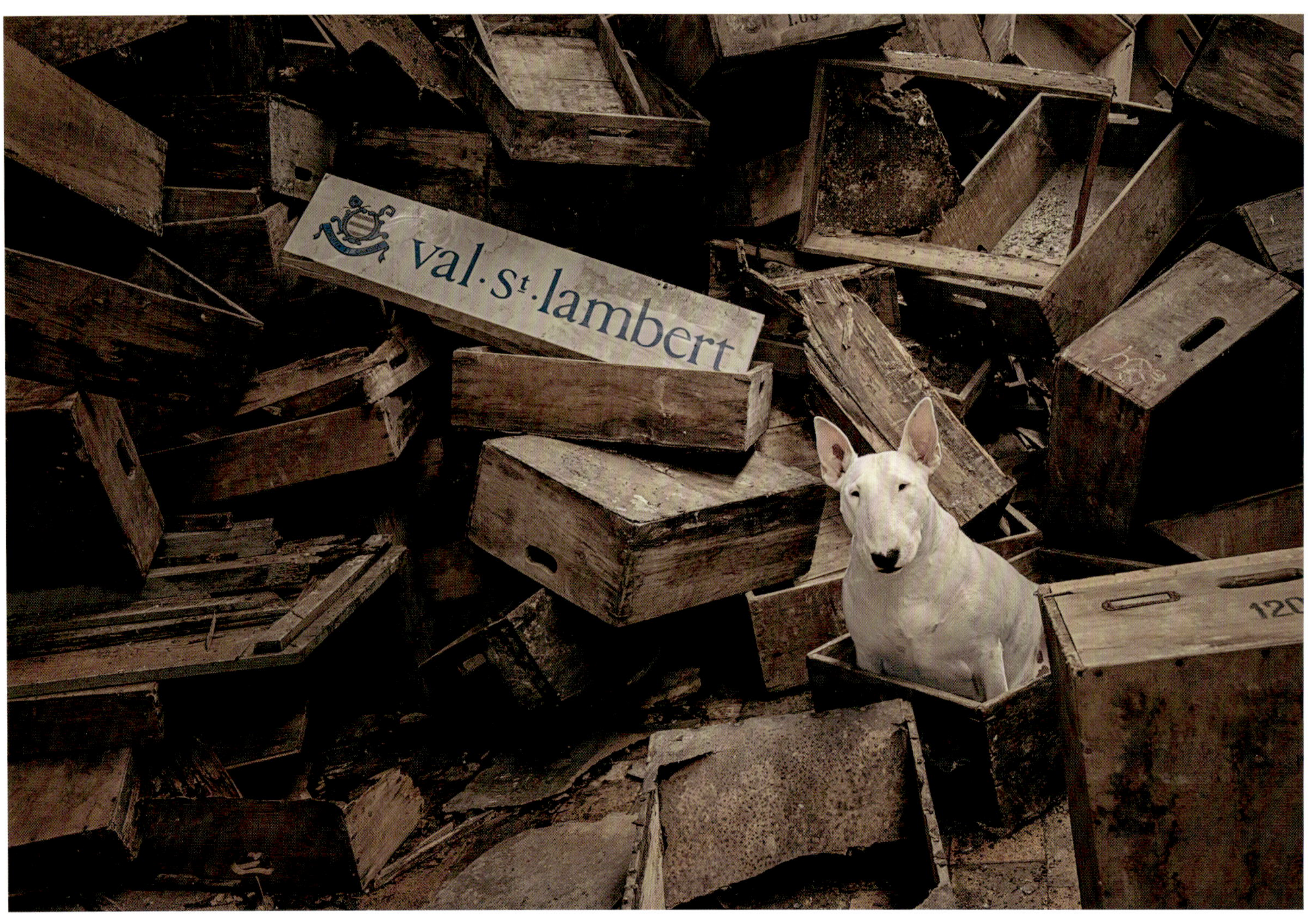
val·st·lambert

In 1826 the furnace of the crystal factory at Seraing fired up, establishing the first – and to date only – crystal glassware factory in Belgium. Originally produced in an old Cistercian abbey, the glassware, which is characterized by complex geometric patterns across the entire surface, turned Val Saint Lambert into a global brand. By the end of the 19th century it had customers worldwide, including the Russian tsars of the House of Romanov. In the early 1900s, Val Saint Lambert created two crystal chandeliers for the hall of the Jai Vilas Palace in Gwalior, India. With a weight of almost 8,000lb (3.5 tons) and a height of more than 40ft (12.5m), they are said to be the world's largest crystal chandeliers; the story goes that the architect had the strength and solidity of the ceiling tested by bringing 10 elephants to the first floor.

The company's more recent history is marked by restructurings and takeovers, which began in the 1970s. A new factory was built beside the old one in 1979, and this is still in full operation, as we found out during our first visit. We thought we had found the right entry point to the old buildings, but having lifted Claire and her half-sister Pip over the wall and started walking towards the building we suddenly saw smoke coming from a chimney. As fast as we could, we jumped back over the fence.

After a thorough inspection of the area, we find the right spot, but it is surrounded by razor wire. We follow the wire round to a 10ft (3m) high wall, hoping to find an entrance somewhere. It seems there is no end to the wall, but then it turns a corner and stops abruptly. Beyond, we see a path of trampled grass – an urbex path, without a doubt. We follow the path, which ends at a row of metal fences, some of which have already been lifted slightly. We only just fit underneath, but we're in.

The old factory buildings were simply abandoned when the new factory was opened. Old tools were left behind, as were prototypes of crystal glasses and vases. Some of the halls are empty, but thanks to the beautiful light streaming through the many windows there is still plenty to photograph, and we end up staying for a couple of hours.

A few years later we visit again, but this time access is easy: the buildings are about to be demolished and all the razor wire and fences have been removed.

Travel Gallery

Have dog, will travel...

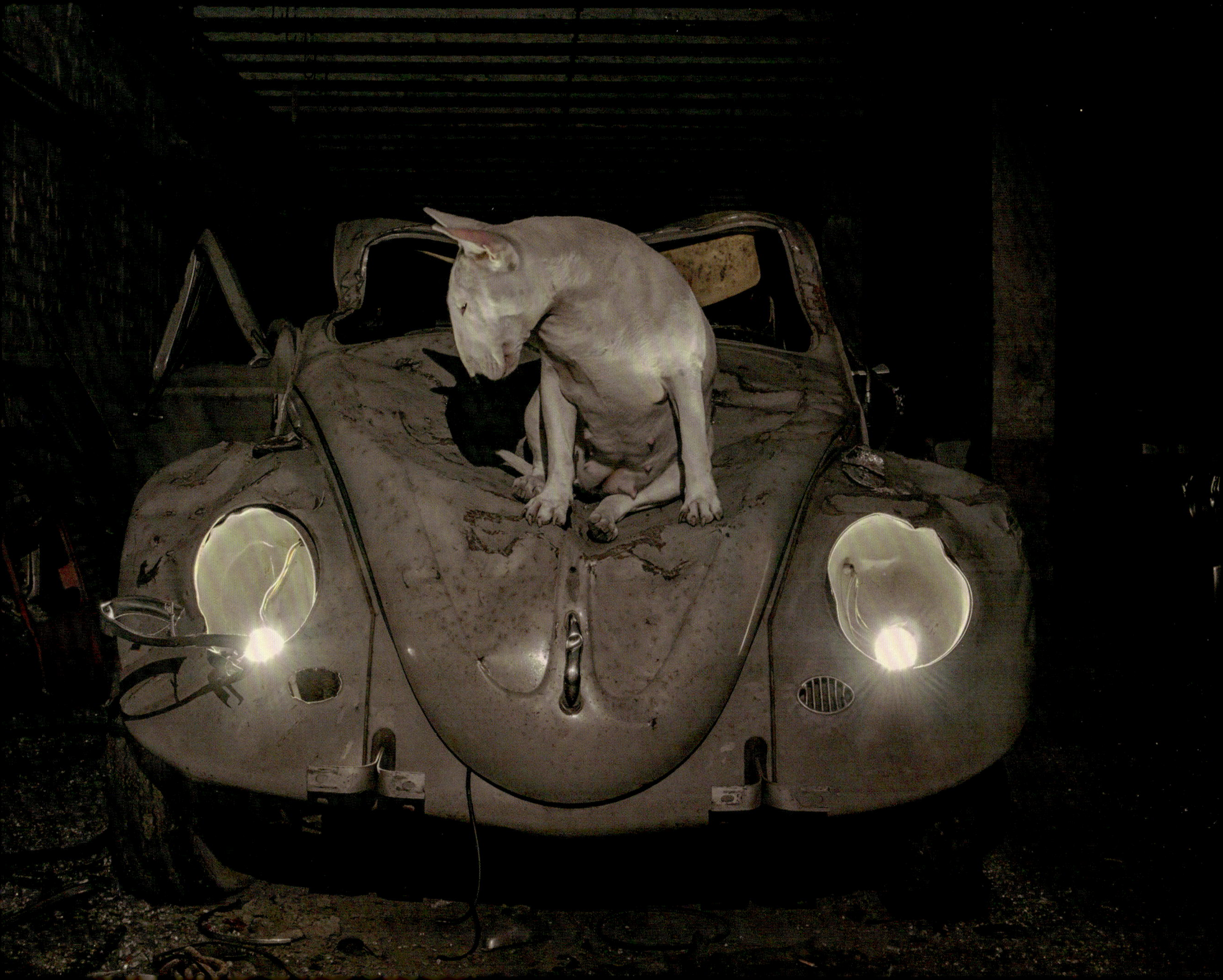

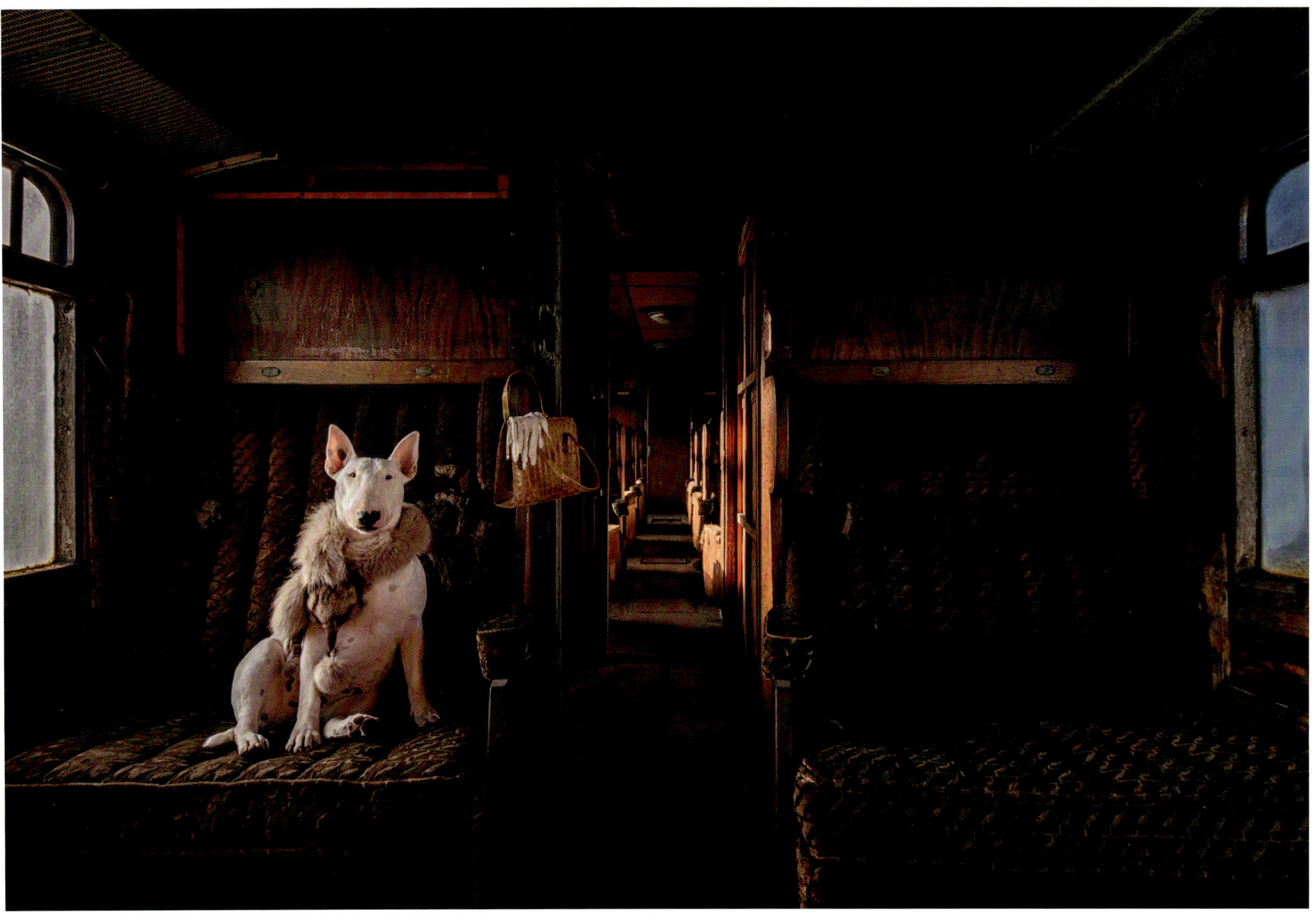

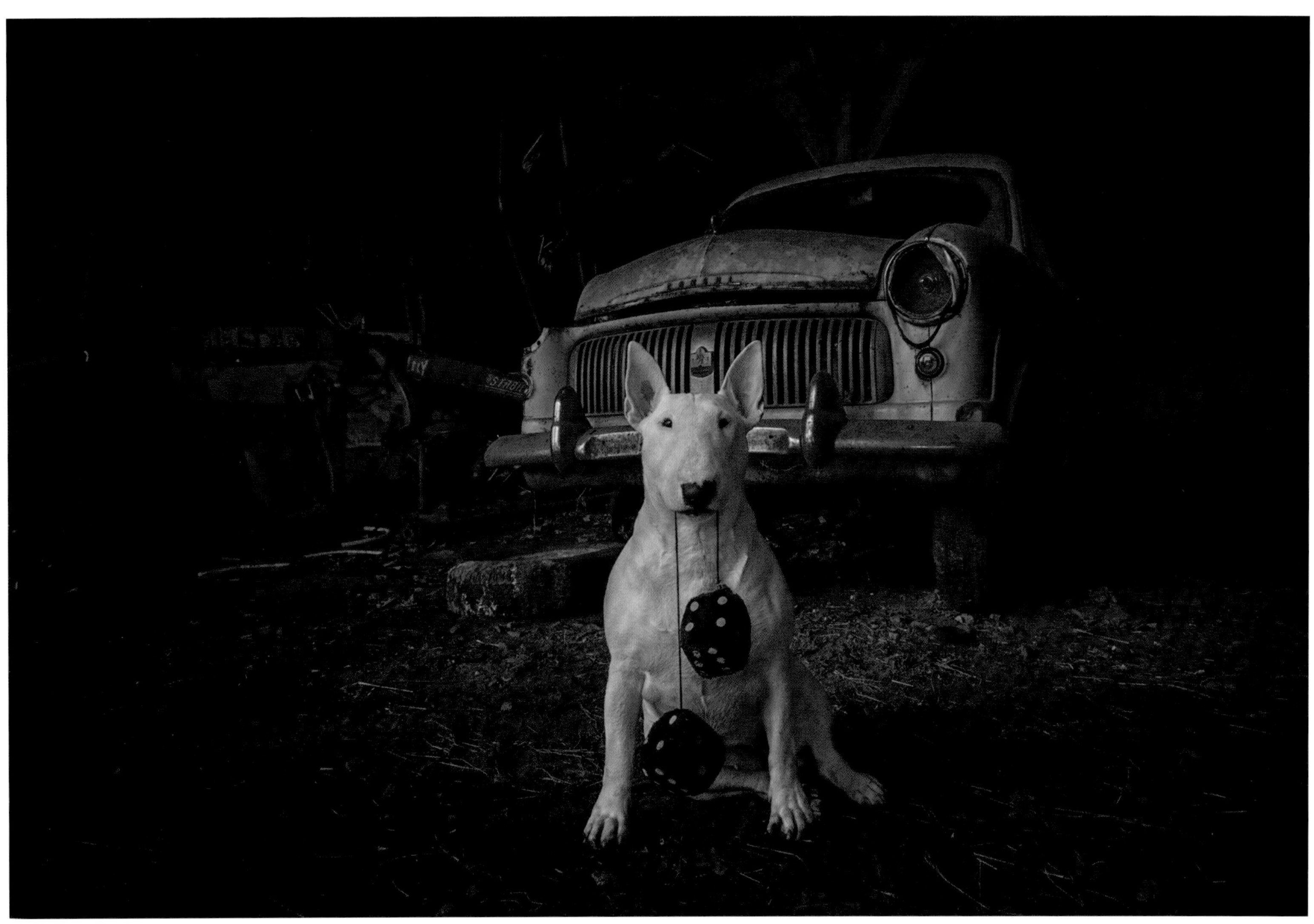

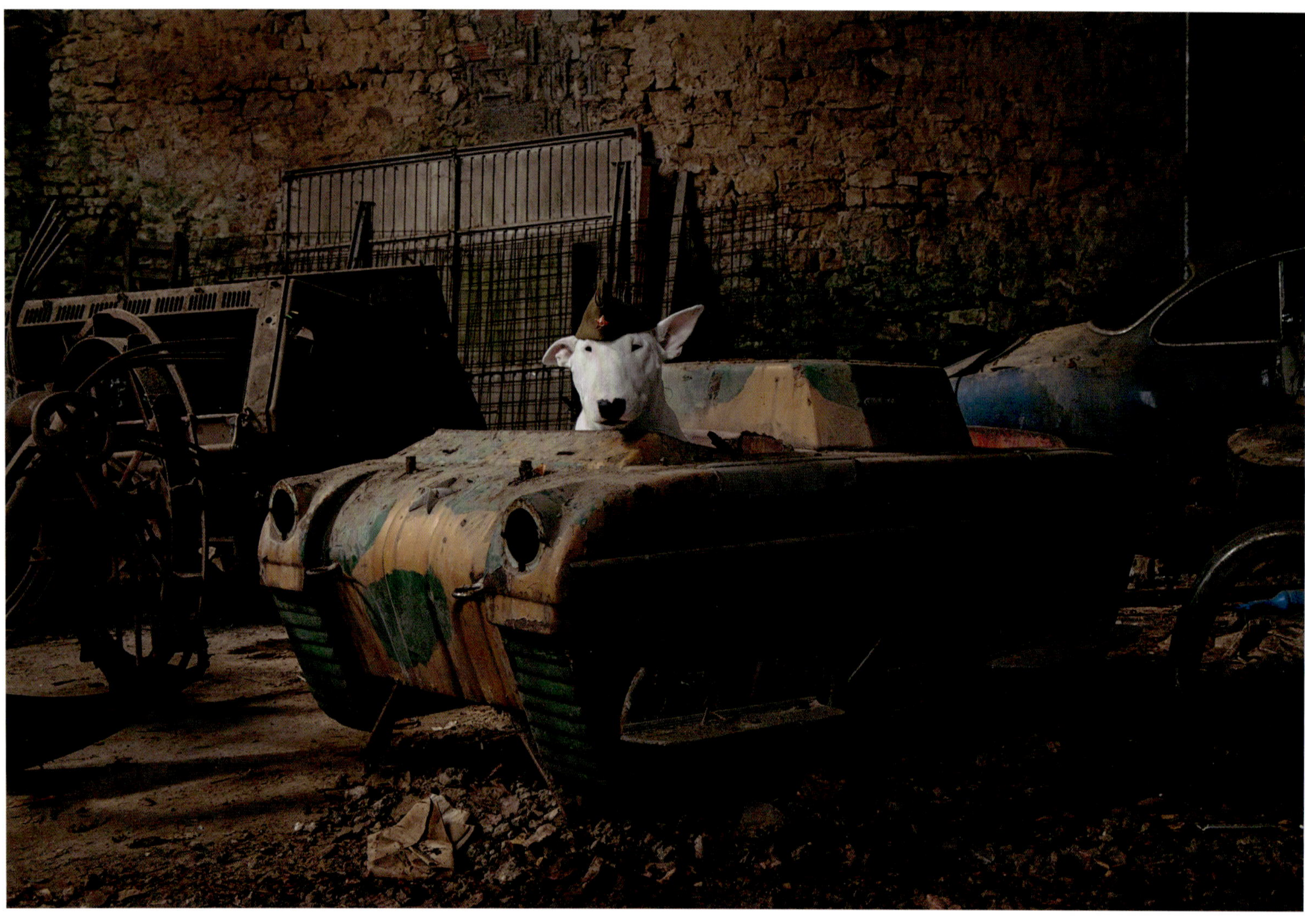

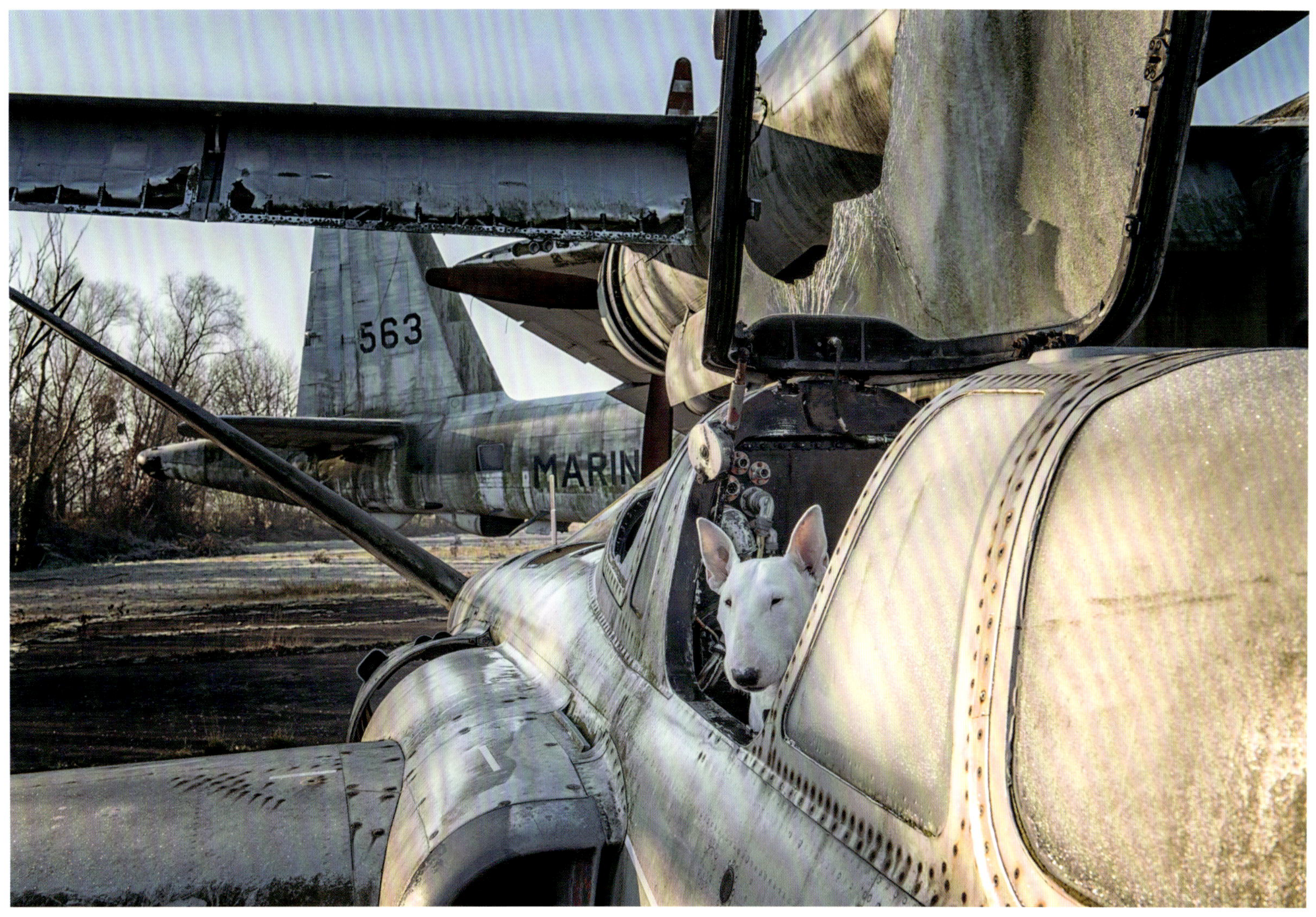

563
MARIN

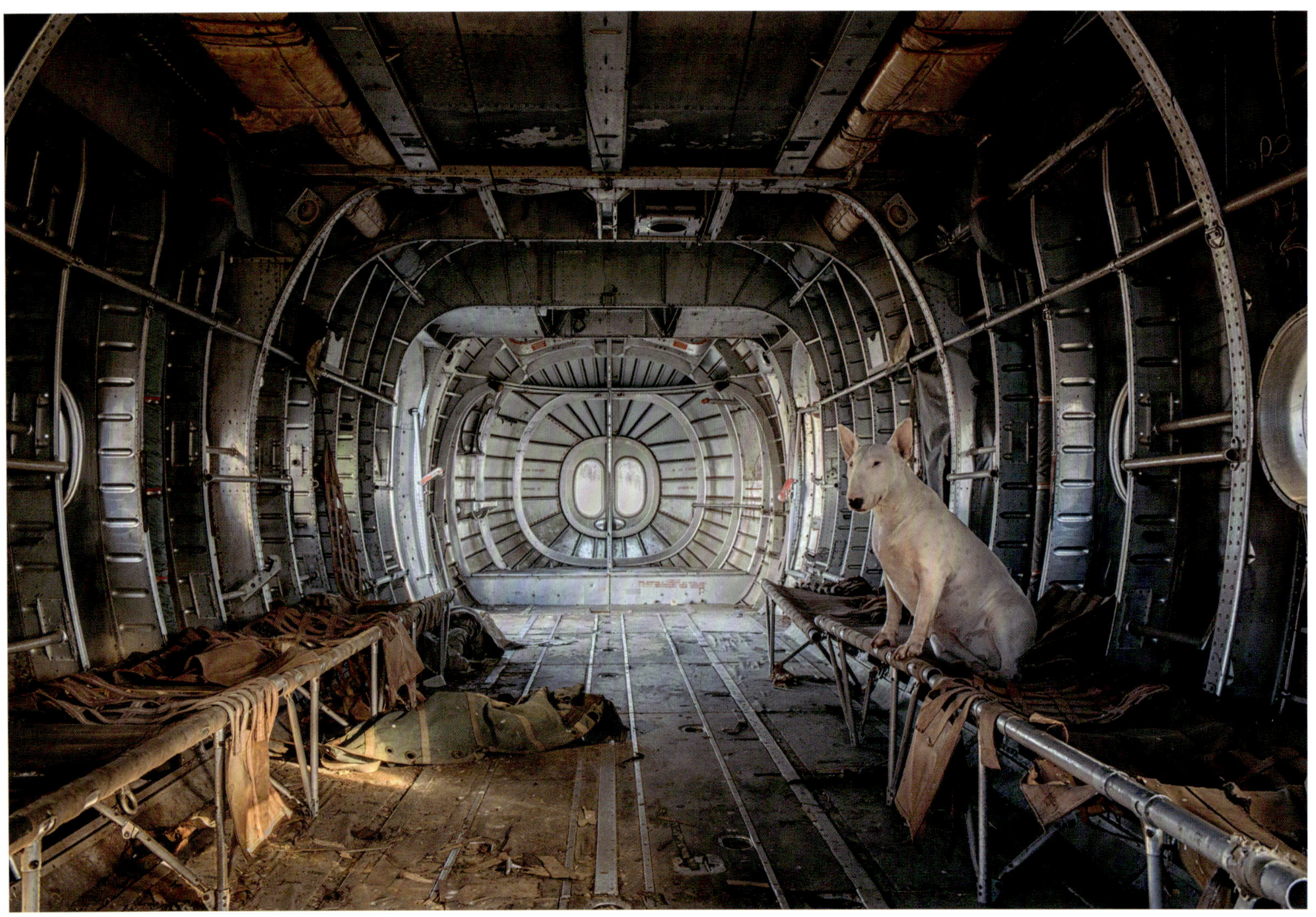

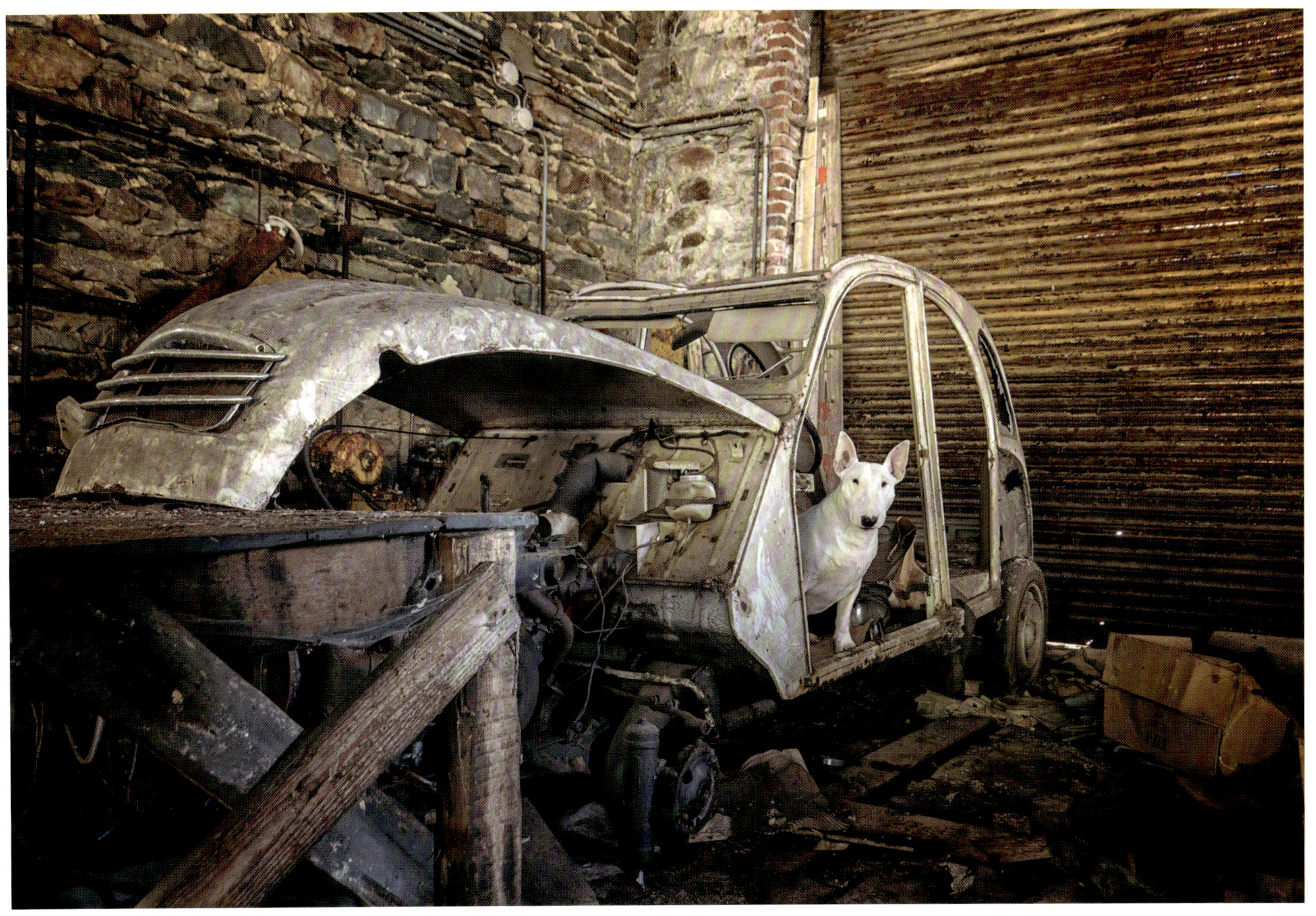

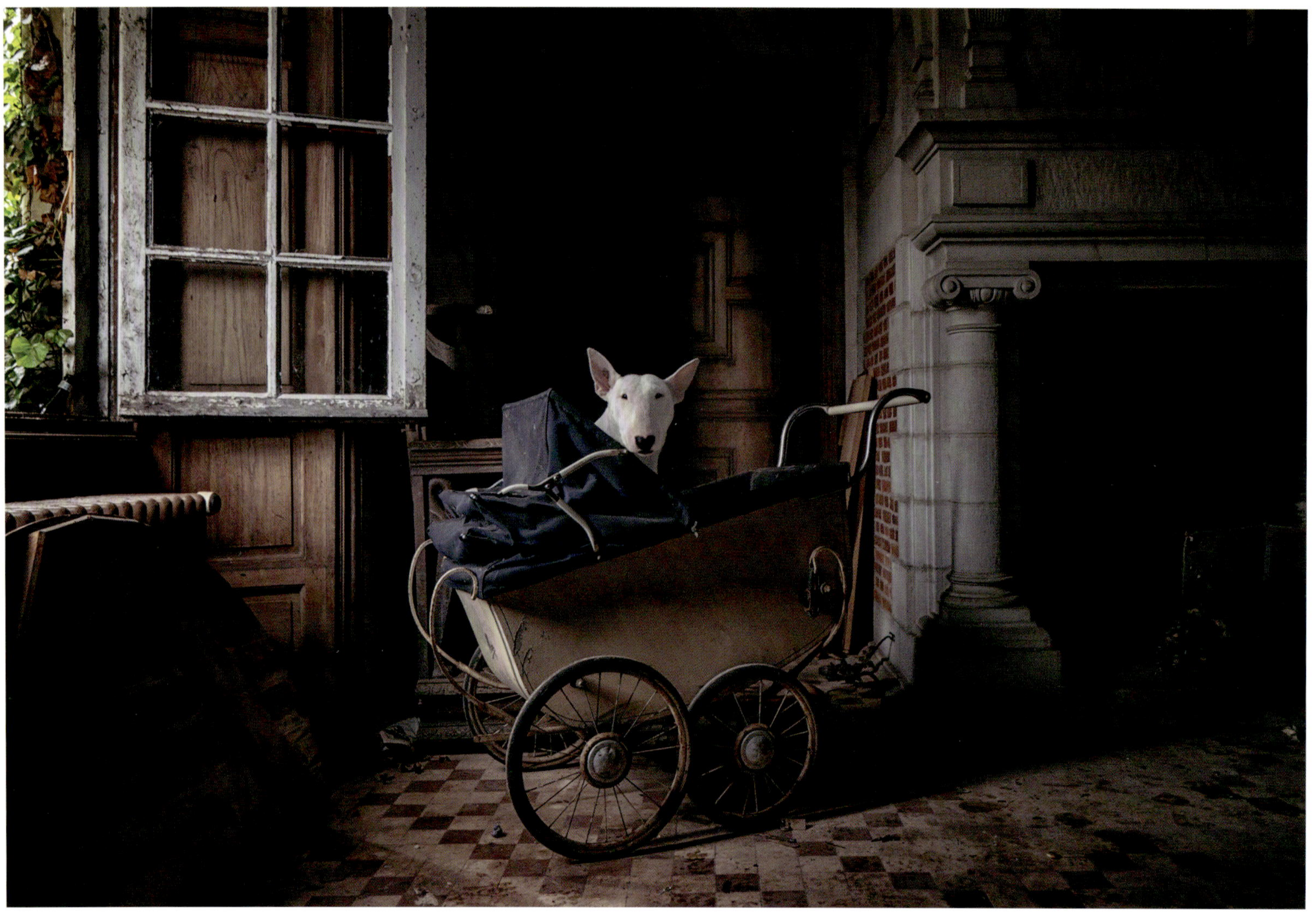

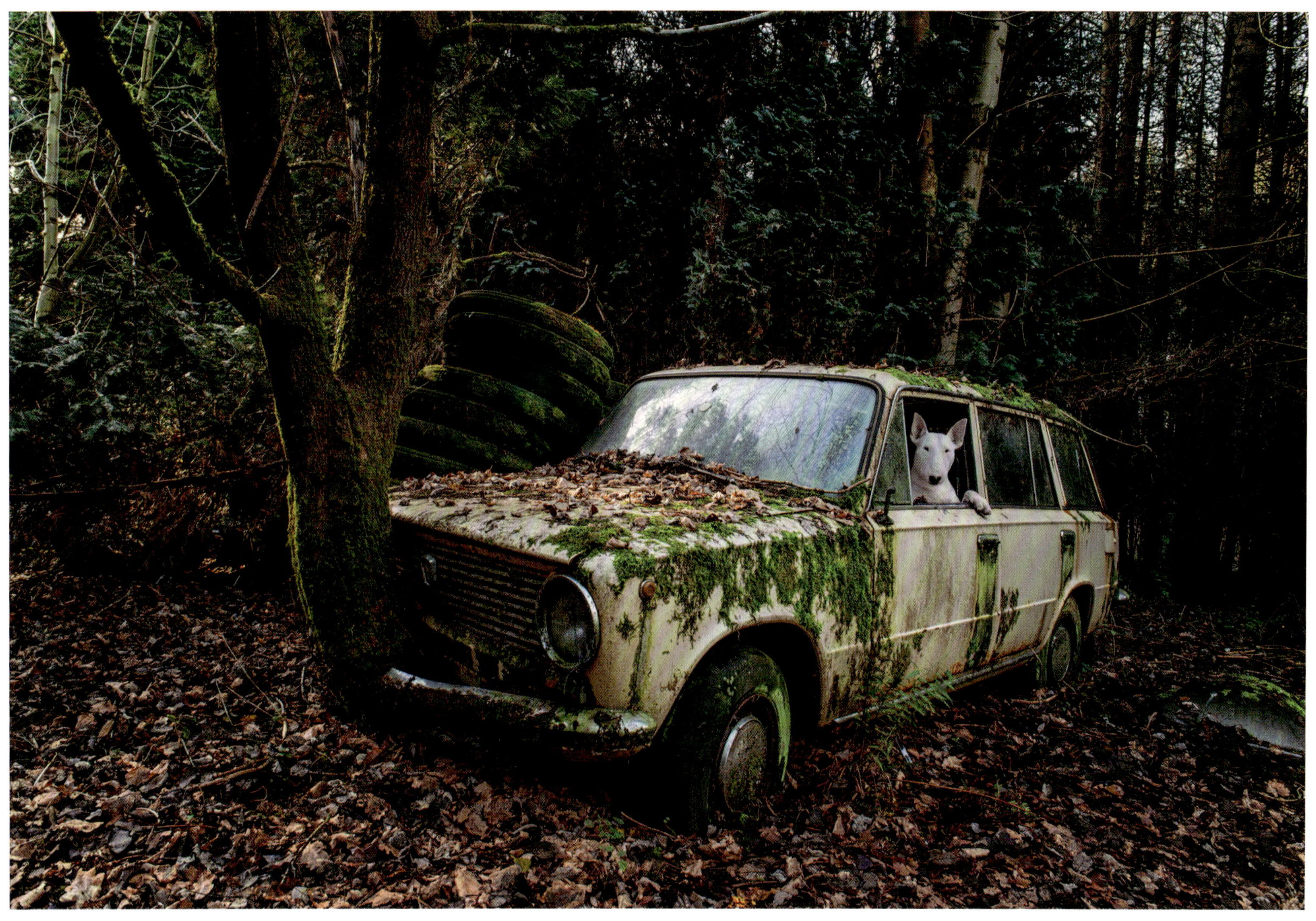

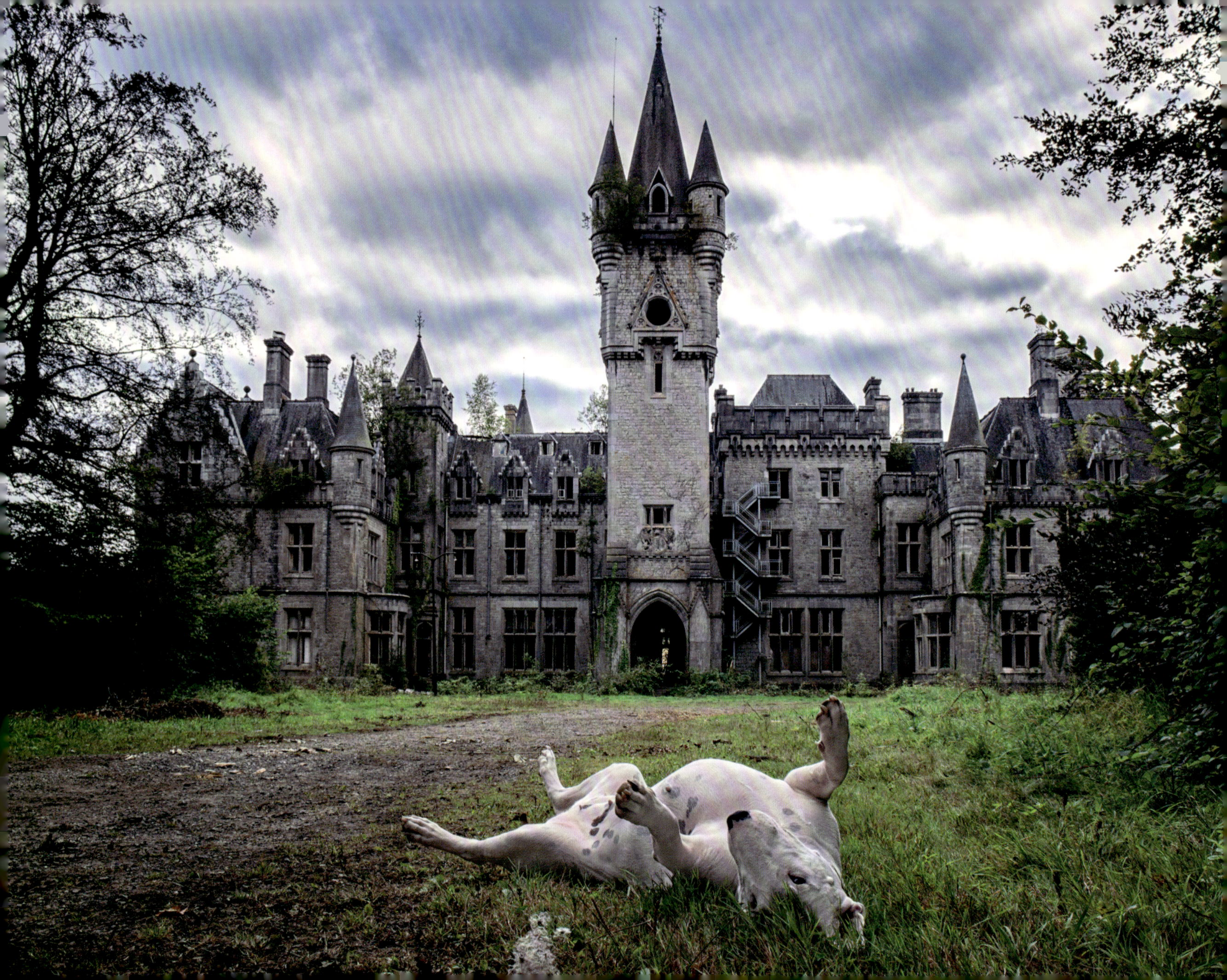

Château de Noisy

Belgium

Left Château de Noisy, ranked among the most beautiful forgotten places in the world, was considered by its owner as "neither more nor less than a folly of a great-great-grandfather."

n the beautiful southern corner of Belgium, forested hills are divided by deep, lush green valleys. The scenery is breathtaking and the wildlife is abundant; in the vast forests deer, wild boar, badgers and foxes all roam freely. In this fairytale landscape there are hundreds of castles open to the public, but one particular château used to attract a special kind of visitor: the urbexer.

The imposing neo-Gothic Château Miranda (or Château de Noisy as it was also previously known) was owned and constructed by the aristocratic Liedekerke-Beaufort family. During the French Revolution the family lost its home – Château de Vêves – and took refuge at a nearby farm. It was on the grounds of this farm that the descendants engaged the English architect Edward Milner to build Château Miranda. Milner was commissioned to build the castle in 1866, but died before it was completed, leaving a French architect named Pelchner to finish the project. This saw the Château extended and the addition of the famous tower. Construction was finally completed in 1907, at which point the castle became the summer residence for the aristocratic family.

Like many castles during Second World War, Château de Noisy was confiscated and occupied by the Nazis. Post-war, through to the late 1970s, it was used as an orphanage and holiday camp for children of employees of the National Railway Company of Belgium, before serving as a school in the 1980s. However, the castle was slowly starting to crumble and fungus was nibbling the wooden structure from the inside out. In 1991 the castle was abandoned and started its transition from a beautiful architectural masterpiece into a ruin.

The castle soon came to the attention of a small group of people who started to visit the building to capture the beauty of its decay. These first visitors probably went unnoticed by the castle's owner – Count Hadelin Liedekerke-Beaufort – and his gamekeeper, but as urban exploration gained popularity, urbexers from across Europe started making the pilgrimage to photograph the "fairytale Château".

As the number of visitors increased so too did the "scare stories" – some true, others less so. According to some, the heir and his gamekeeper would hunt for urbexers all day long, hiding in the park

"The castle was abandoned and started its transition from a beautiful architectural masterpiece into a ruin."

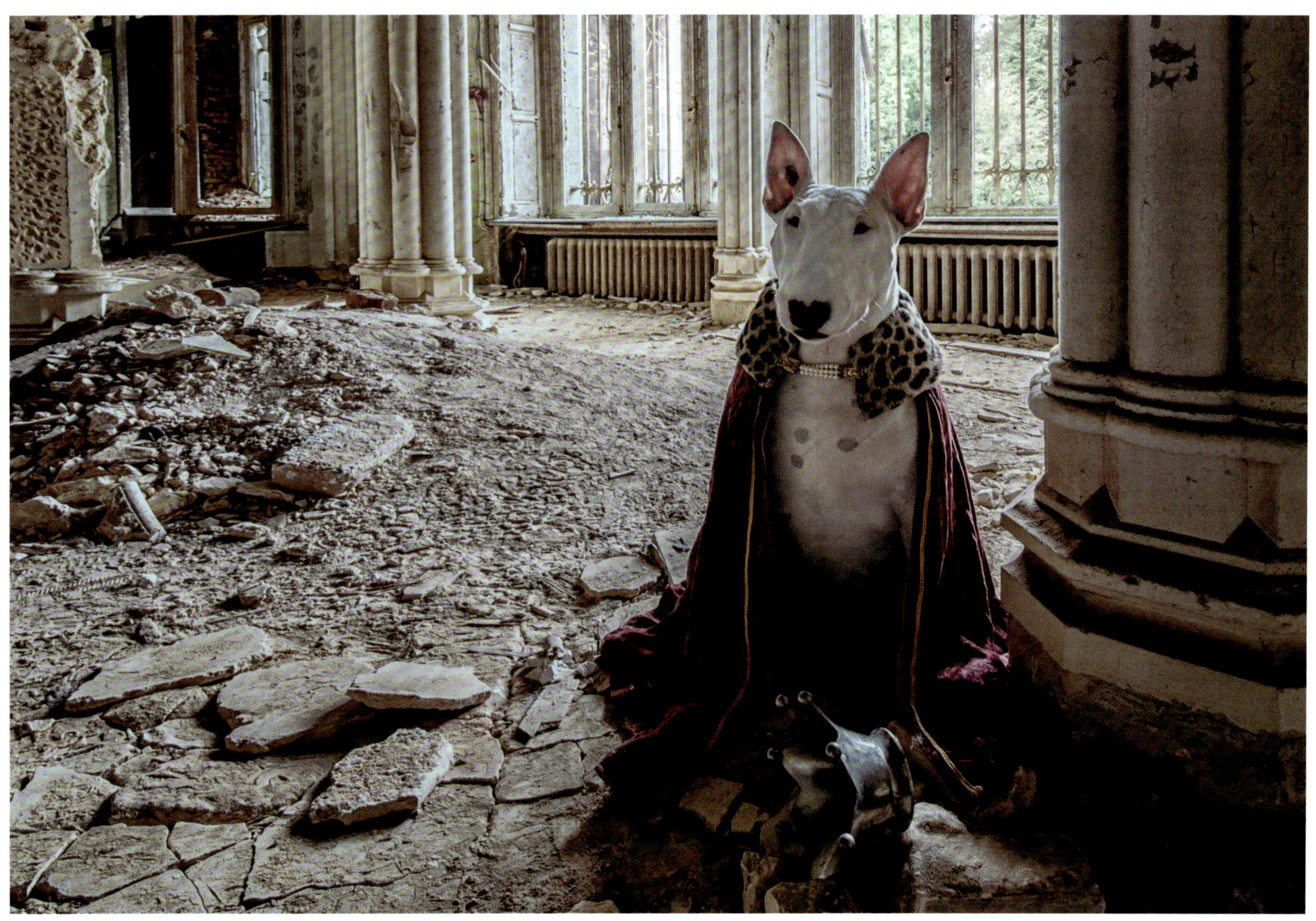

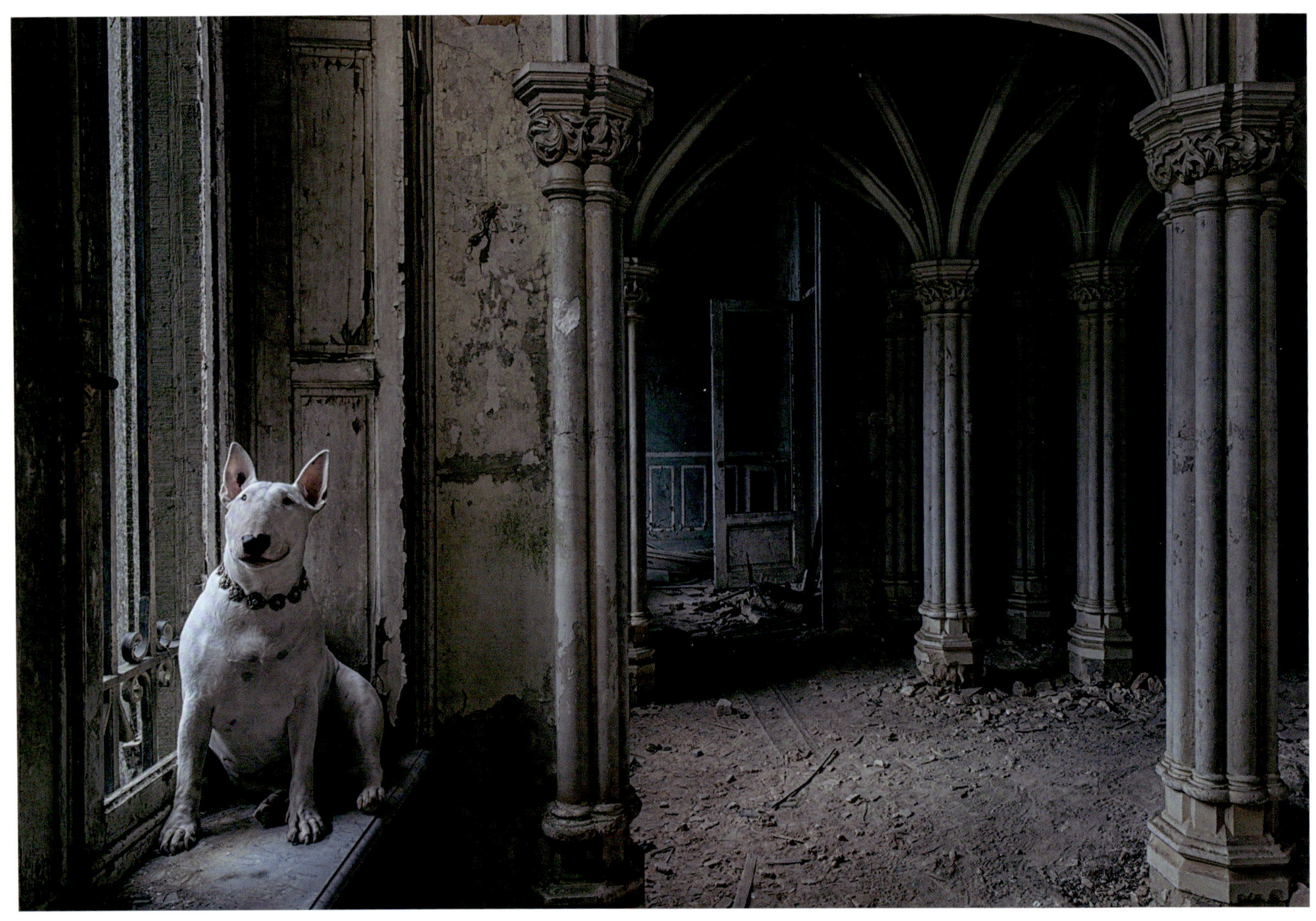

and shooting at trespassers with their hunting rifles. One of these stories even made the local newspaper, although how much of it was based on fact is impossible to ascertain.

What is true is that the gamekeeper would drive around the estate in his Jeep. If you were unfortunate to get caught by him, he would immediately eject you from the grounds, usually downhill and on the steepest side of a very steep hill, much to his own amusement. Introducing himself as "the police of the woods", the gamekeeper developed quite a reputation, so much so that he multiplied; there are stories of two gamekeepers, sometimes four and even eight. His dog also underwent transformations, turning from a friendly medium-sized dog into at least four pit bull terriers or three Rottweilers, depending on who was telling the tale.

Yet despite the stories, explorers continued to find their way to the castle. The exterior was as beautiful as ever, even though almost all of the 500 windows were broken and the walls had become a playground for young trees. However, inside the fungus continued eating the wooden structure; ceilings came tumbling down, there were no doors left to separate the rooms, and without a roof or windows the building was hit increasingly hard by wind, rain and snow, year after year.

In the years after the castle was abandoned, Count Liedekerke-Beaufort tried to find investors to save the building, but no one came forward. Finally, at the end of 2013, he applied for a demolition permit for the castle, citing increased illegal visits to the property: not only was there the very real risk of someone getting injured in the increasingly unstable property, but his gamekeeper had been assaulted and beaten by trespassers, resulting in him going to the hospital emergency room.

The permit was issued in July 2015 and demolition eventually started on 31 October 2016. One year later the process was complete; nothing remained of the once-glorious Château.

> *"The exterior was as beautiful as ever, even though almost all of the 500 windows were broken and the walls had become a playground for young trees."*

Villa Falconetti
The Netherlands

Right Claire poses in the doorway that leads into the kitchen. It was here, on the evening of 26 April 1994, that the villa's final owner, Antonio Brizzi, was found dead.

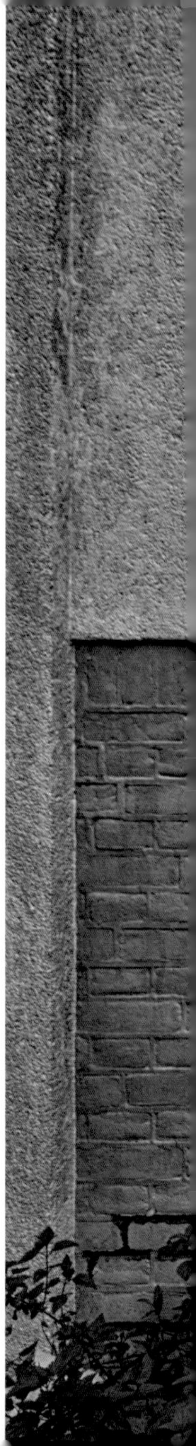

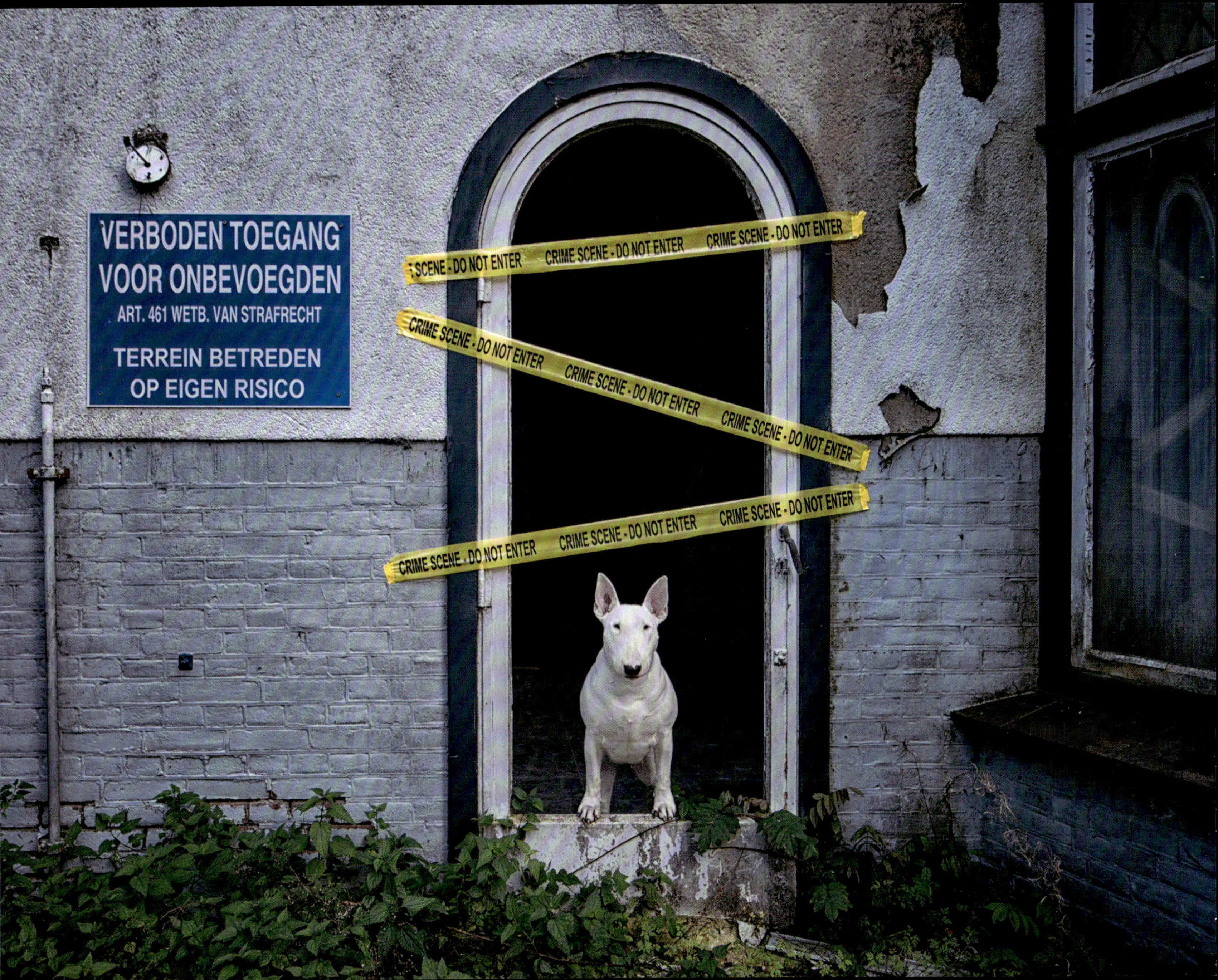

VERBODEN TOEGANG
VOOR ONBEVOEGDEN
ART. 461 WETB. VAN STRAFRECHT
TERREIN BETREDEN
OP EIGEN RISICO
CRIME SCENE - DO NOT ENTER

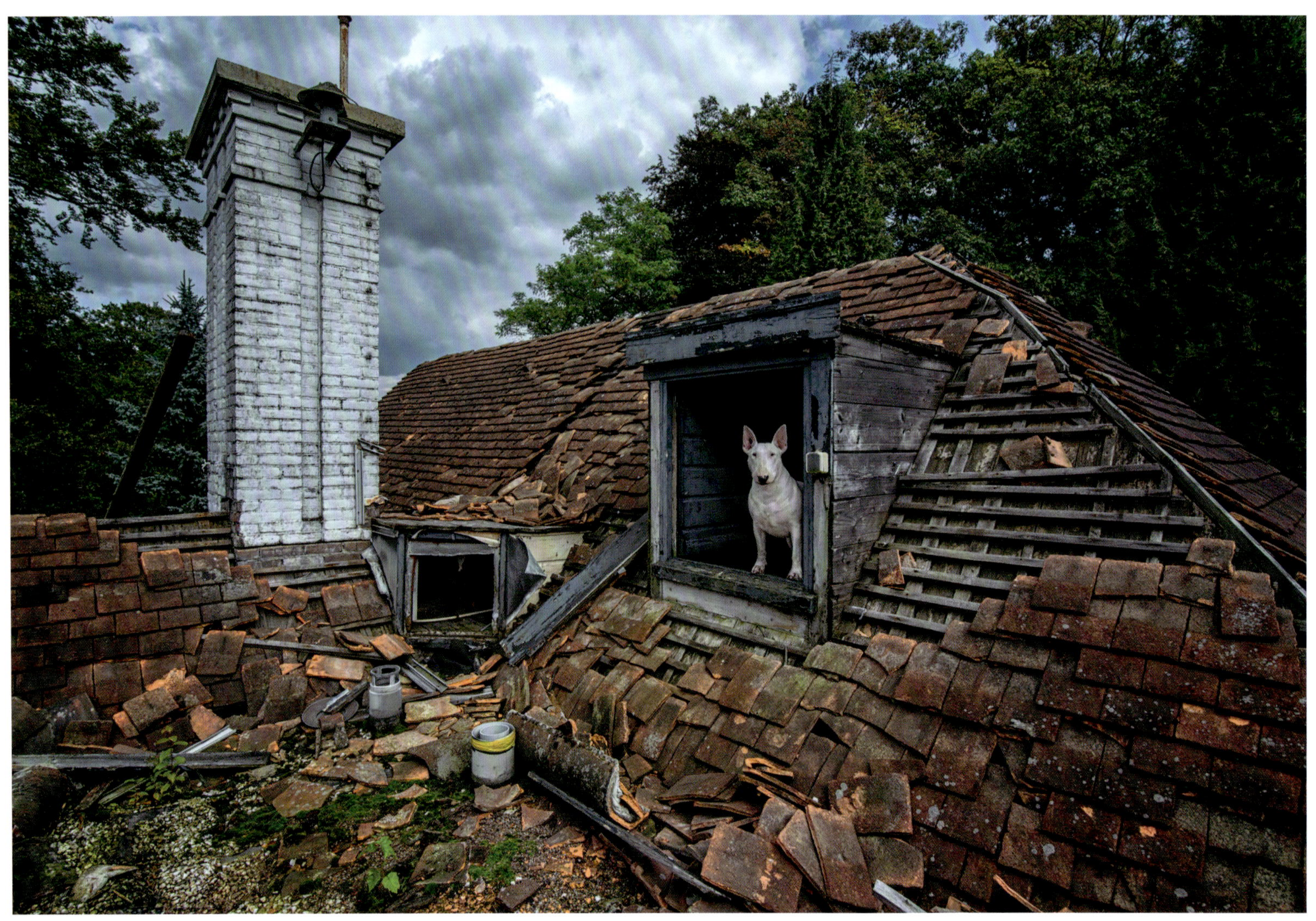

It is Tuesday evening on 26 April 1994 and a white Fiat Panda has got stuck in the mud on a dirt road in North Brabant. The man walks to the nearest house, Villa Falconetti, where Antonio Brizzi is watching television. Brizzi doesn't know the man standing at his gate, but he starts up his tractor and pulls the stranger's car out of the mud, before inviting him inside for a drink.

While the men talk and drink beer at the large kitchen table, Brizzi's girlfriend – Simone – enters the room; she's going to call the doctor, as their young daughter is complaining of earache. The doctor tells Simone to come over with her daughter and the pair leave at 10:15pm, at around the same time that Brizzi tells his guest he wants to watch the sports news on television. As Simone drives towards the villa's large gate she sees the stranger in the white Fiat Panda in her rear-view mirror, following her down the driveway; when she returns home at around 11pm, she will find Brizzi lying dead on the kitchen floor, shot three times and covered in blood.

Antonio Brizzi was born on 15 July 1953 to a blue-collar family, but didn't finish his education. Instead, he embarked on a life of crime that was rumoured to involve drug trafficking, illegal gambling, illegal cigarette trade, extortion and prostitution. He became a leading figure in the underworld in the southern part of the Netherlands and was convicted at least once.

However, in the early 1990s Brizzi decided to leave his criminal past behind, buying Villa Falconetti for one and a half million guilders in cash. His luxury villa included an indoor swimming pool, horse stables and a small zoo with 32 kangaroos (among other animals). But his new-found life came to an abrupt end on that fateful April evening. The villa was subsequently abandoned around 2010 and fell into decline. Fire destroyed several of the empty property's outbuildings in 2013, as well as damaging the villa itself in what some considered to be a deliberate arson attack.

If Brizzi were still alive, I would never have dared to enter his property, but now I step through a big hole in the fence without hesitation. The house and the outbuildings are completely trashed, so I decide to put Claire's boots on; four special shoes with leather soles that are designed to protect her feet from glass and other sharp objects. Within minutes we're standing in the kitchen where Brizzi was murdered. It feels a bit weird to be here, but the only thing that remains from the former resident is the large kitchen table where Brizzi and his supposed murderer – who has never been identified – drank a beer together.

Claire poses in a couple of spots, but there's nothing that special to find in the house; everything is trashed and much has been destroyed by fire. Ultimately, the story behind the villa is far more interesting than the location itself.

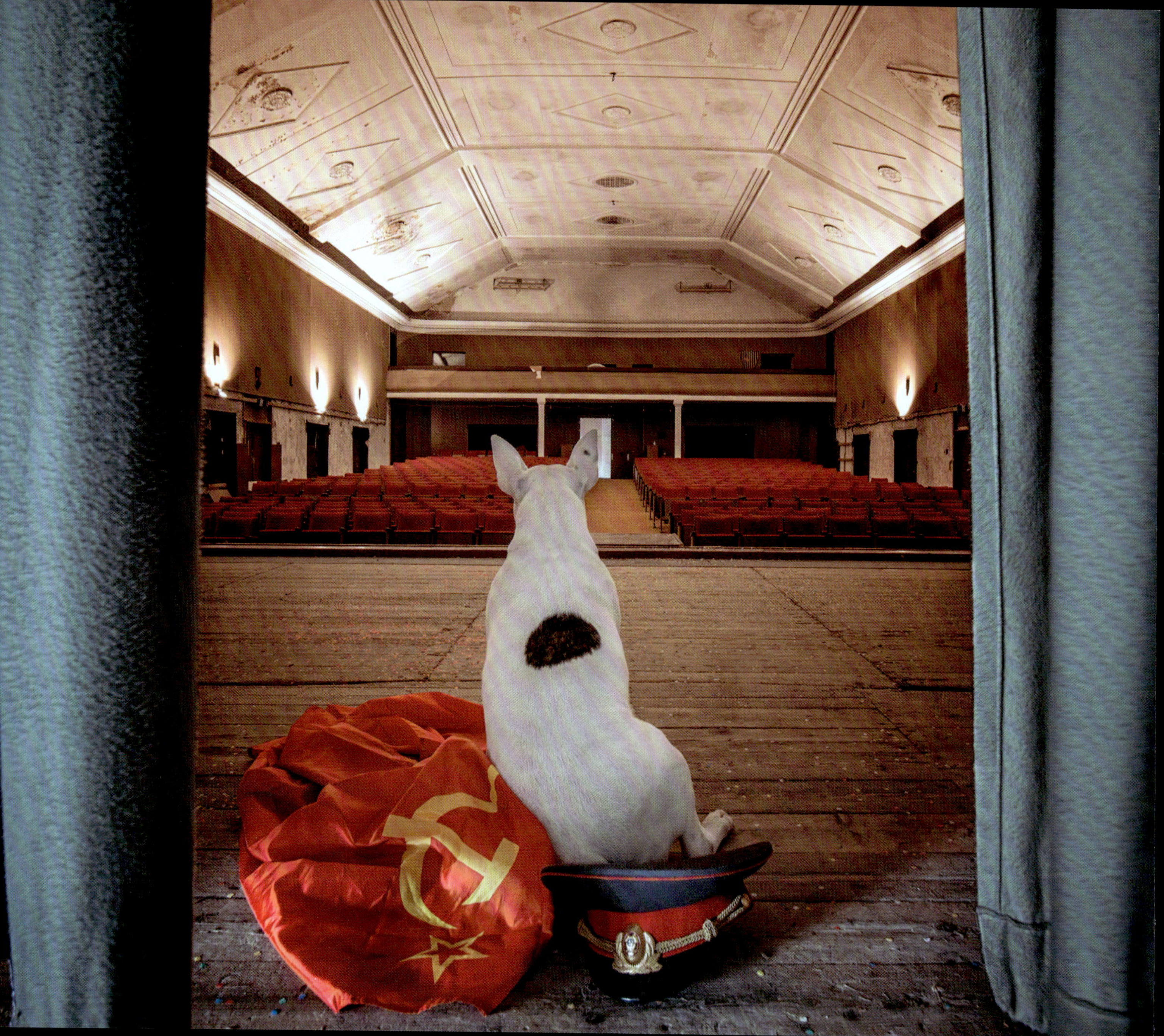

The Forbidden City
Germany

Left Claire's performance is as brilliant as ever; she sits still for almost two seconds while I take her photograph looking out over an imaginary audience.

Once surrounded by almost 75,000 comrades, Lenin now stares across an abandoned, overgrown sports field where Soviet soldiers used to march. After the German reunification almost every statue of Vladimir Lenin was melted, demolished, buried or sold abroad. A few of them survived, though, including this one, which stands in front of the Haus der Offiziere in the town of Wünsdorf, near Berlin.

The town has a long military history. The area was first militarized after the German Empire was founded on 18 January 1871, and then became the headquarters of the Wehrmacht – the unified armed forces of Nazi Germany – shortly before the outbreak of the Second World War.

After the war, Wünsdorf fell under Soviet control. The Red Army high command moved in and expanded the military complex to create the largest Soviet military camp outside Russia. Closed off from the outside world and encircled by an 11-mile (18km) long concrete wall, people referred to Wünsdorf as "Little Moscow" – a Soviet city in the heart of Germany. The city was completely self-sufficient; it had its own schools, hotels, stadiums, bakeries, hairdressers, gyms, a swimming pool, a theatre and a hospital. It even had its own direct railway line to Moscow, and every Thursday night a train would leave for the Russian capital.

"Although it should have been completely inaccessible there were always ways in," says Jurgen Naumann, who now takes care of the buildings and the surrounding area, checking for damage, arranging repairs and keeping an eye out for unwanted visitors. "Soviet soldiers were bribed by East German consumers who wanted to shop at the stores; it was cheap and you could buy things that you couldn't get outside. You had to be very careful to be back out by around 4pm, though. If you were too late you would be held for 24 hours and made to peel potatoes for the troops."

Naumann can talk for hours and hours and he is very entertaining, but we are here to take photographs. He hands us a map with all the buildings drawn on it and points out each building that we are allowed to visit, which includes the swimming pool. I am so sad about the decline of this beautiful pool; the original ceramic tiles and murals date back to 1890 and it was in pristine condition when the Russians left in September 1994. Naumann also suggests we visit the theatre, where the Bolshoi Ballet performed, telling us "there is a light switch just around the left corner where you come in."

As we part company with Naumann, my friends head for the swimming pool, while I decide to check the theatre first. It feels kind of strange to switch the light on at an abandoned location, but this is a legal visit and without the light it is pitch-black. Even with the lights turned on it is still dark inside, but you can imagine how it would have been.

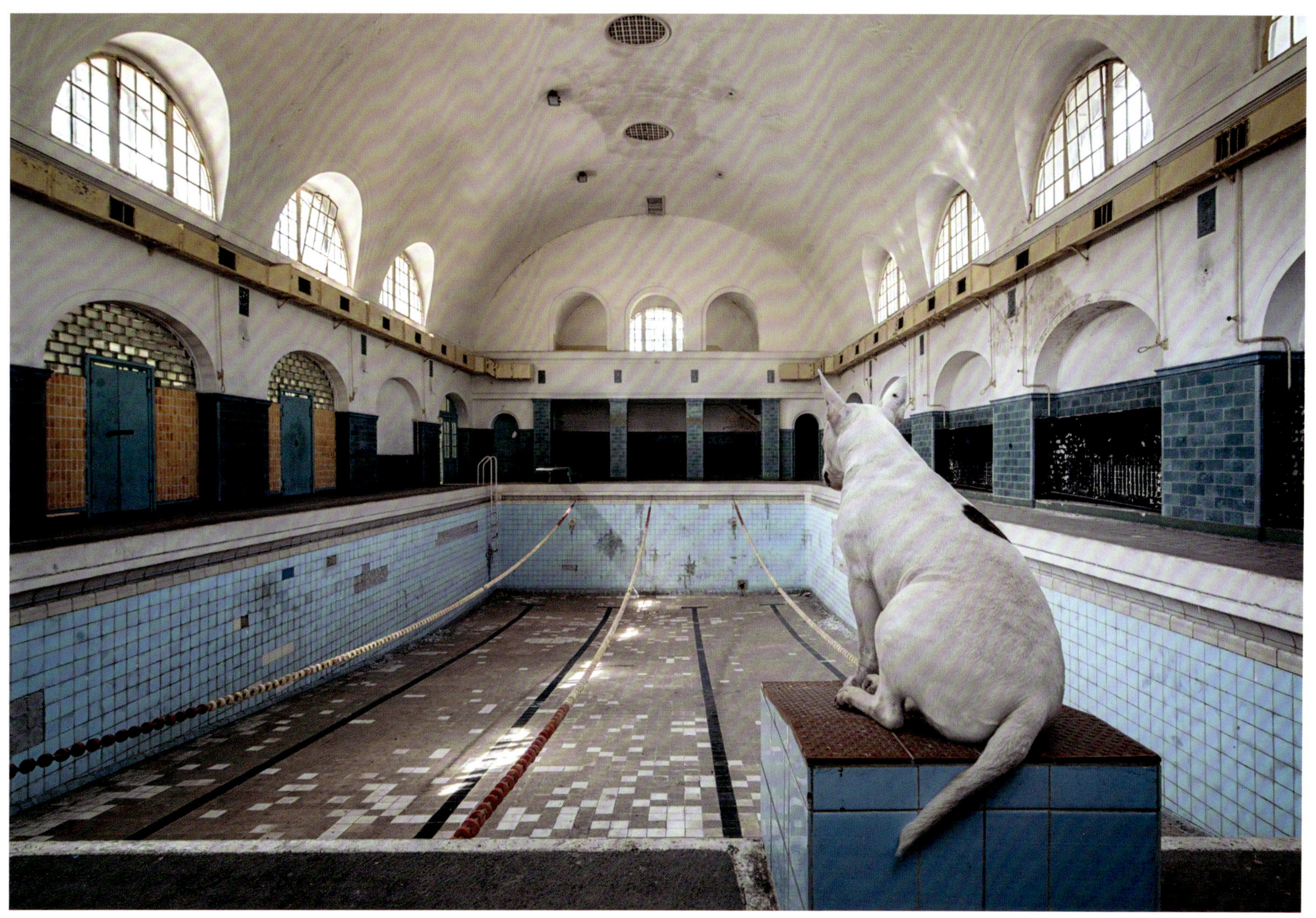

Manoir Colimaçon
France

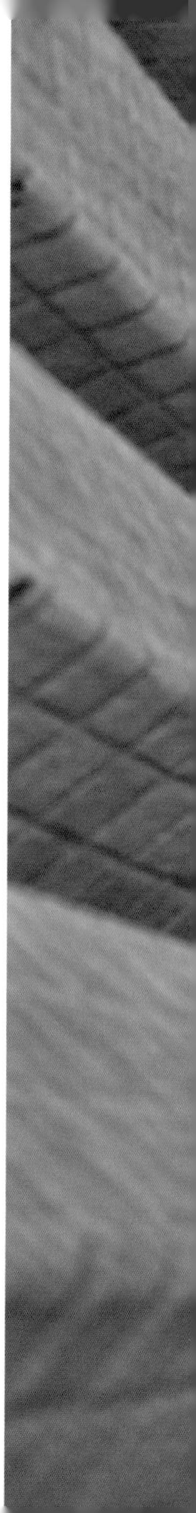

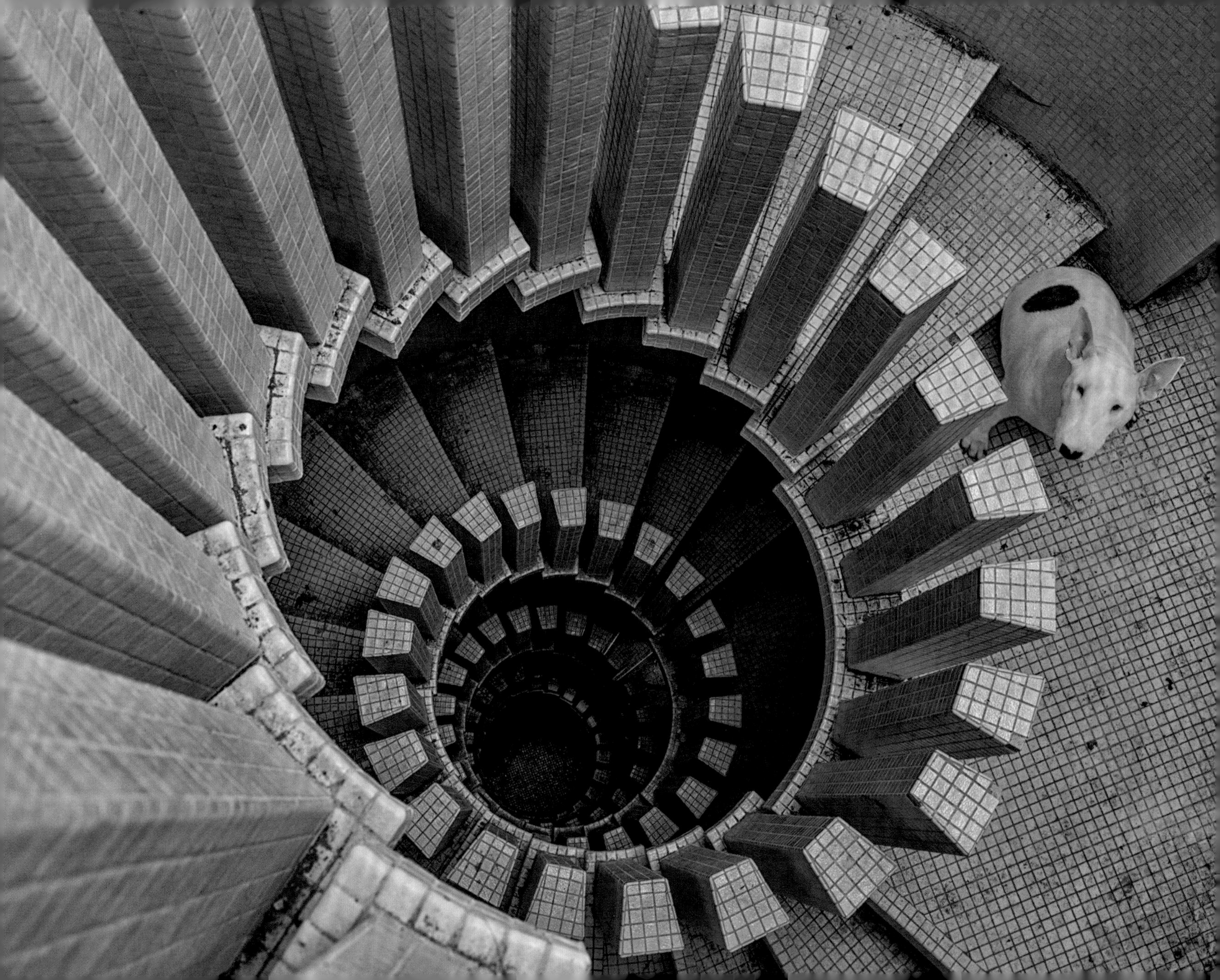

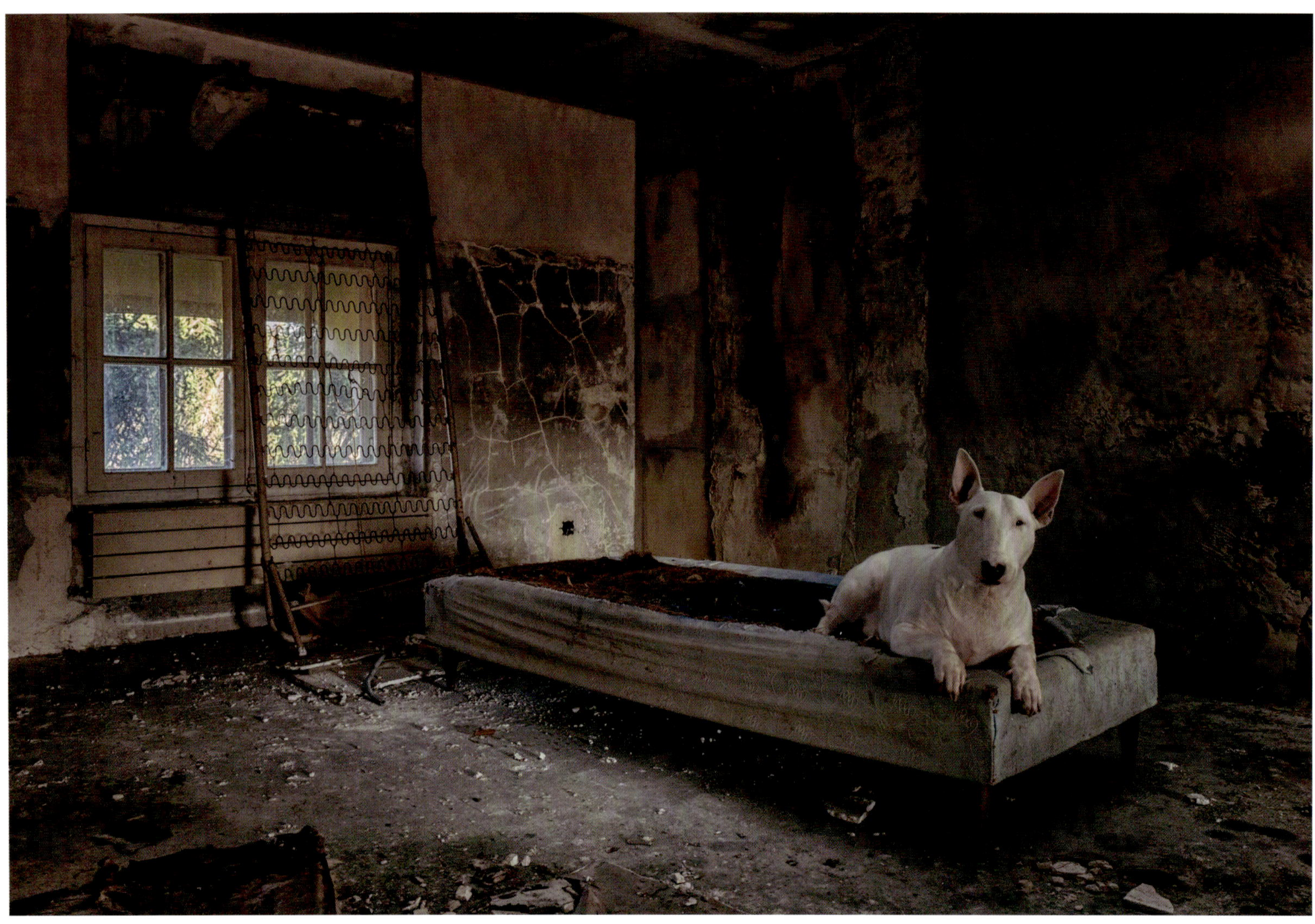

There are some locations that you hear the wildest stories about. Sometimes the stories are made up, sometimes they are grossly exaggerated, but in the case of this mansion I really believe the stories are true.

The house is built on the foundations of an old castle and was designed by the well-known French architect Marcel Oudin, even though its Victorian look is very different to the Art Deco designs he is known for. In 1976, an Iranian engineer bought the house and lived there for three years while he undertook extensive renovation work. During this time his neighbour reportedly made his life unbearable and the new owner eventually abandoned the house without putting it up for sale. The Iranian – who now lives in the United States – has subsequently informed the local mayor that he has no desire to live in his house, and nor does he intend to sell it; he's obviously content with the fact that it is gradually decaying.

Now, if someone manages to make the rightful owner of a property abandon a house that he has been painstakingly renovating for three years, there's a very strong possibility that other "horror stories" are true as well. Before we head to the house I have already heard that the neighbour slashes the tyres of any car parked in the vacant property's driveway and that he even shoots at people with his shotgun. It is claimed that he keeps sheep on his neighbour's land, which act as "guard sheep", bleating loudly when they see strangers on the premises, signalling him to pick up his shotgun and go in search of intruders…

Whether this is an urban myth or not, my friends and I decide to park our car far away from our destination, completely out of sight. As soon as possible we get off the road and walk across farmland towards the mansion. We climb over a fence and then we see them: the sheep. Fortunately, they are grazing on the opposite side of the premises, but we are now super-alert, in case the neighbour is prowling around somewhere. When I spot empty red shotgun shells lying on the ground I decide to keep quiet so I don't scare my friends.

The house is old and dilapidated, and while it must have been beautiful once, I see very few beautiful places to photograph. The only thing that draws me is the spiral staircase running up five floors from the basement; I take some photos of Claire at the staircase and wait for the others to be finished.

As we are about to leave, one of my friends looks out of the window and, clearly startled, whispers "The sheep are right outside!" We have no option, but to wait while they slowly pass the house, grazing, hoping they aren't alerted to our presence. When we think it's safe we leave the building and we don't hang around!

Left The old villa was completely empty except for this old bed. Claire caused a huge dust cloud by jumping on it.

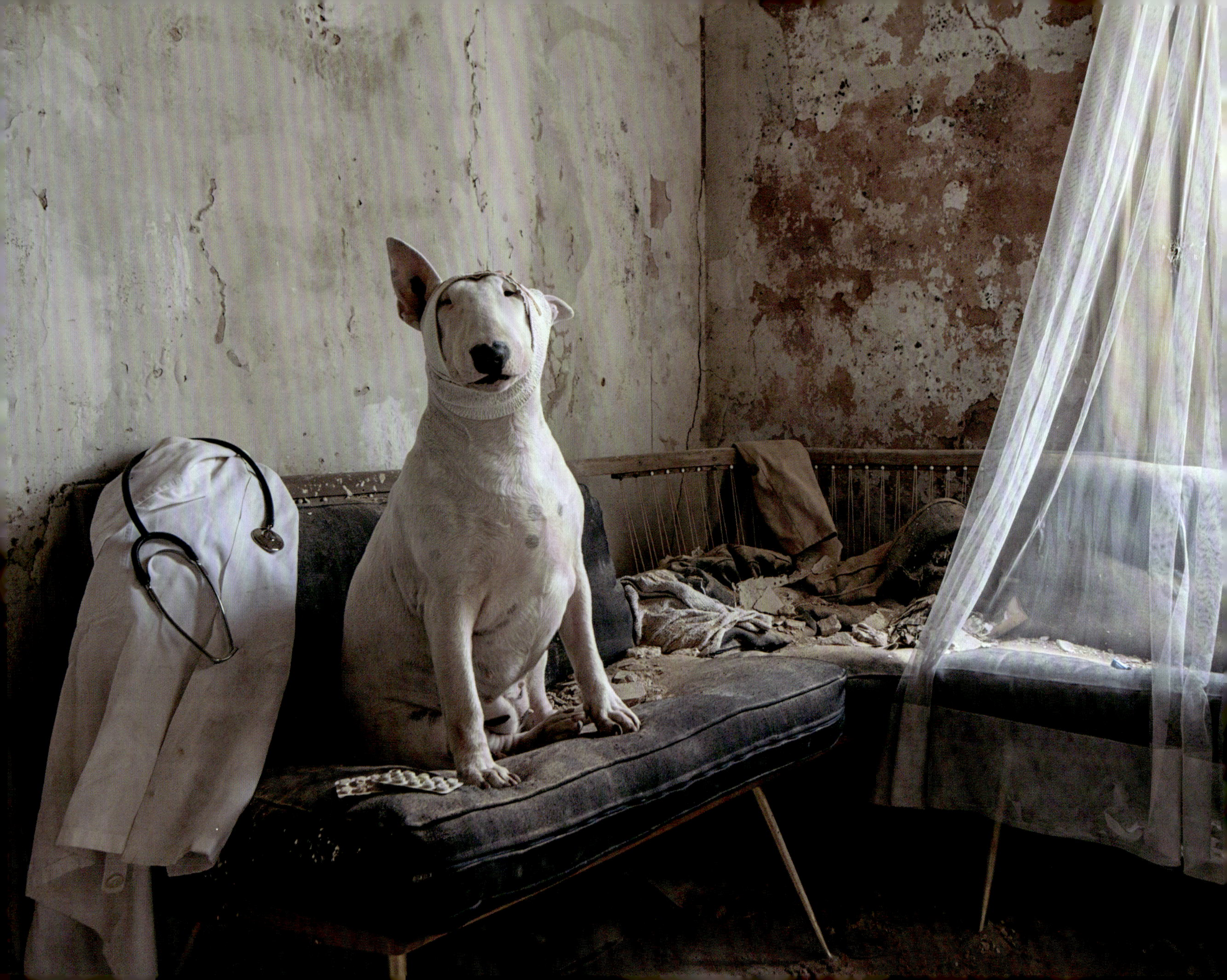

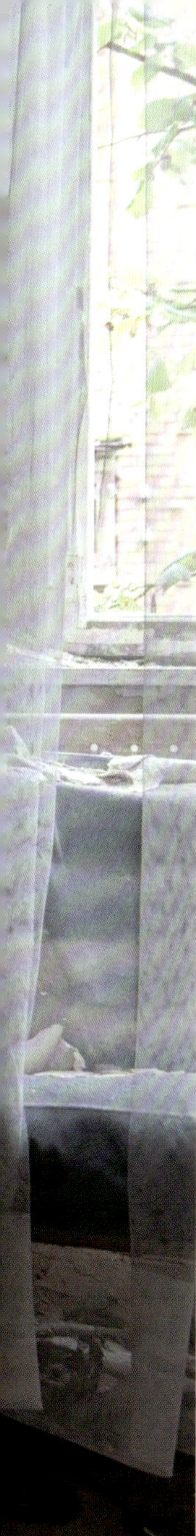

Dr Anna L
Germany

Left There are no signs of "Dr Anna",
and that's because she never lived here.
Instead she occupied the house next door
and her stepson, Dr Klaus K, lived and
worked in the practice.

Mention a Grotrian-Steinweg piano and human organs in formaldehyde, and urbexers worldwide will simultaneously think of Dr Anna L. For almost 30 years the house and its practice were abandoned, although it was not until early 2012 that the first photos of this furnished house – still full of personal belongings – appeared on the internet. Since then it has become one of the most popular destinations in Germany for urban explorers from around the globe.

Looking at those very first photos it is noticeable that the house was already extremely messy – presumably, one or more burglars gained access to the property before explorers discovered it. There is also considerable decay caused by years of abandonment: wallpaper hangs in shreds, walls are covered in mould and plaster ceilings have crumbled to the ground.

Nevertheless, you can tell it must have been a delightful home: the living areas on the upper floors are decorated with style, with lots of interesting art and stuffed animals; wardrobes are filled with classy clothes; and the library overlooking the garden is well-stocked. The doctor's practice is housed in the basement and all the equipment and furniture is still present.

However, over the years the house has been "redecorated" by visitors several times. Very personal belongings have been displayed, photographed and published on the internet, while stuffed animals have "walked" from one room to another and back again, a mummified raccoon accompanying them on their journey. At the same time valuable items and artworks have disappeared entirely, including a set of silkscreen prints by Leonor Fini, entitled *Metamorphosis of a Woman*.

Finding the place was easy: loads of photographs have been published since the property's discovery and these gave me enough clues to trace the location. Getting there was more of a problem, though, as I couldn't find anyone willing to come with Claire and me. Eventually, I decided I didn't want to wait any longer and got up in the middle of the night to drive with Claire to Dr Anna L.

> *"The living areas on the upper floors are decorated with style, with lots of interesting art and stuffed animals."*

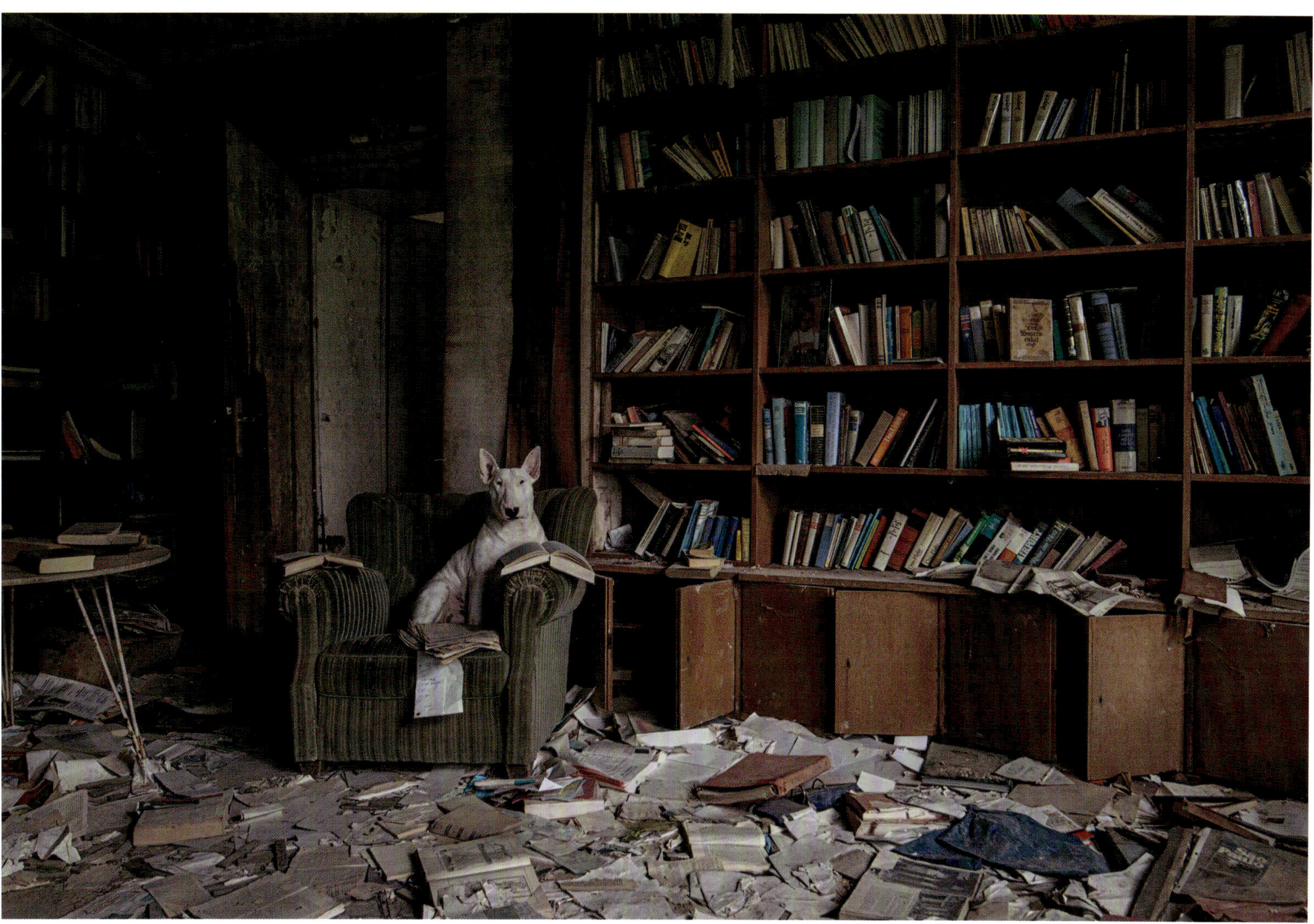

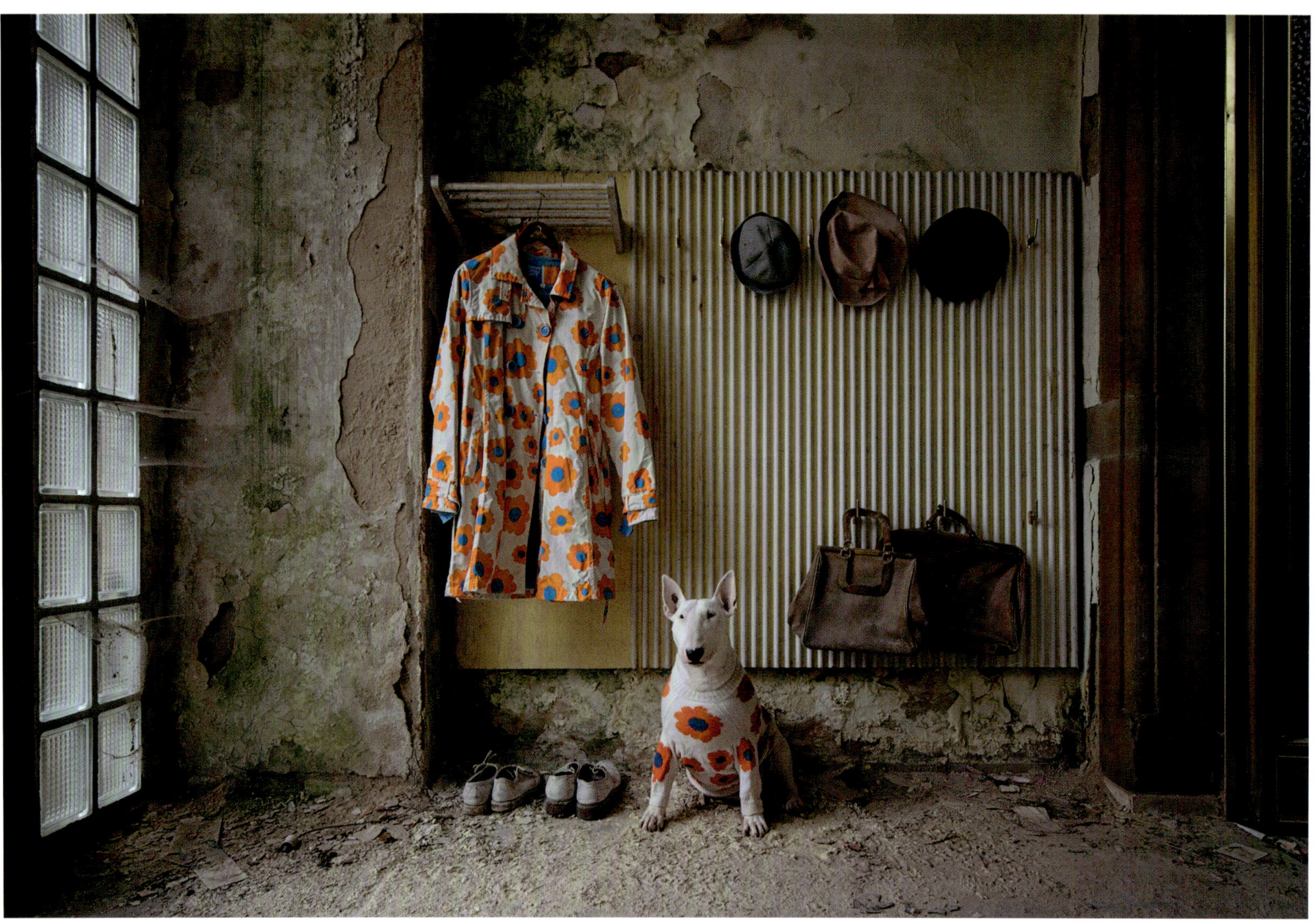

We arrive just before dawn and step over the fence and on to the property without being noticed. We walk through the open back door and into the library. The whole place is a mess and I definitely think I waited too long to visit. However, looking through the ruins I can see some interesting spots where I can photograph Claire; the piano is beautiful, as is the hall, and even the surgery room offers the potential for a nice picture. Claire and I spend five hours in the house before we start the 300-mile (500km) journey back home.

After my visit I come up with several new ideas that I want to photograph, so a second visit to Dr Anna L takes place a few months later. This time, I make a four-day trip through Germany with a friend and this is the first location we visit. We arrive at night and park our camper in the vicinity of the building, planning to visit very early, as construction workers are working in the building next door. We needn't have worried though – the construction workers do not even look up when we walk through the bushes to the back of the house. They are probably used to the daily pilgrimages.

As well as my camera bag and tripod I am carrying a number of props this time round. One of the ideas I came up with required some preparation, as I had to find a very specific coat. After a few weeks of searching online I found what I wanted on eBay and Pauline, a Facebook friend of mine, then knitted a beautiful sweater for Claire in the exact same pattern as the coat.

This "coat" photograph is the first one I am going to make. I know the way, so I'm off to the hall at the front of the house. There are now two pairs of white shoes beneath the coat rail in the hallway – they weren't there on my first visit, but they look great. I put my raincoat on the hanger, get Claire dressed in her new sweater and take the picture I had in mind.

> *"…the piano is beautiful, as is the hall, and even the surgery room offers the potential for a nice picture."*

Left This photo won first prize in the Pets category in the prestigious International Photography Awards (IPA), 2017. I also received honourable mentions for another photograph and a series in "Advertising."

Green Valley Hotel
Germany

Right Almost as if Claire understands, she sits down in exactly the right spot waiting for the lift to come. The Queen has arrived.

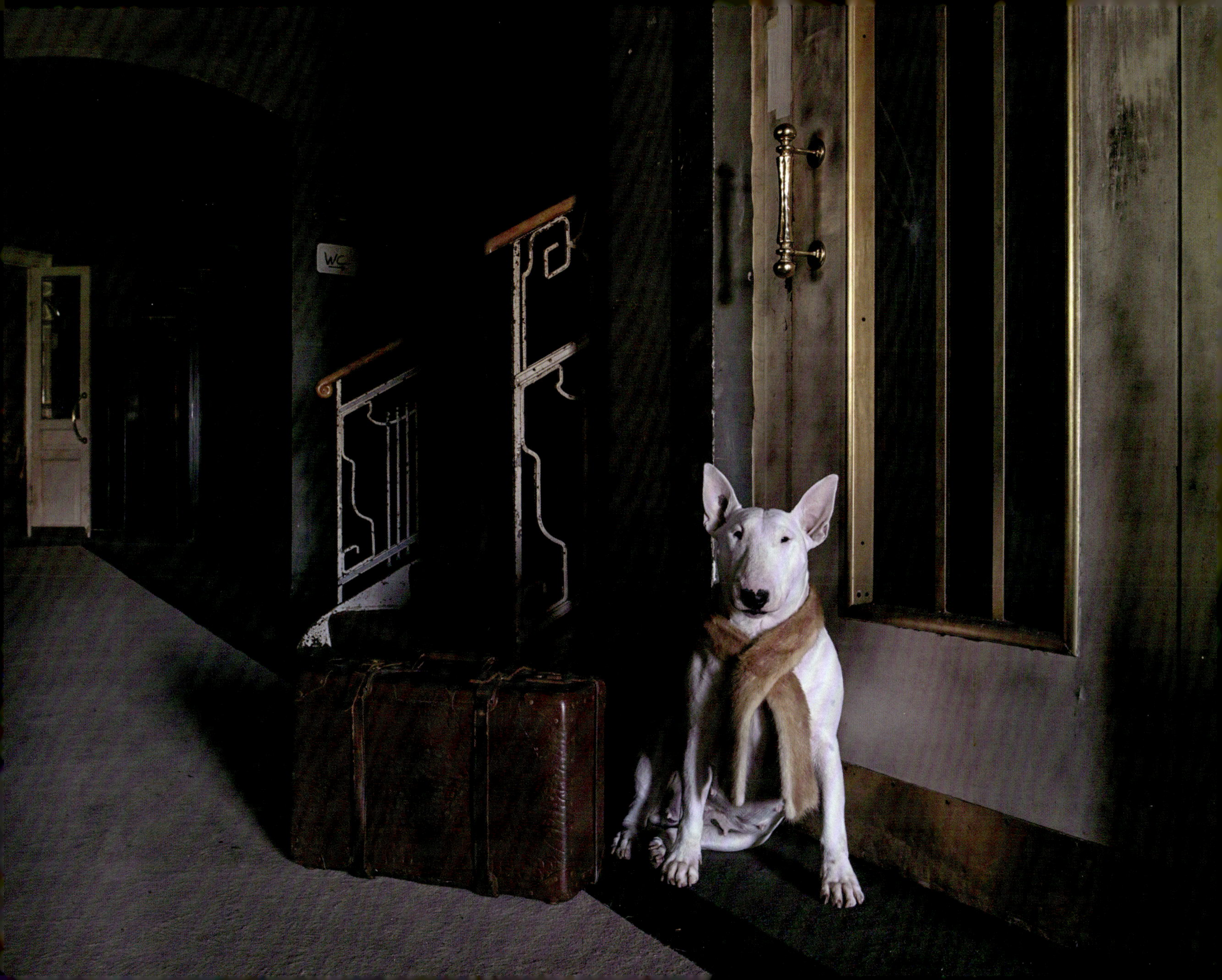

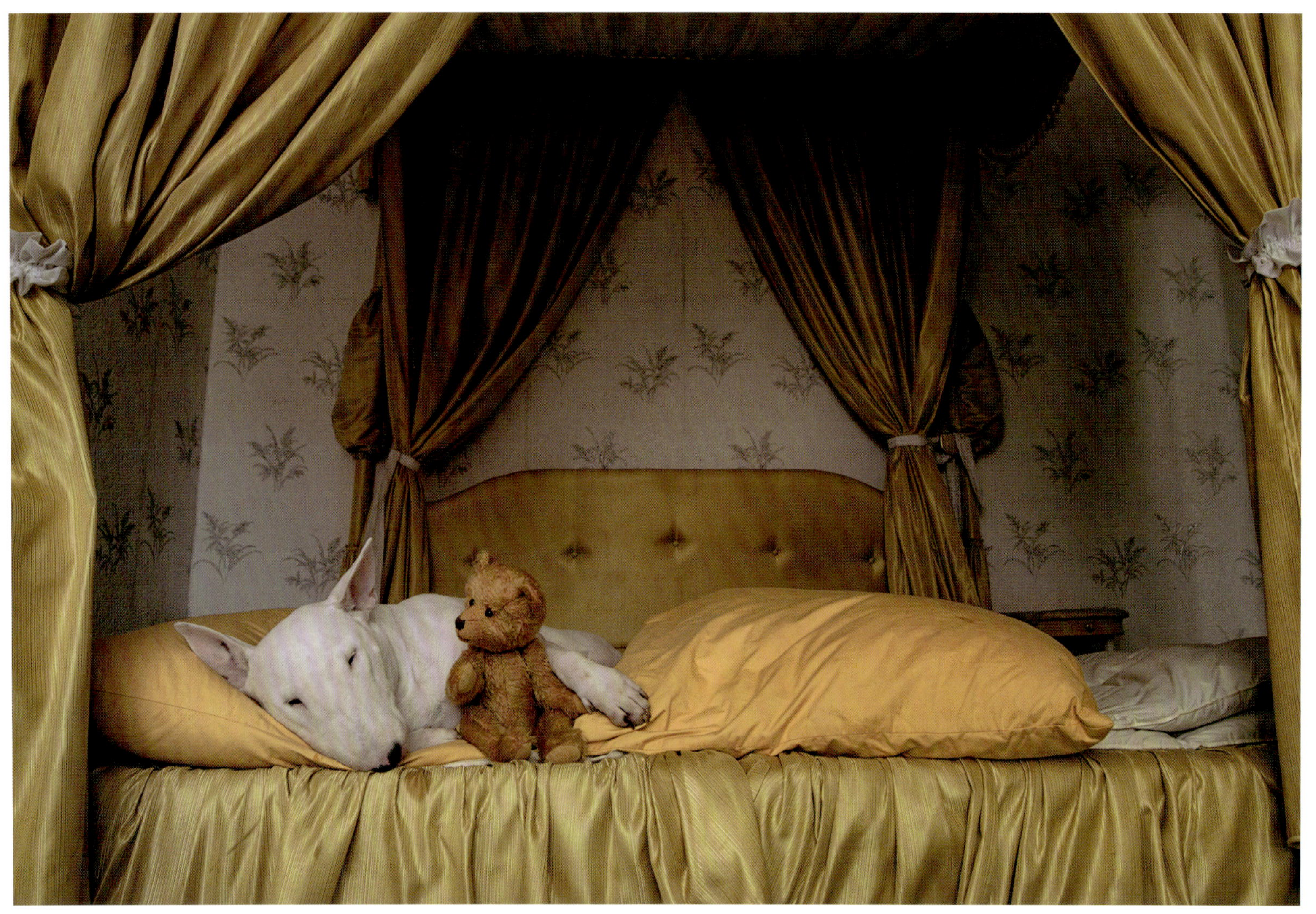

The Green Valley Hotel opened its doors in 1903, and with booking agencies in London and New York the Black Forest schlosshotel quickly became a popular destination for the rich and famous. Kings, queens, sultans, famous actors, artists and other celebrities all found their way to this beautiful Art Nouveau building; King Gustav V of Sweden, Queen Mother Emma of the Netherlands, the Prince of Wales and actors Douglas Fairbanks and Mary Pickford (among others) are known to have stayed in what was one of the most distinguished establishments in Europe.

The hotel experienced its most fantastic period shortly after the First World War, during which time it was extended, but with the onset of the Second World War (and shortly after) it found itself converted into a military hospital. Although it managed to rekindle some of its former allure in later years, several changes of ownership followed and with tourist numbers declining and temporary closures for renovations and repairs, the lustre faded. In 2005, Green Valley closed its doors for the final time.

Today, the hotel is abandoned, apart from its widely reported ghosts. According to employees, the hotel became a place of "unredeemed souls" stuck on their way to the afterlife. The list of otherworldly experiences is long: electrical appliances suddenly stopped working, but later ran without any problem; portrait paintings had changed facial expressions; glasses moved; beer bottles were found half empty, yet still sealed; a wandering woman wearing a white veil was seen regularly; and the elevator would constantly move up and down between floors without guests or employees in it or calling it. On two occasions paranormal researchers investigated the building, but the only conclusion was that it provided the optimal conditions for perceptual illusions.

For our visit, Claire and I have an appointment with the caretaker of the building, who arrives exactly on time to open the door and invite us in. She provides a brief history of the hotel and explains where we can and cannot go, what we can and cannot do and then we each go our own way. I am on my way to one of the bedrooms with a canopy bed when I pass the long corridor where the elevator is located. We don't detect any unexplained or invisible presence, but the light is fantastic. I have to act quickly, though, because I know that this sort of light can be short-lived. As if Claire understands, she sits down in exactly the right spot and pulls a face as if she's the queen herself. I know right away that this will be my favourite shot in this abandoned place. All of the other photos I'm going to make will be a bonus.

Relaxation Gallery

Let sleeping dogs lie...

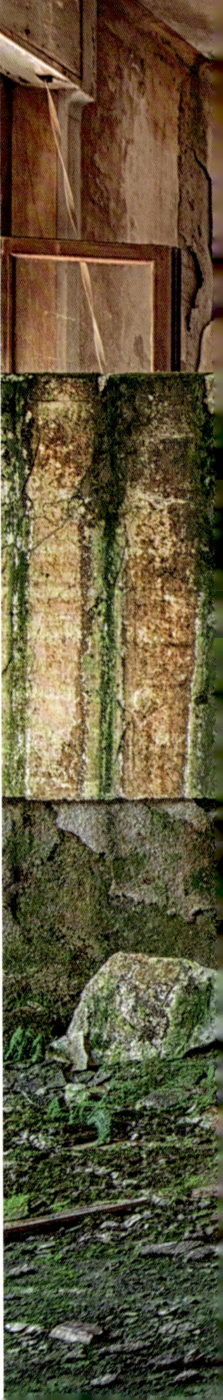

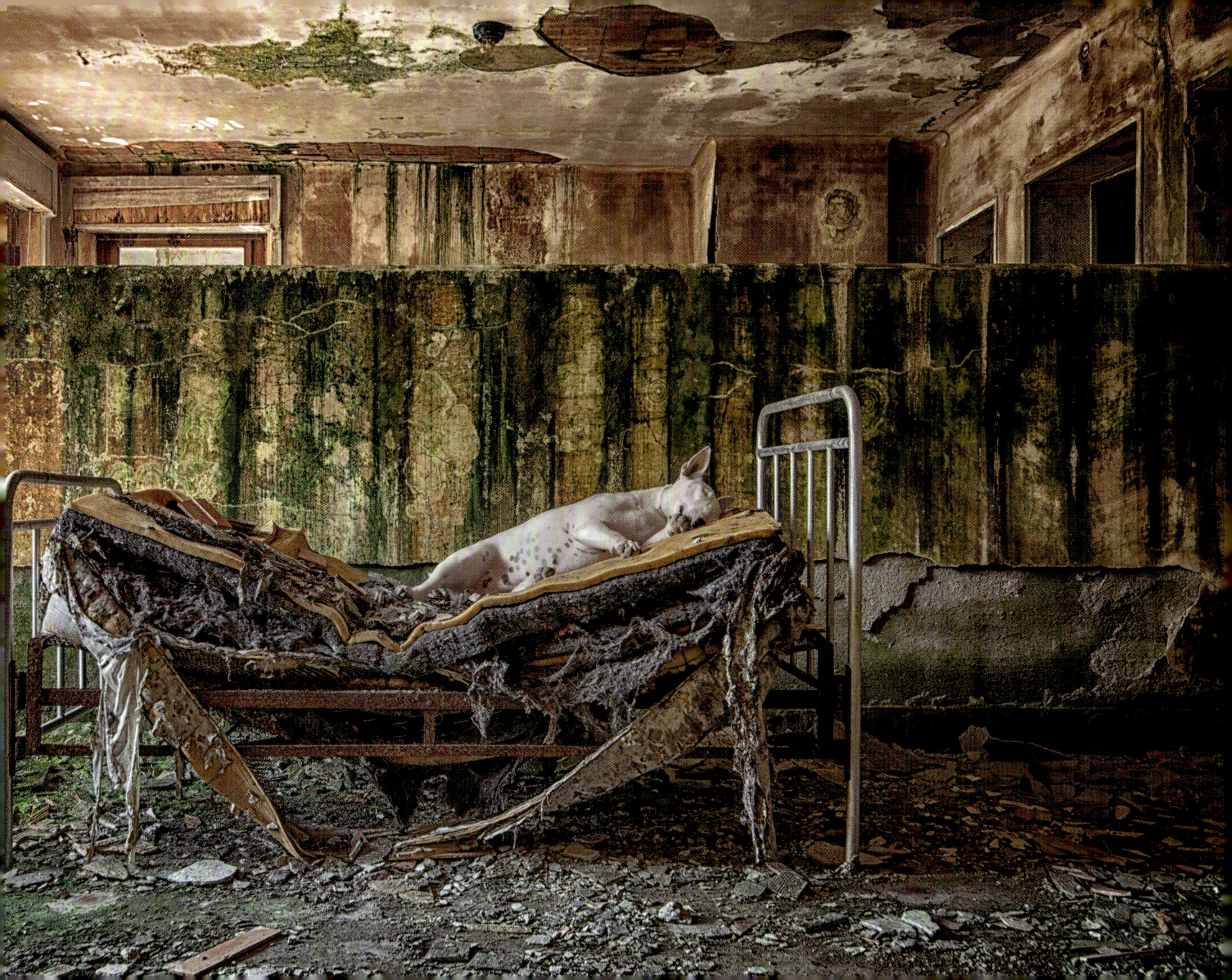

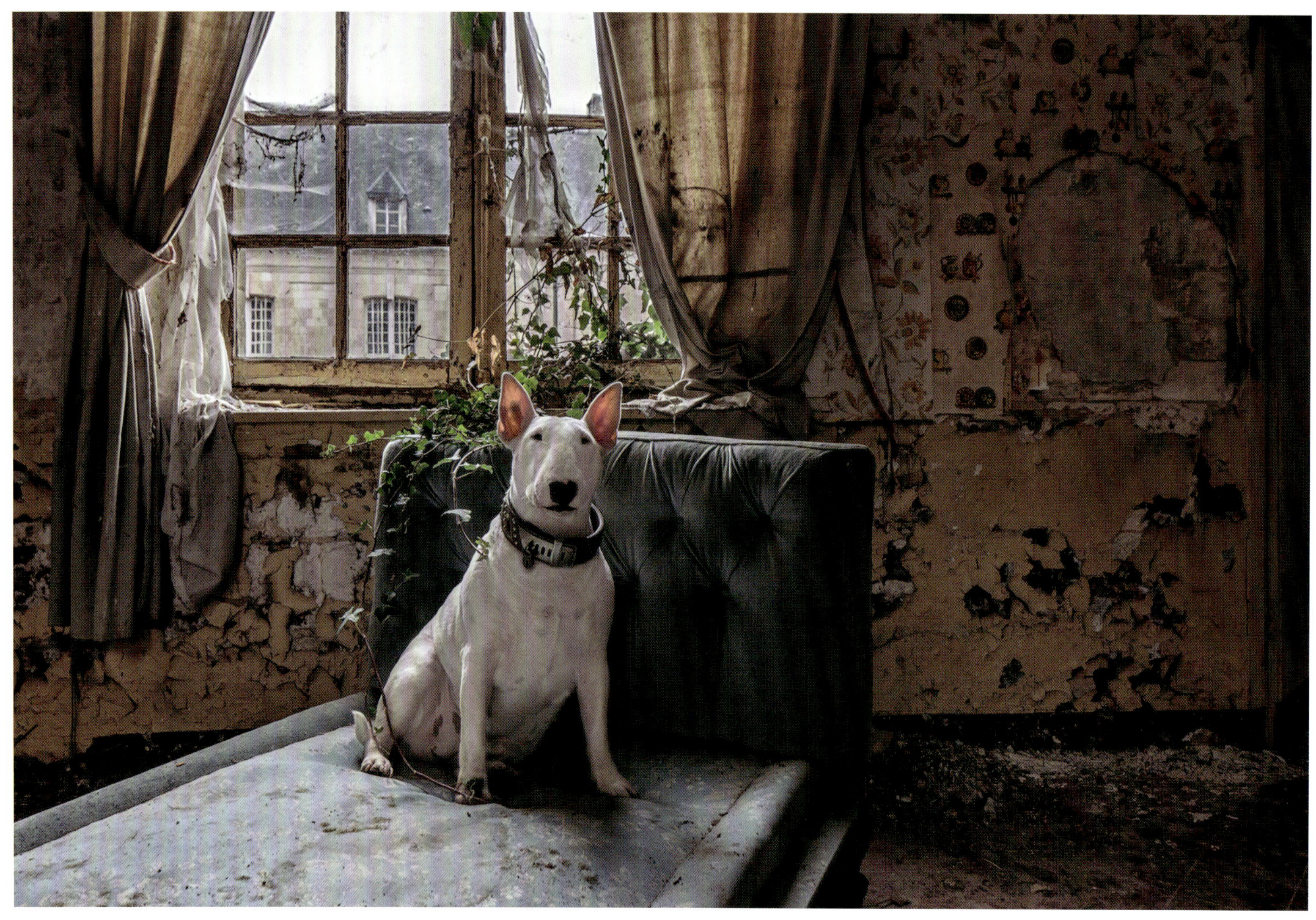

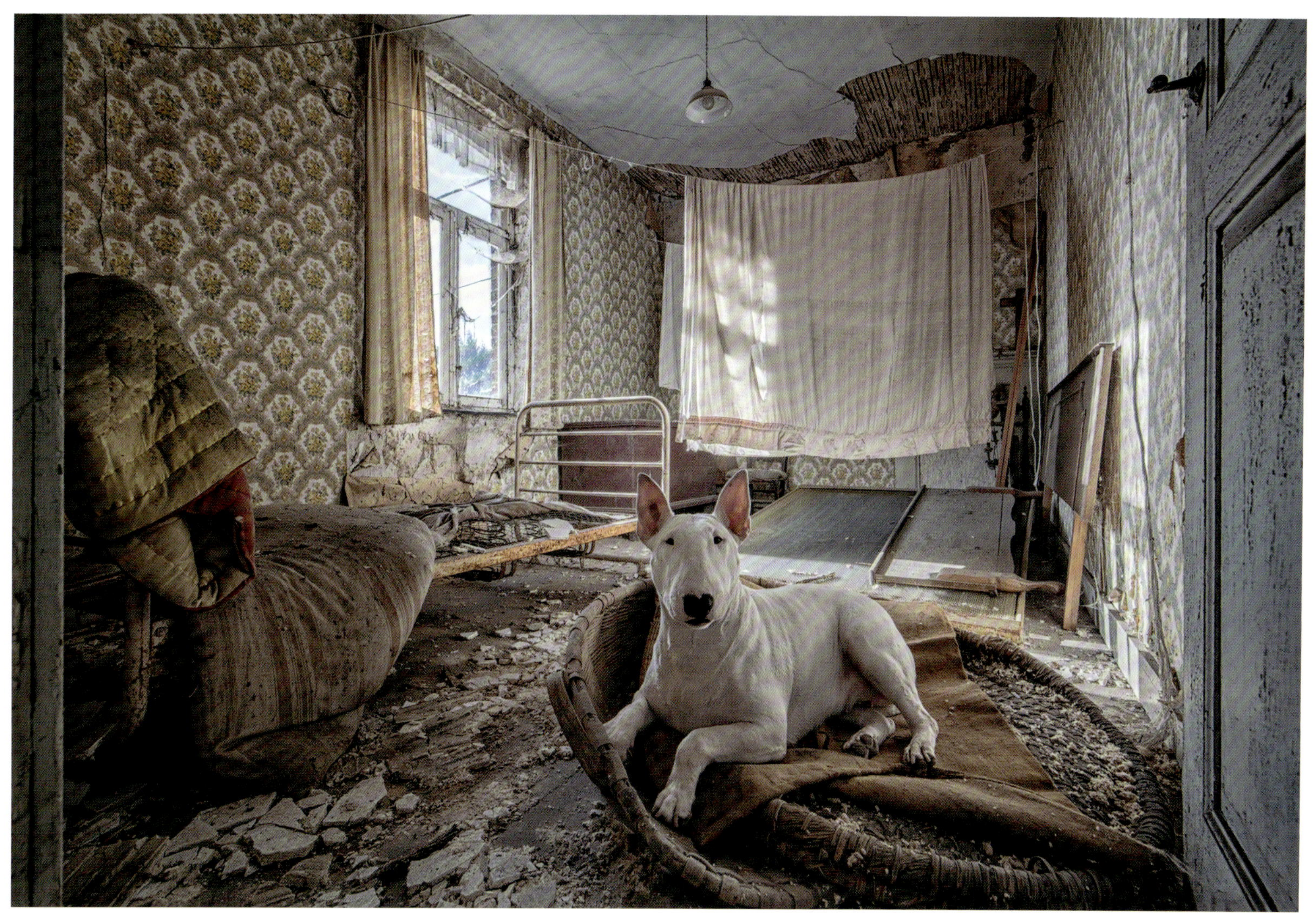

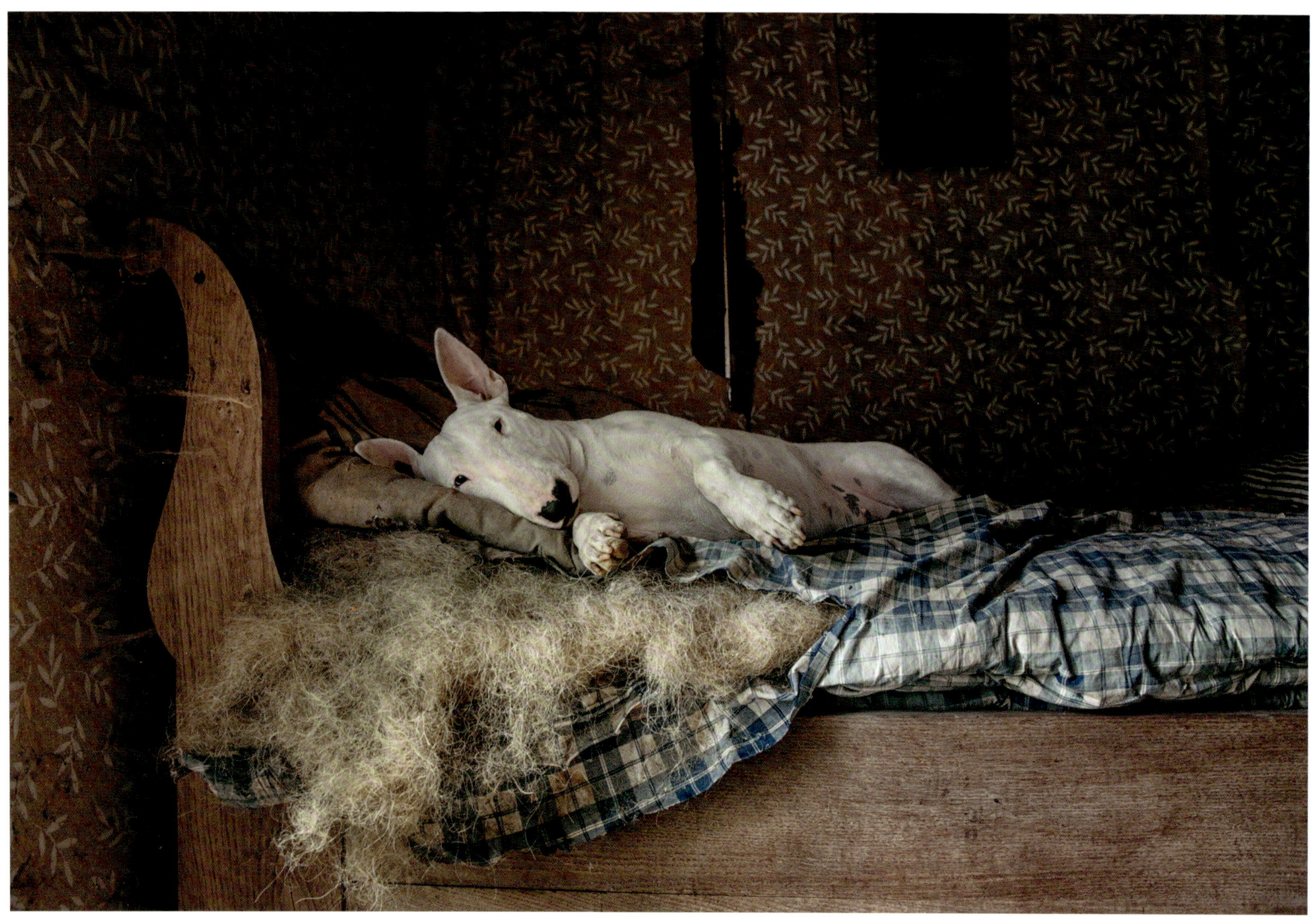

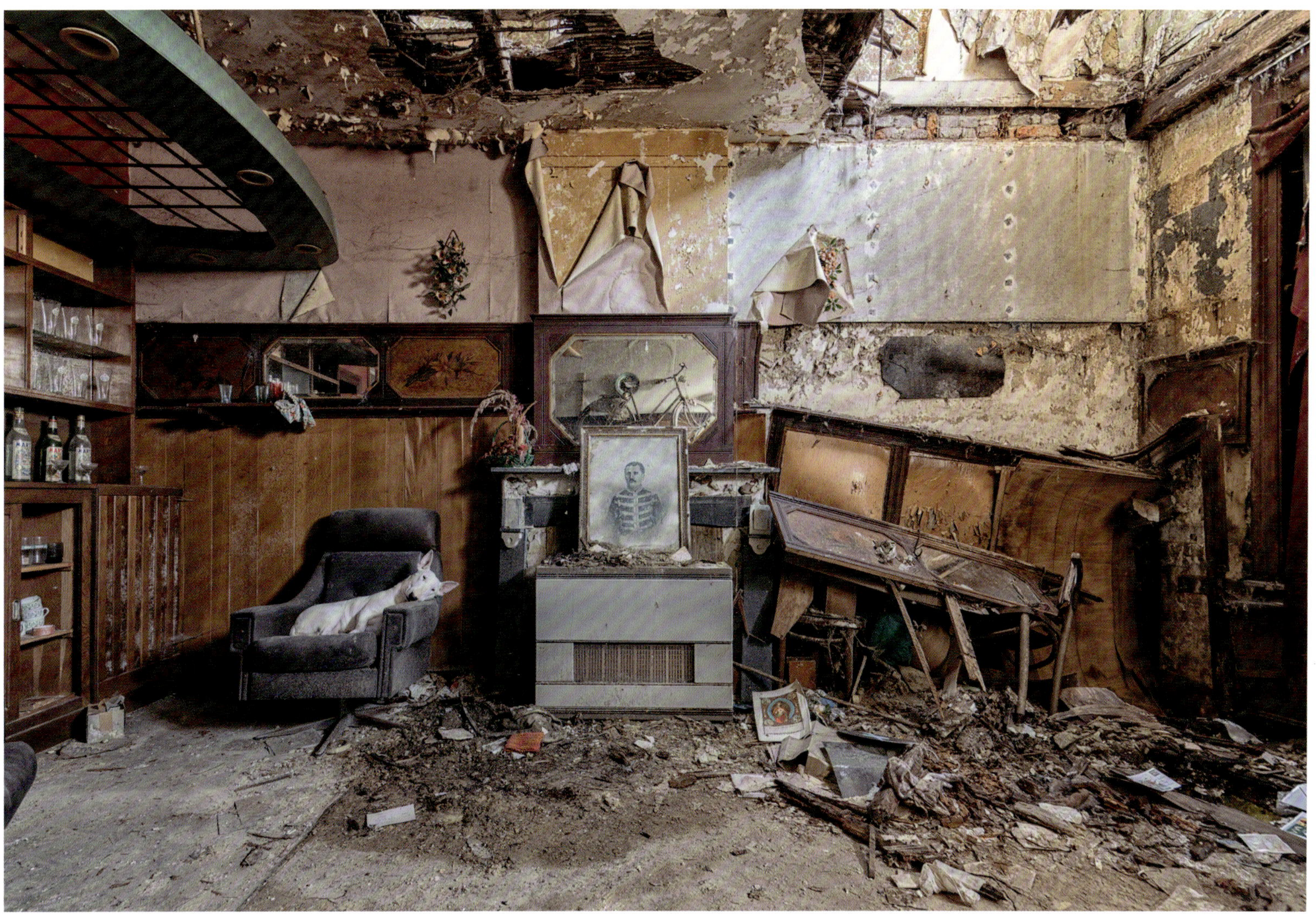

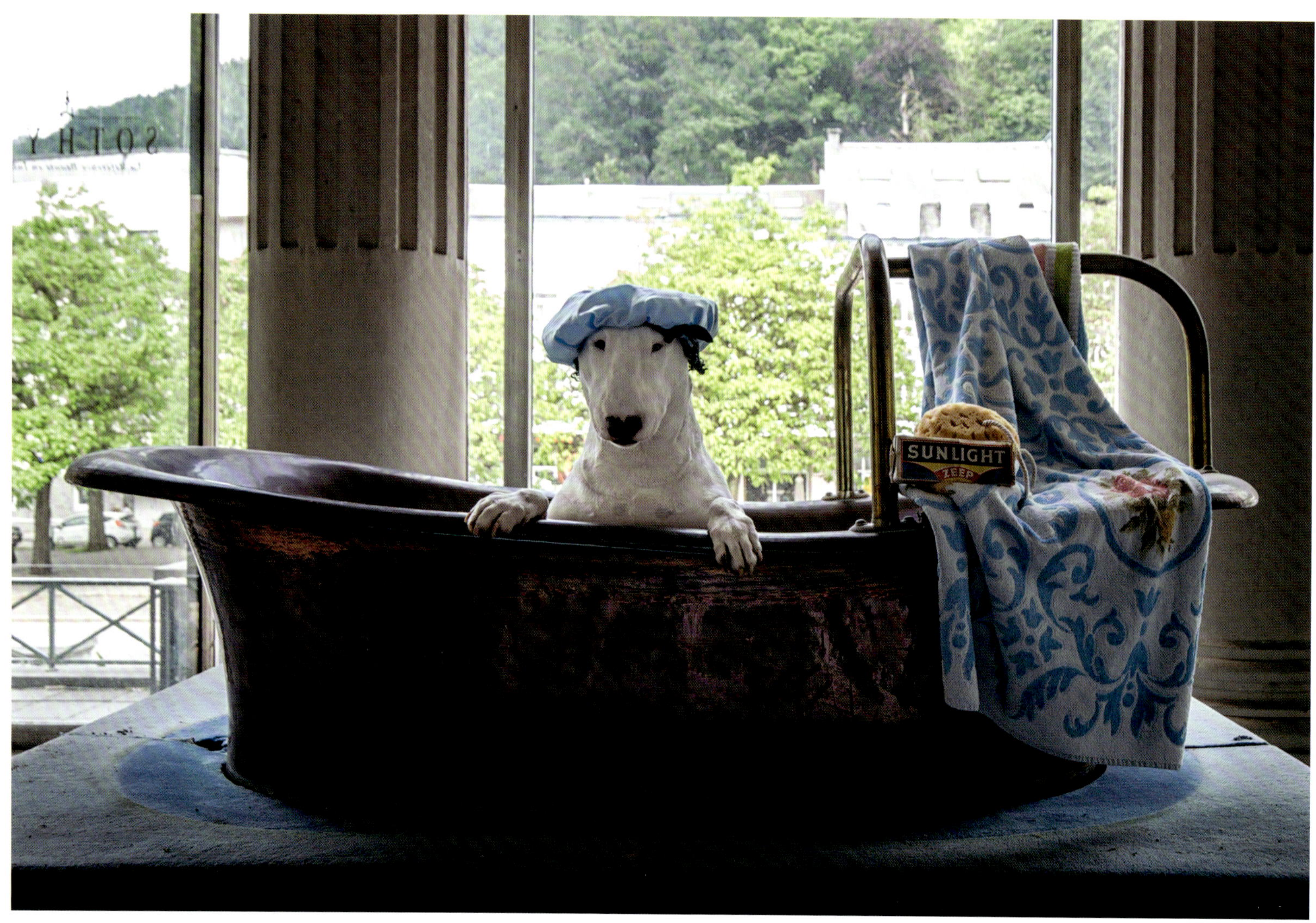

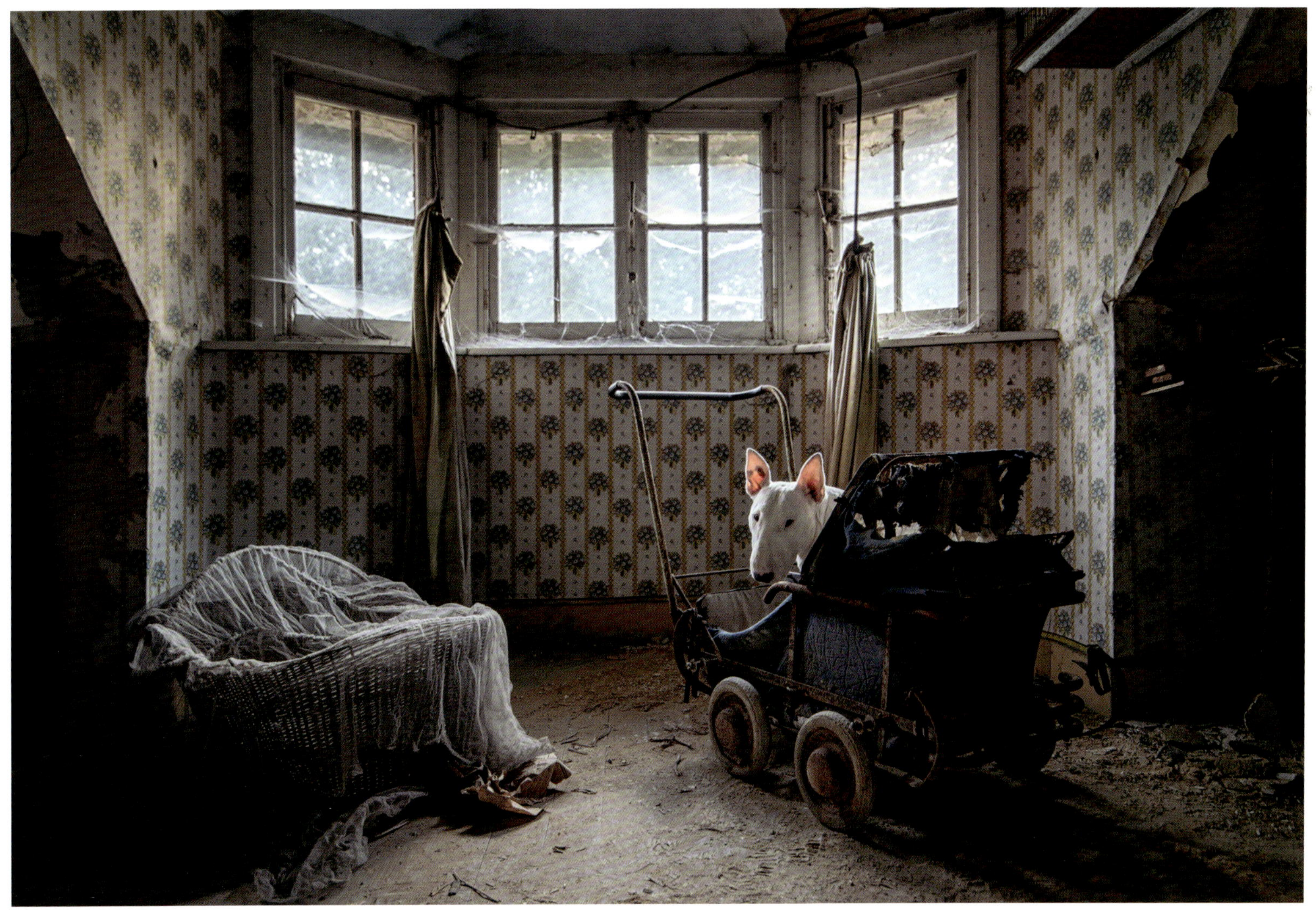

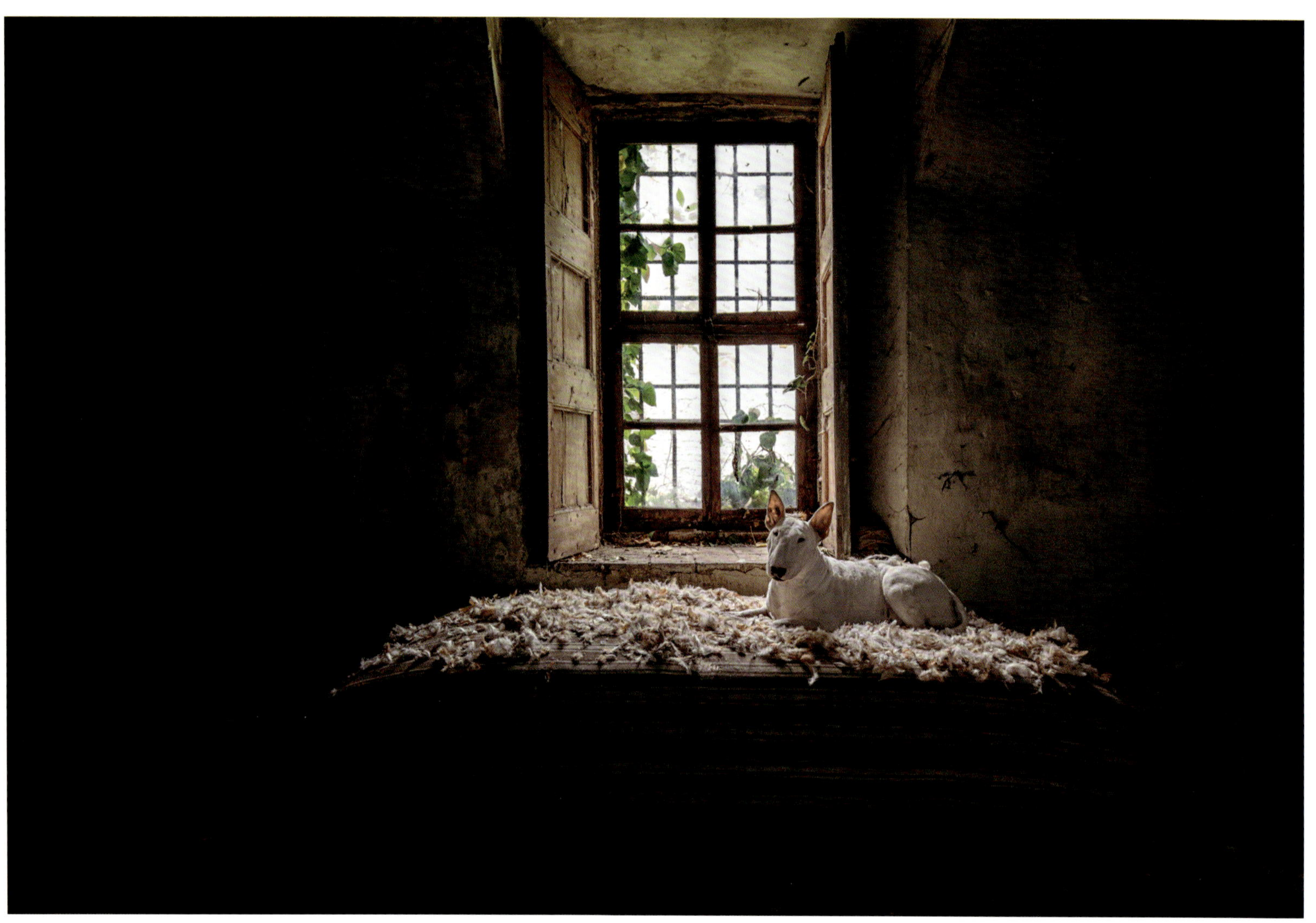

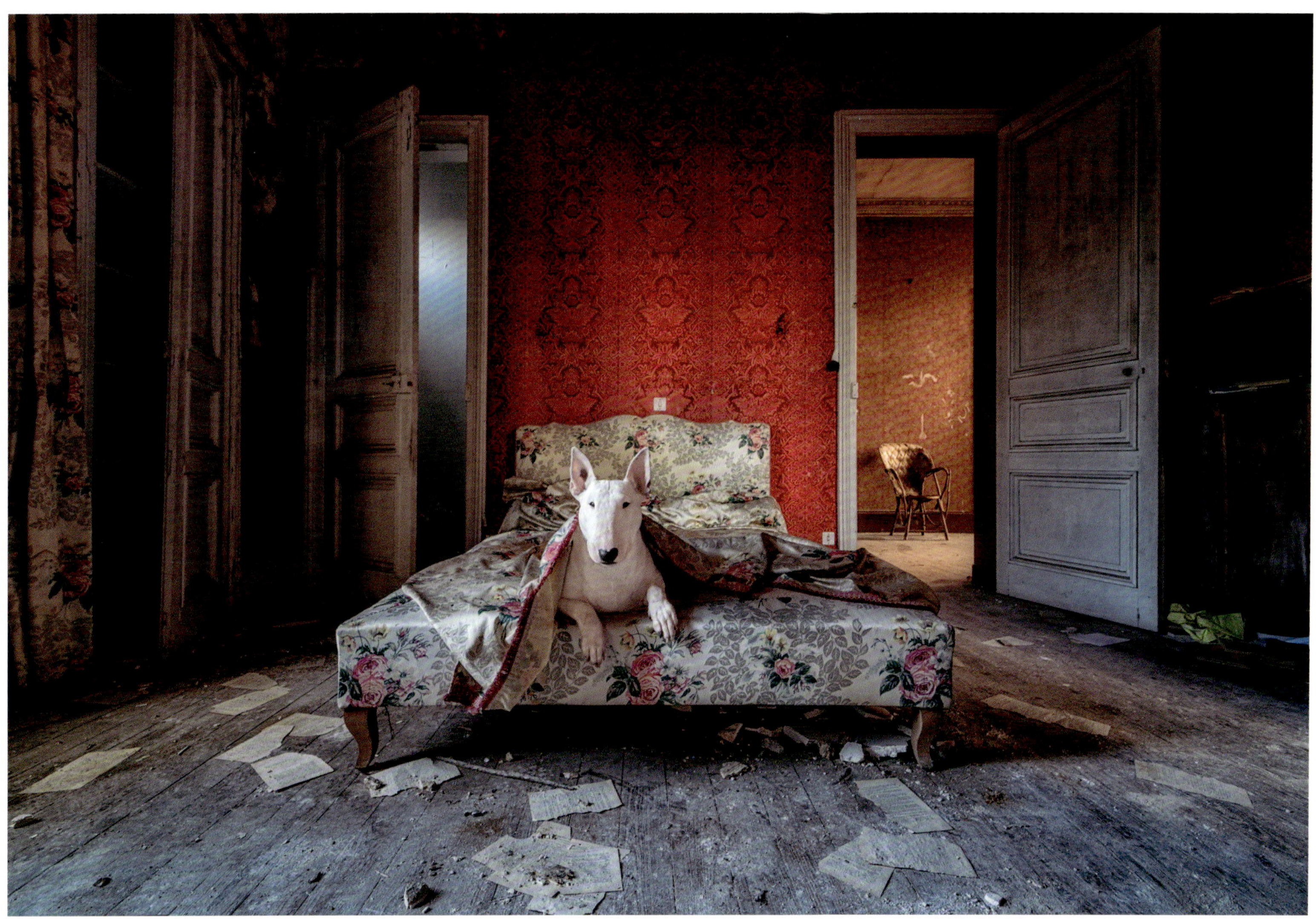

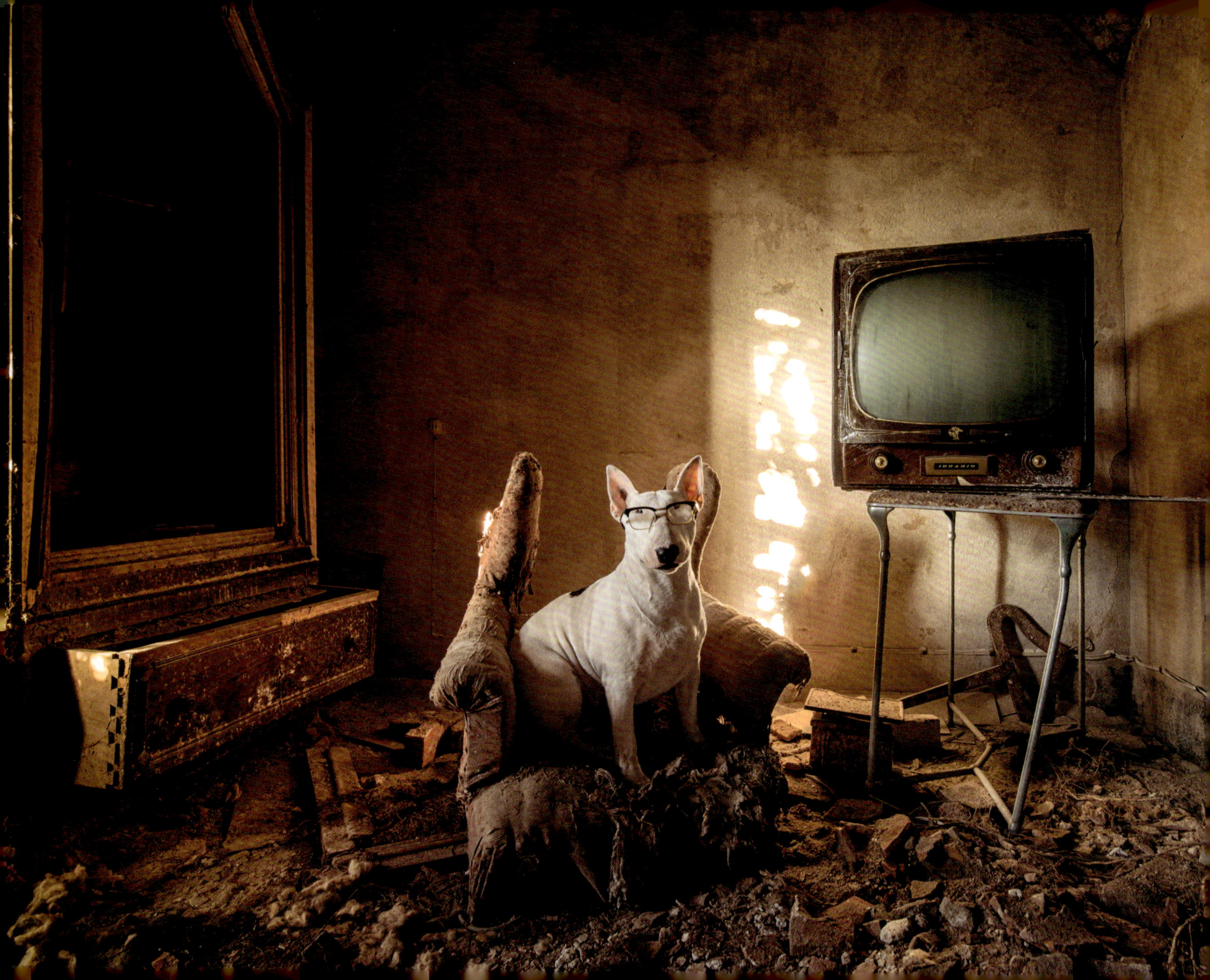

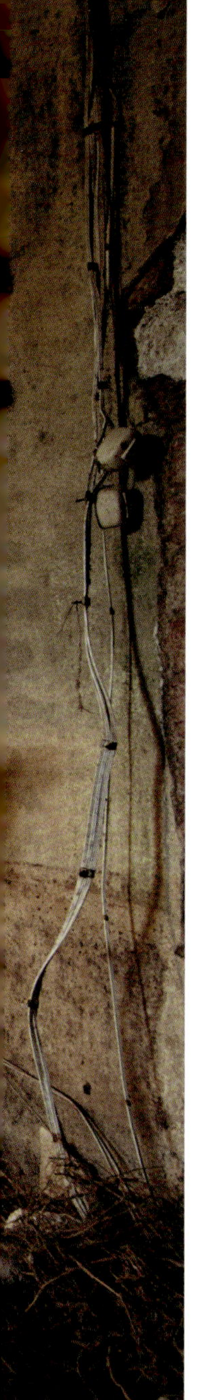

Castello dell'Apicoltore
Italy

Left The orange rays of the early sunlight peek through the windows, illuminating the room. There isn't much time to capture the scene before the light changes.

When we arrive in Italy we are welcomed by our Facebook friends, Luca and Oxana. After a sightseeing tour through Genoa they invite us out for dinner, where we get the full introduction to Italian cuisine, from aperitivo to digestivo and everything in between. It is excellent food, excellent company, and the perfect start to our Italian road trip. At 8am the next morning Luca and Oxana pick us up to visit some abandoned buildings including an ancient church, but the first stop is a bar next to our first location; for breakfast and coffee while we talk urbex.

Later, over lunch, we discuss a number of places we want to visit during our trip and our hosts tell us the best ways to enter, where we have to be careful as there's a risk of being caught, the history of the places and why some locations have been abandoned. Luca knows a lot about history and we love listening to his stories about the nobility of Italy; the duchi, marchesi, conta, visconti and baroni.

One of the locations we want to visit is a castle that dates back to the 10th century, when Ottone III became the Holy Roman Emperor at the age of three. Since then it has been under the reign of noble families such as the House of Savoy, Barbarossa, Biandrate and De Albano, but now sits empty. However, Luca warns us that the castle's current owners have a house right next to the castle, so we'll have to park our car at a graveyard and walk across fields to access the castle from the back. Apparently, getting in is easy, as the doors are open.

When we reach our destination the next evening, we explore the castle's surroundings on foot. Just opposite the castle is a small, family-owned restaurant where we decide to have something to eat. The waitress explains they only use the very best locally grown products, including meat from local farmers, cheese made in the region and "honey produced over there".

The following morning we crawl through a small opening in the fence and walk through the fields towards the castle. The first part of the field is covered with stinging nettles; there are too many for Claire's liking so I have to carry her while the nettles sting through my trousers. When we reach the castle we realize what the waitress was

> *"We crawl through a small opening in the fence and walk through the fields towards the castle."*

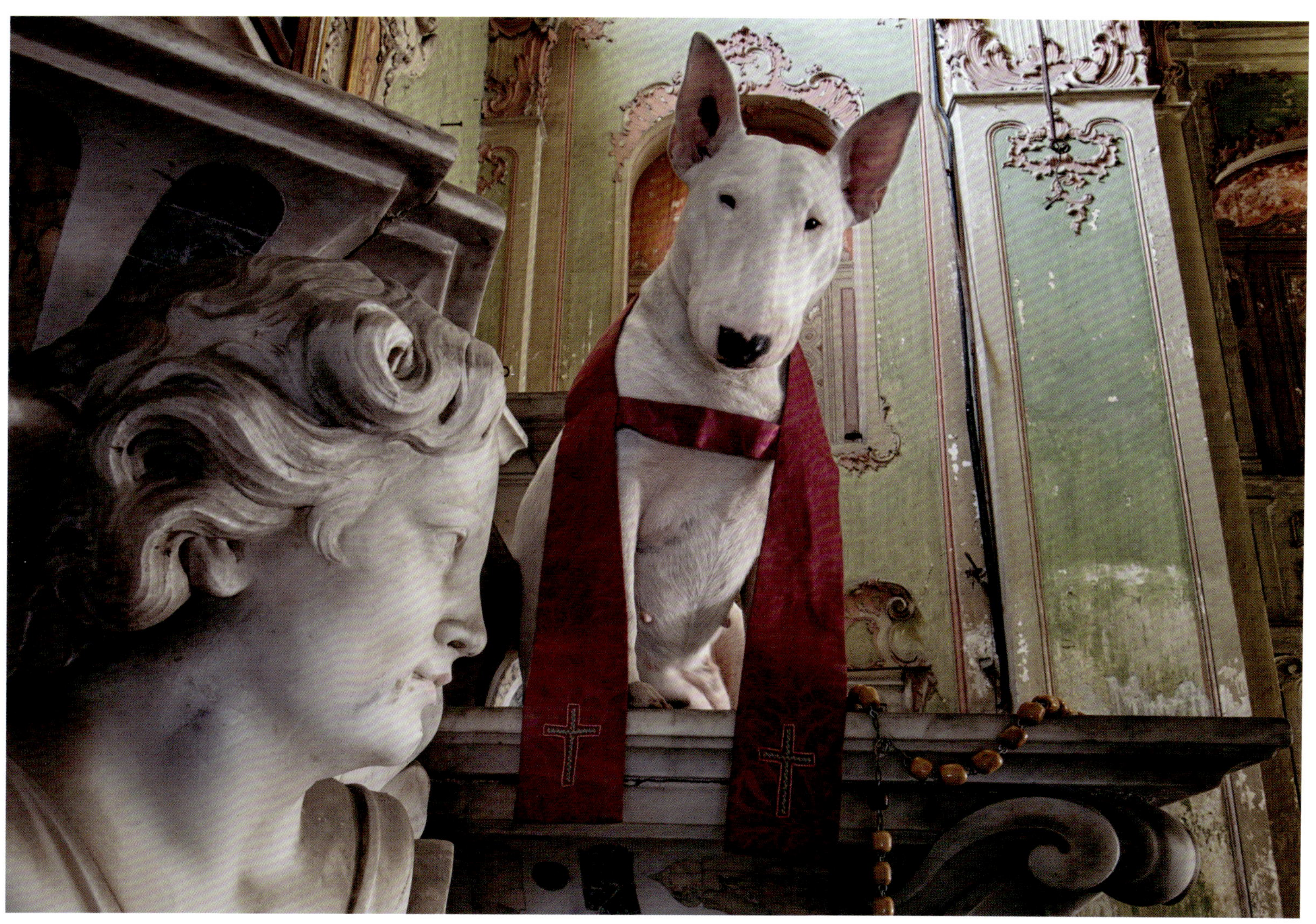

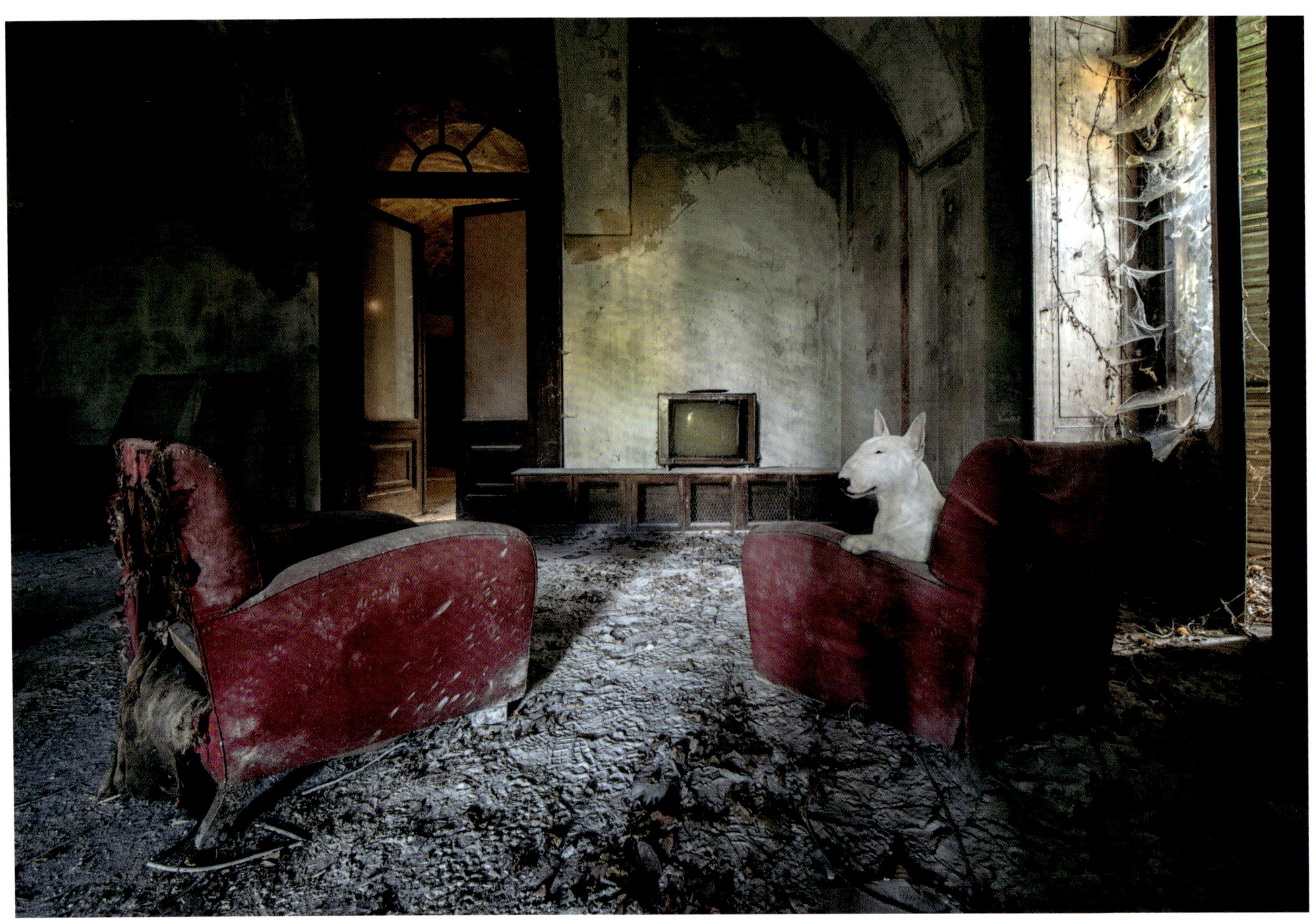

referring to the previous evening. About 30 wooden beehives sit neatly in a long row in front of the castle – the honey at the restaurant is produced in the castle grounds. Thankfully, the bees are not yet active, which means we don't have to worry about the bee-keeper turning up to inspect his hives.

As Luca said, the doors to the castle stand invitingly open. We make our way through piles of wood, stone and other rubble, all covered with a very thick layer of dust, until we reach the room I have seen in other urbexers' photographs. I watch as the orange rays of the early sunlight peek through the windows. The warmth of the light is stunning, but I have to act quickly, before the sun rises too high and the glow is gone.

Claire has already positioned herself – she knows what to do – but I'm only halfway through my series of photos when I hear a loud noise. Very carefully, without making any sound myself, I walk to the window and peer around the corner, only to see a woman with a Jack Russell – the neighbours Luca warned us about. I hope her dog doesn't bark, because that might trigger Claire. She never usually barks, but they are so close to us that I can hear her talking to her dog. Quieter than

before, I try to finish the other half of my photo series, but the Jack Russell suddenly barks. Luckily Claire's too focused to react; she sits stock-still in the mouldy chair. "One more" I whisper, and then we're done in this room.

We walk downstairs, knowing we need to be even more careful, as we're now on the same level as the neighbour's garden, which borders the wall of the house where we are. The windows are draped with cobwebs, and years of dust cover two red chairs and an old television. This is an easy one, as the more comfortable the chair, the more relaxed Claire is. It only takes 10 minutes to take the necessary shots and then it's time to go: we don't want to stay any longer and risk getting caught.

"The doors to the castle stand invitingly open. We make our way through piles of wood, stone and other rubble, all covered with a very thick layer of dust"

Left In one room we find two red armchairs covered by years of dust, facing towards the old television – the perfect setting for another shot.

Château Lumière

France

Right The large skylight in the centre of
the building allows the natural light to
illuminate all three floors.

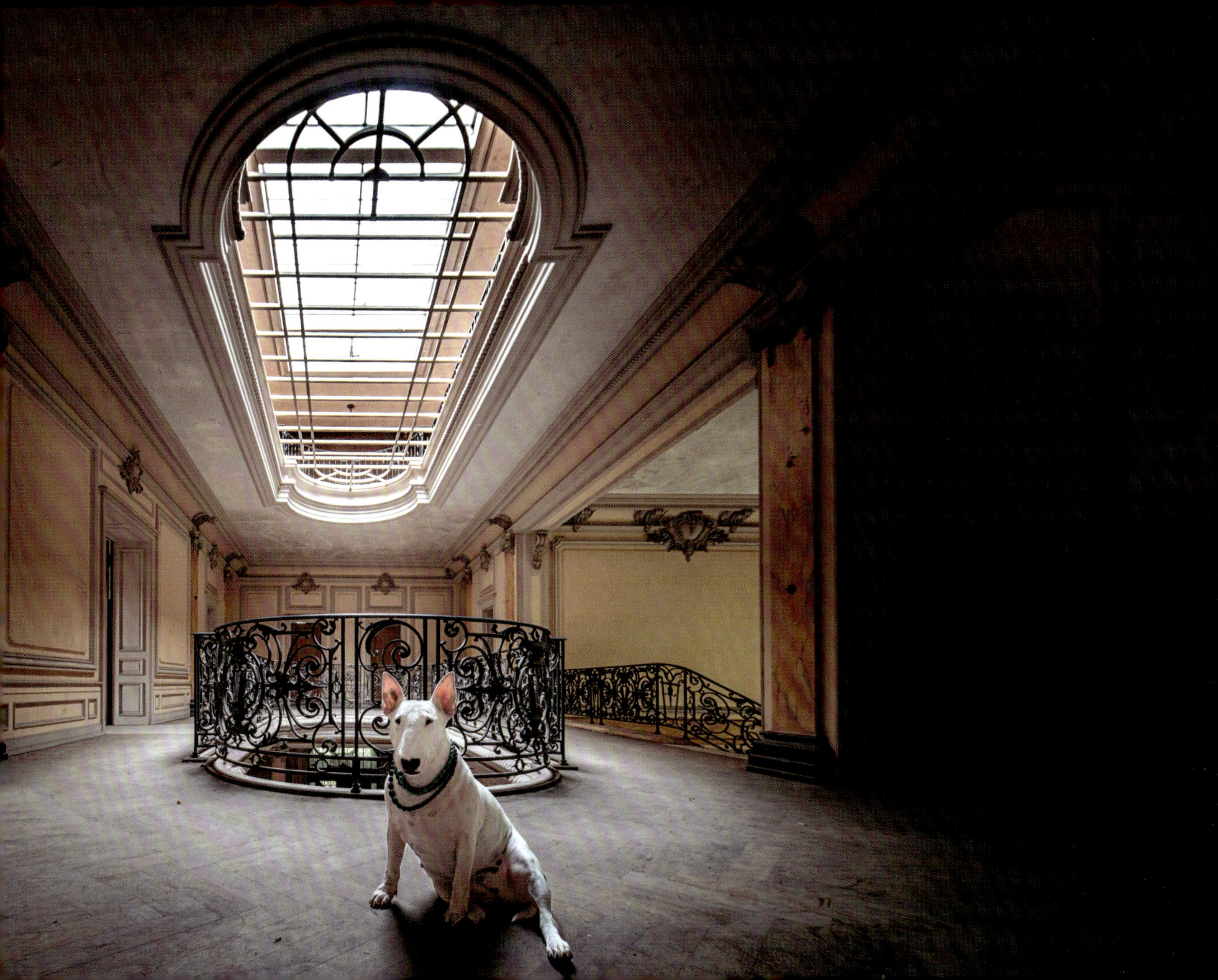

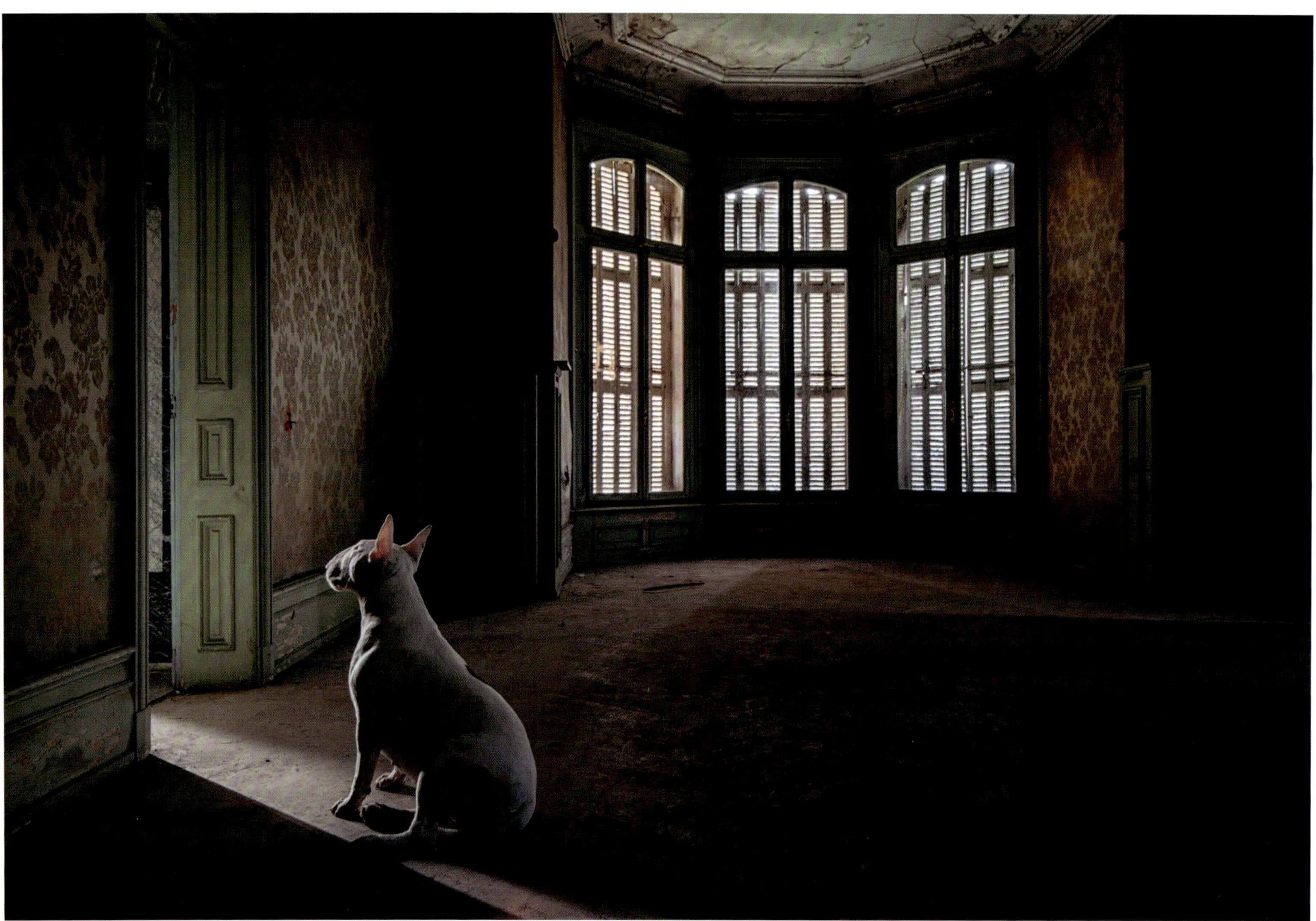

I am in the abandoned castle of "a man with taste", as the former owner was described by auction house Christie's. Built in 1900 in the neo-Baroque style, the castle was originally the property of a very rich tobacco industrialist, whose son inherited it in 1911. Today it is little more than an empty shell; apart from the beautiful marble floor and staircase, and the remnants of a few lavish embellishments, there is little left of its former splendour.

As I sit in an abandoned room with my friend Lies, Claire and her half-sister Pip, I try to imagine what the building might have looked like when it was still fully furnished. It is quite possible that we could be sitting in the former library, and I imagine a wealthy resident in a comfortable leather chair admiring his book collection. We know it was a very special collection, because part of it sold at auction for almost €2.5 million ($3 million). In another room he probably kept his stamp collection: seated behind a beautiful wooden desk he could admire his rarest acquisitions with a magnifying glass, including some of the most desirable stamps in philately.

During the First World War, the owner was forced to house a number of German officers in his immaculate castle. In a letter to his sister, who lived in Switzerland, he complained about the behaviour of one of the officers during a party where alcohol was flowing abundantly.

The Germans intercepted this letter and their host was sentenced to 10 months imprisonment. That must have been very uncomfortable for a man who had spent his entire life in great luxury, but while he lost 30 pounds during his incarceration he was relatively lucky: many other Alsatians were simply shot.

We have been waiting in the castle for a little over two hours when the sun starts to rise. It's breathtaking to see the early morning light pour in through the skylight and illuminate the entire building. The castle certainly lives up to its urbex name – Château Lumière, or "Castle of Light".

After three hours of photography we decide to leave, but don't dare take the same route back; to get here we crossed a business park that is now crowded with workers and we will be spotted immediately if we climb over the wall with two bull terriers. Instead, we head to the back of the castle. Although we knew that it was built against a mountain, we hadn't realized how steep that mountain was. We soon find ourselves having to hold on to trees, pulling Claire and Pip up, and then moving a few steps up, repeating this ritual until we reach the top. When I revisit the castle two years later, I decide to take the easy way out, despite the curious looks of the office workers. I am never climbing that mountain again, with or without a bull terrier!

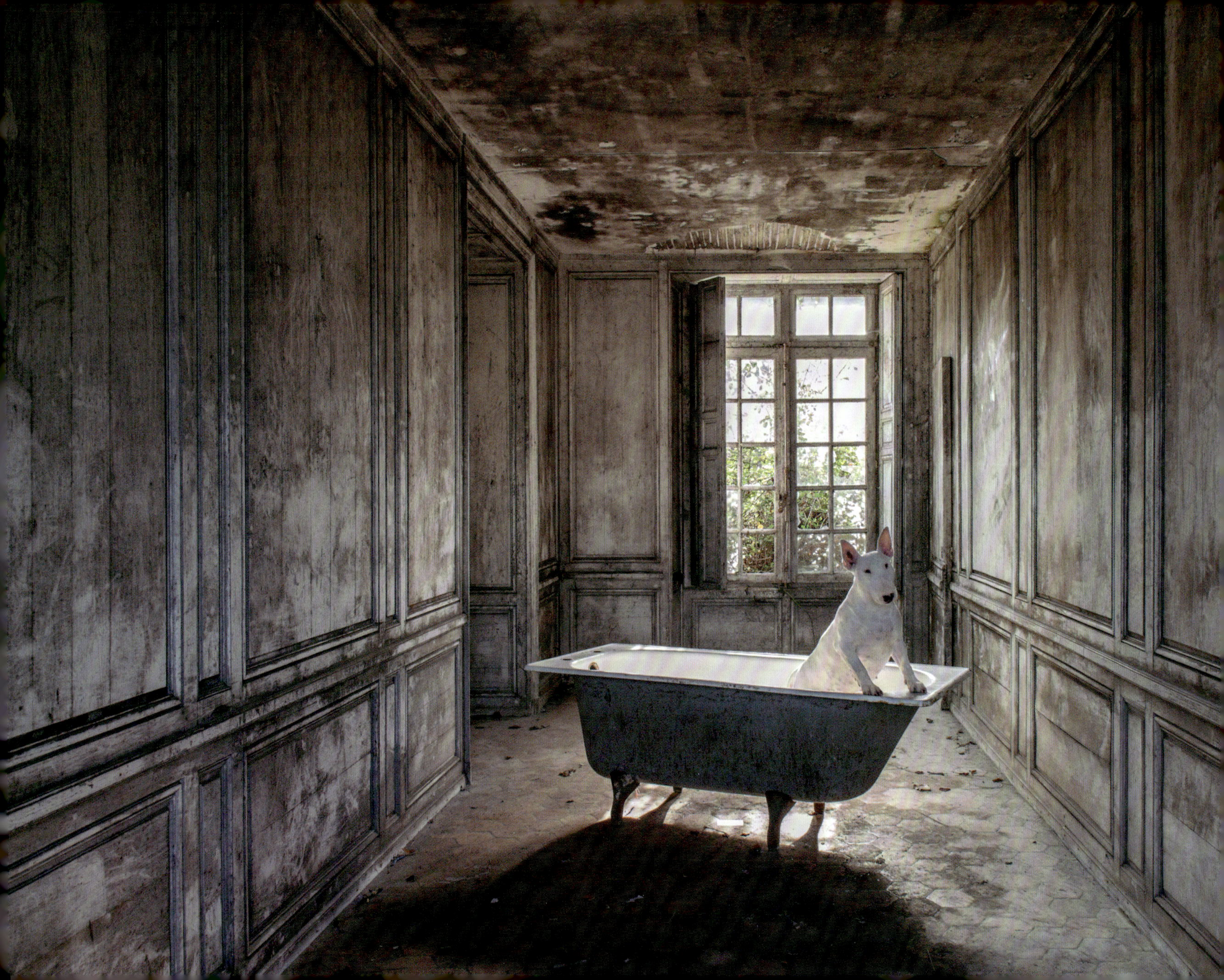

Château de Singes
France

Left Before I know it, Claire jumps into
the bathtub and looks at me as if to say,
"Hurry up before that beautiful light is gone".
I don't want to miss this opportunity.

When I heard of an abandoned castle near Paris that once belonged to an African dictator, my interest was immediately aroused, and when I found out that it had a beautiful spiral staircase with a red carpet I knew it would be perfect for a particular photograph I had in mind. Most successful explores start with good preparation and in this instance there was plenty of information available. This is usually the case when it concerns dictators, especially this one: Jean-Bédel Bokassa, the self-declared "Emperor of Central Africa", whose grand coronation was rumoured to have almost bankrupted his country.

At home I print out photographs of Bokassa's coronation. The plan is to drop them randomly on the stairs in his former castle and have Claire sit among them, wearing a red robe with ermine lining and a crown. I am convinced it will turn out to be a brilliant photograph.

We leave in the middle of the night and arrive in the village on the River Seine early on Sunday morning while everyone is still fast asleep. I drive around the corner and we get our first sight of the castle: a beautiful, almost renovated building with cars on its new driveway and a castle garden in the making. It is definitely not the neglected castle and overgrown garden we were expecting to see! There's no other option but to go to plan B.

Plan B is a ruin known as the Château de Singes: "Castle of Monkeys". It gets its name from one of its rooms, which has beautiful painted panels decorated with monkeys and other figures. We decide to park the car in the castle grounds, completely out of sight, rather than parking it by one of the surrounding roads where everyone can see our foreign number plates and guess where we've gone. Claire jumps from the car and sets off through the weeds and coarse grass, creating a narrow path for us to follow.

We get inside and I'm amazed. The long, narrow rooms are drenched in early morning sunlight and there's a beautiful staircase just inside the entrance. In one of the small rooms there's a bathtub and the light falls through the window right into the tub. After a few shots we continue to explore, taking pictures wherever the sunlight is best.

Upstairs we find the room where the castle's final resident lived for several years. Empty heating oil containers lay scattered across the wooden floor, among piles of stacked newspapers and horse-racing results. The castle's last "king" was eventually unable to afford the upkeep of his castle, so retreated into a single room with a portable heater to keep him warm during the cold winters. He lived like this for many years, refusing to leave his beloved castle, even as it crumbled around him.

Right The Château de Singes is just one room deep, but it has large windows on both sides, creating the illusion of space.

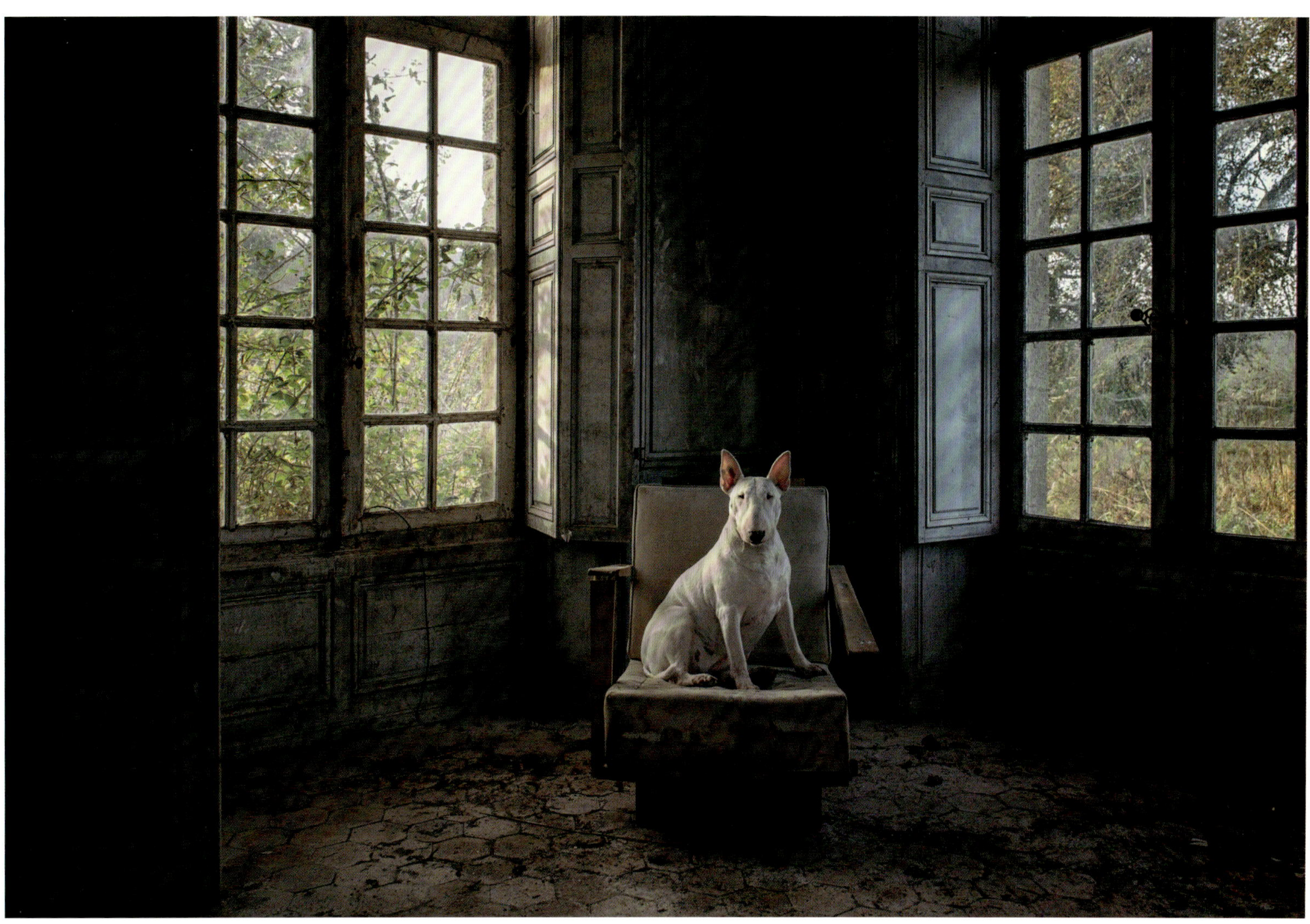

Maison Kirsch

Luxembourg

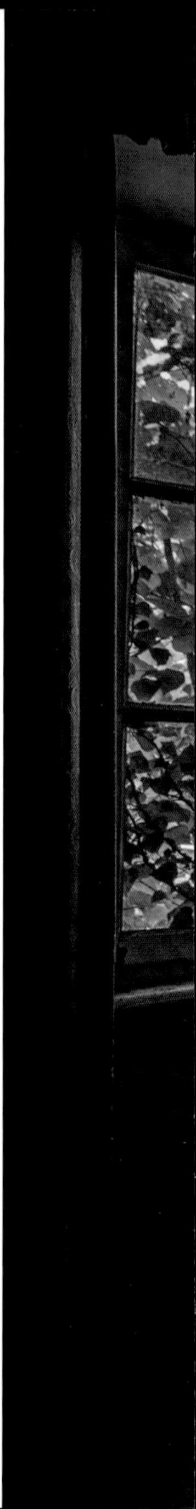

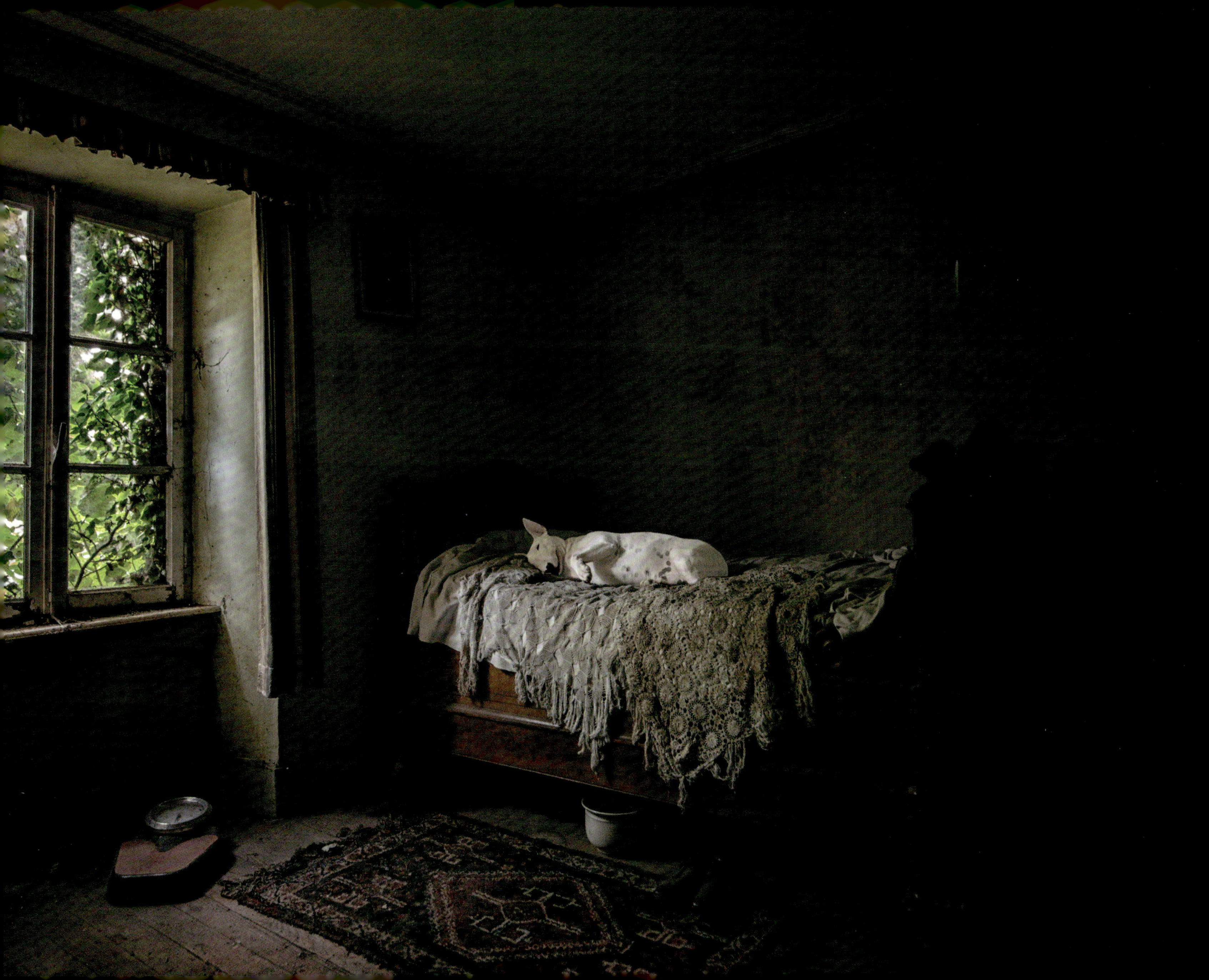

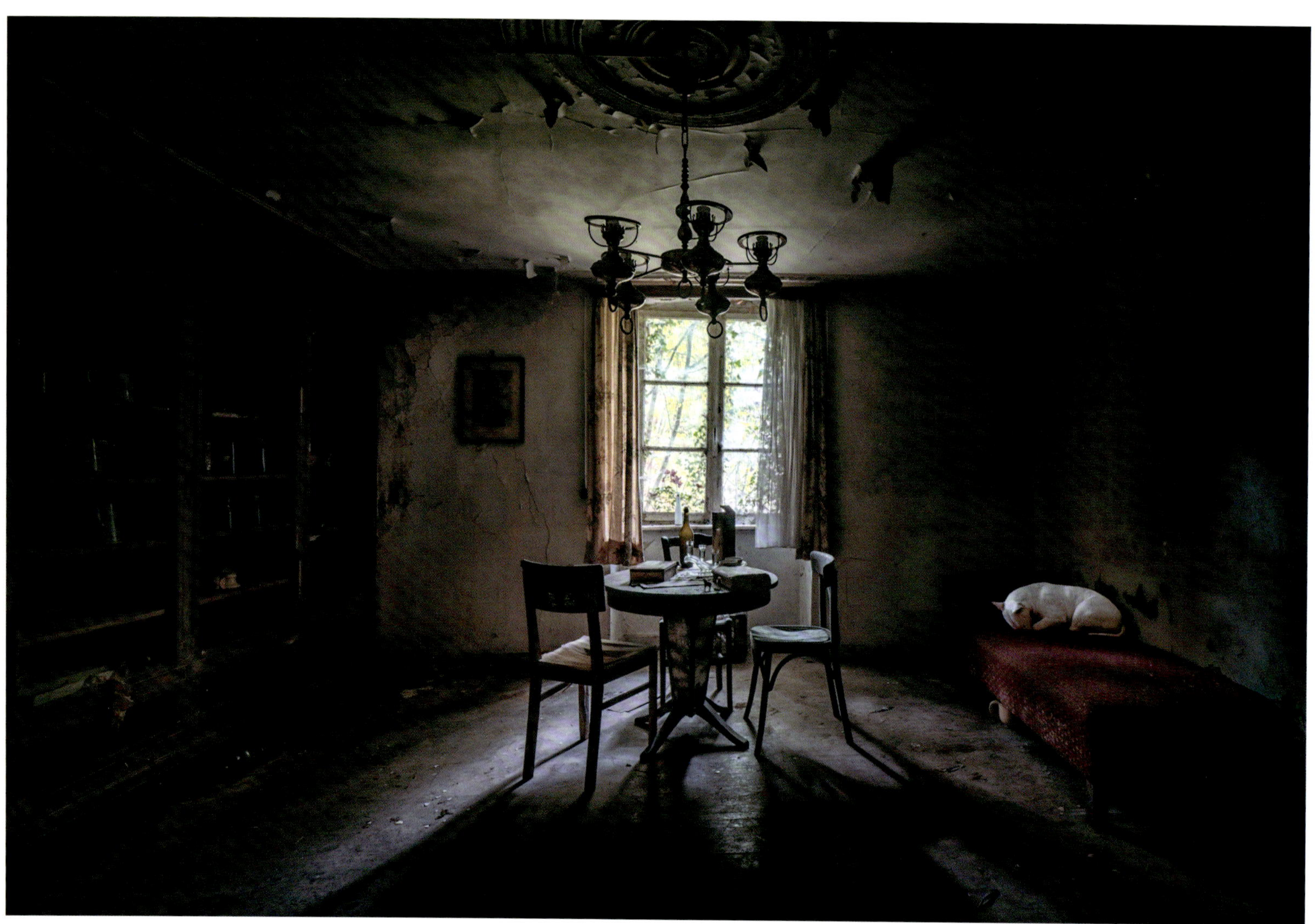

There is the usual smell of decay accompanying my first step through the door into a house that was built in the late 1700s. I don't know the exact story of Maison Kirsch, but it used to be a distillery; there are still large numbers of bottles and preserved fruits in the cellar and barns, which have probably been abandoned for more than 30 years. In this time capsule, everything appears perfectly preserved and untouched, with rooms full of old furniture and authentic relics. However, if I compare photos taken by various explorers over the years it is clear that some items – including the furniture – have been moved around, while other items have been removed. Despite this, it is still a very rare gem.

We wanted to enter the house while it was still dark outside, to prevent local residents from seeing us, but our entrance does not go as smoothly as we planned. Just before we disappear between the bushes in search of an entrance, a local bus arrives and parks right in front of the house. We quickly hide out of sight and wait. And wait. And wait. Fifteen long minutes pass before the driver starts the bus and pulls away, at which point we walk quickly to the house, dodging blackberry bushes and crawling under low-hanging branches. The back door is open and Claire is first to enter, turning to look at me as if to say: "What are you waiting for? We've waited long enough!"

It is incredibly dark inside. Not only are the windows overgrowing with ivy, but the house is surrounded by trees and shrubs that prevent the light from reaching the panes to start with. The gloomy weather outside isn't helping either. However, I get all excited – I love to play with light and shadow, and this is just so beautiful.

This type of location requires a lot of concentration from Claire, as I have to use shutter speeds of at least one second; the exposure time for the shot of Claire lying on the bed is two seconds and downstairs in another room I need an exposure time of just over one minute. Fortunately, my co-explorer works silently, so Claire is not distracted by noises elsewhere in the house. On the couch she lies down and pretends to sleep. Who knows, maybe she is sleeping?

When we are ready to leave, I notice the front door is open. This happens to us all the time: why take the easy way in when there's a much more difficult route to be found?

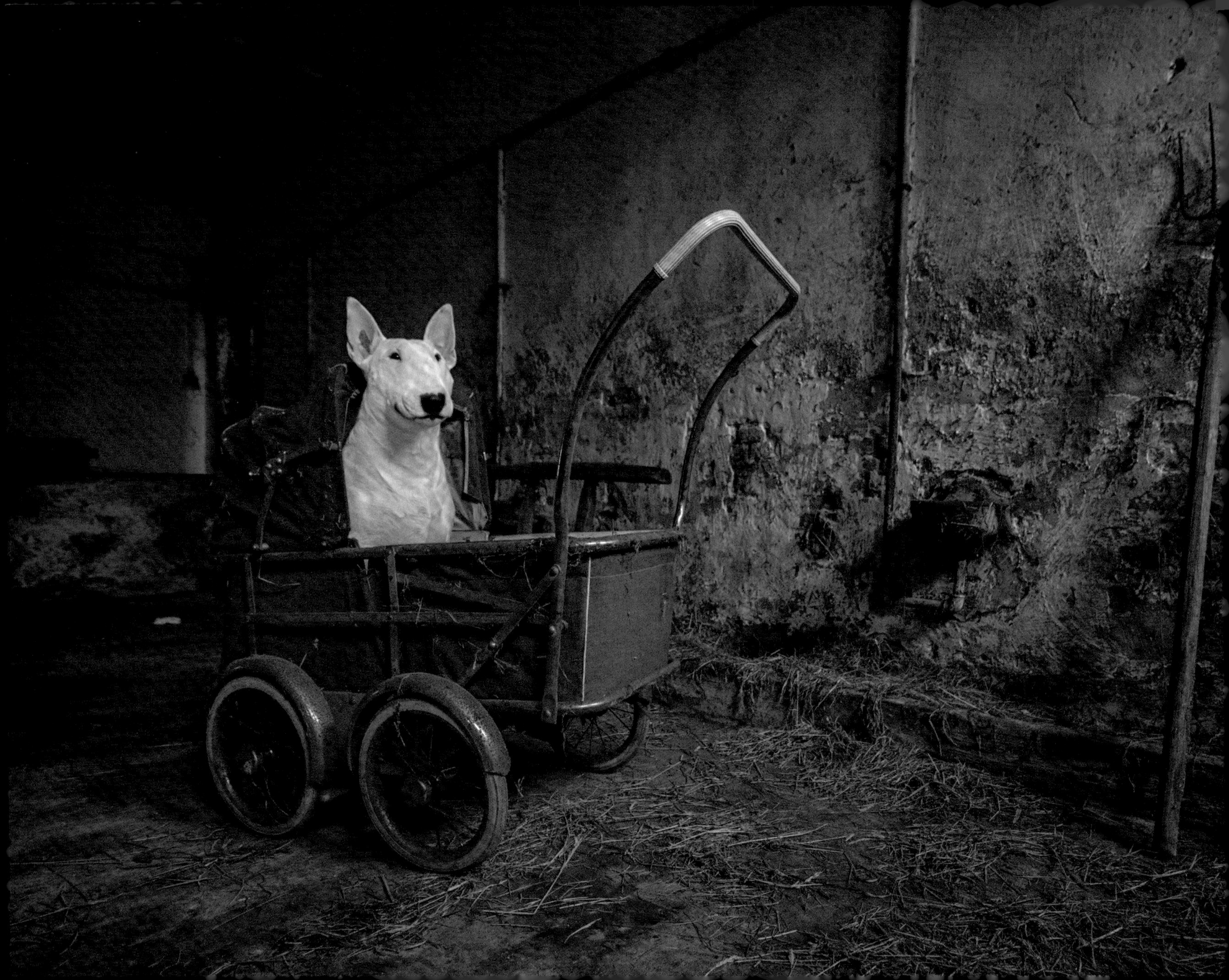

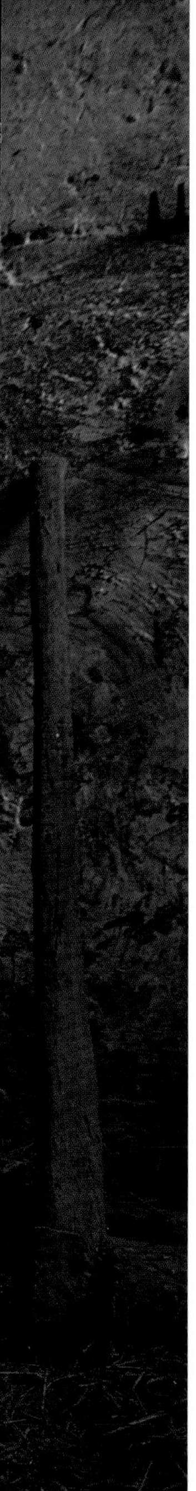

Rosary Farm

Belgium

This farm is like all the others in this small, quiet, rural community. It's a typical long gable farm where the house, stable and barn are built together, with all the doors placed along the long façade. The inhabitants' scarce possessions consist of a horse, seven cows, a couple of pigs and about a dozen chickens; behind the house stand a number of fruit trees and a modest vegetable garden. It's a hard life. There's heavy physical work to be done every day of the week, all year round, and while the people in this area rely mainly on agriculture, it does not yield much.

It is the early 1950s and a mother puts her baby back in the pram and walks from the living room, through the stable, to a corner in the barn where she fills up the coal-scuttle so she can heat the stoves to cook dinner.

Dinner is prepared in the "stove room", a small space roughly 8ft^2 (2.5m^2), next to the pump room. The pump room is where the "wet" activities are carried out, with water pumped up from the well by hand so the occupants can wash themselves, their children, their clothes, milk cans or anything else that needs to be cleaned.

"The house has religious statues and figurines in every room, framed images of saints hang on the walls."

The tranquillity is broken by the rattling of a horse-drawn farm cart on the hard cobblestones outside; the woman's husband is home from working in the fields all day. He enters the farmhouse and sits down at the table where she joins him so that they can pray together. They are deeply religious people: the house has religious statues and figurines in every room, framed images of saints hang on the walls and rosaries lie around the house, giving the farm its urbex name: "Rosary Farm".

More than 60 years later, Claire and I walk the sandy path to the back of the farm, where I peek through one of the windows. It is as if time has stood still – I can see old-fashioned kitchenware hanging on the wall, with pots and pans standing underneath. The coal stove, where the mother prepared the food for the family, seems ready for use.

The nearest door to us is closed so I try another one; it's open, but I end up in one of the two piggeries. I look over the half-height wall and discover a "long drop" toilet located in the corridor between the two piggeries. I guess the pigs didn't mind the smell too much.

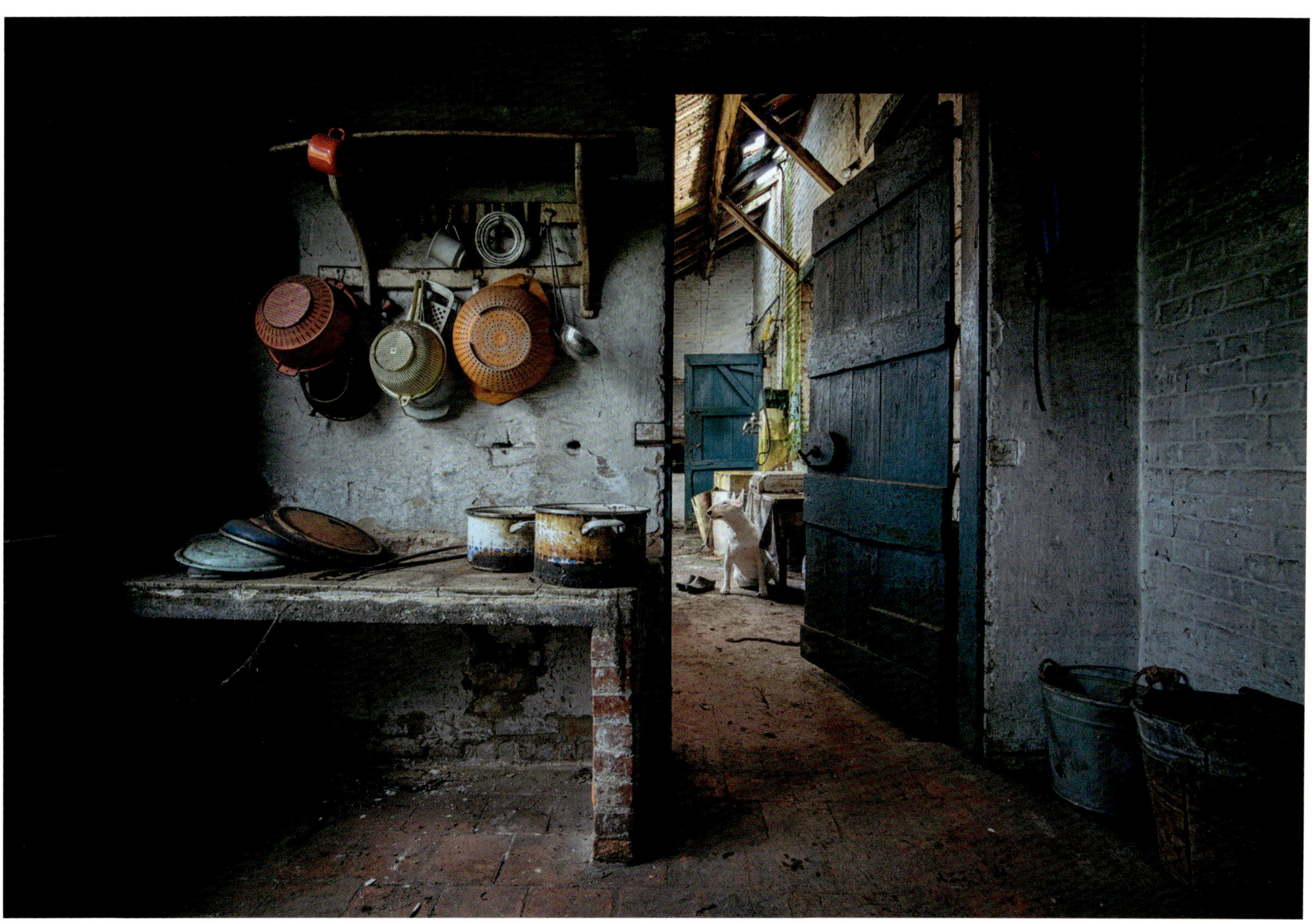

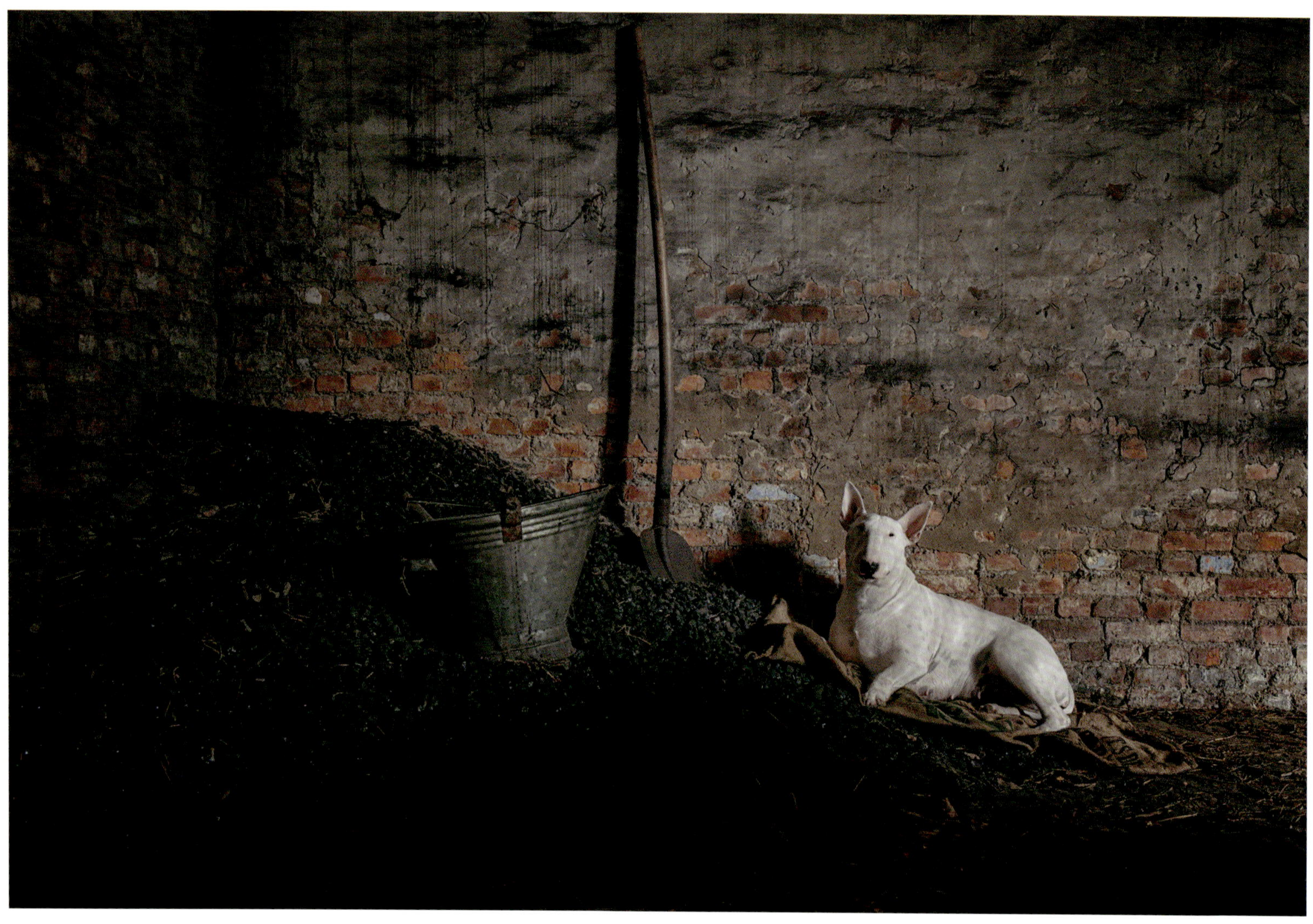

Claire and I eventually enter the main farmhouse through the barn, via a cowshed. It seems that everything is still here. There's absolutely no trace of vandalism, which is unusual nowadays. Today, the urbex motto "Take nothing but photographs, leave nothing but footprints" isn't taken too seriously by some people, so things get stolen or vandalized, and locations are shared openly, which can lead to thieves or graffiti artists visiting abandoned spaces.

Luckily when I am here, the location is in mint condition, although some items have been moved around, as the 1950s pram is found in the cowshed. Apart from that, it is the kind of location that looks as if its inhabitants just walked out. Even the beds are neatly made. Claire takes a special interest in one of them and I quickly see why; the blanket is covered with cat hairs, probably from a stray that found himself a lovely home and warm place to sleep.

Downstairs, the house has three bedrooms and a living room. In the basement we find a number of glass jars filled with green beans and rhubarb. It must have been at least eight years since they were made, but the contents still look tasty.

Upstairs, we find two more small bedrooms and an attic. In one of the rooms there's a calendar from the year 2008, which I guess is the year the residents left. When I checked the location on Google Streetview, the oldest data available was from April 2009, and it was obvious the building was uninhabited at that time. However, it's hard to imagine that people lived like this in the 21st century – without a bathroom, a sink, or running water and with a hole in the ground for a toilet – just a 90-minute drive from my own home.

Claire poses in the old-fashioned pram, next to the supply of coal in the barn, in front of the beautiful old kitchenware and in some other lovely spots. While we are upstairs working in one of the children's rooms I see a drawing lying in the corner of the room. It shows three clouds, the sun and a long row of simplistic trees. A woman in a blue dress is lying flat on her back on the street, while a priest walks past her with a rosary in his hand. Beneath the picture, in a child's hand, are the words: "The priest has no empathy for others".

I don't want to think what has happened here to drive a young child to make such a drawing and it's precisely because of these kinds of things that I prefer to visit locations that are in a greater state of decay; that have been somehow "depersonalized". I still think about that drawing every once in a while and keep wondering what happened there. I will most probably never know. Sometimes it's better that way.

Left Up until the 1960s, coal stoves were used on a large scale, and every household always had a supply of coal.

Entertainment Gallery

The little dog laughed...

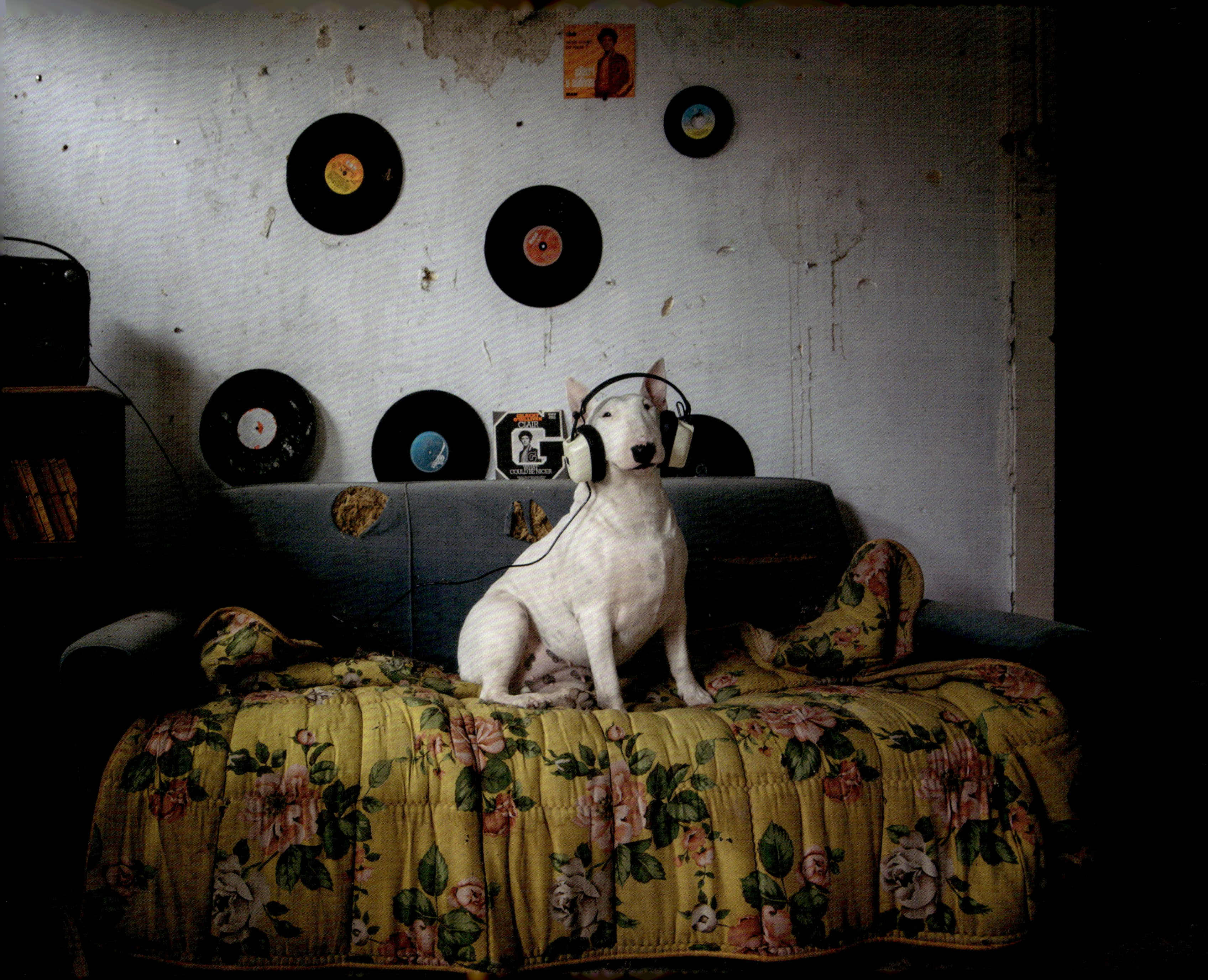

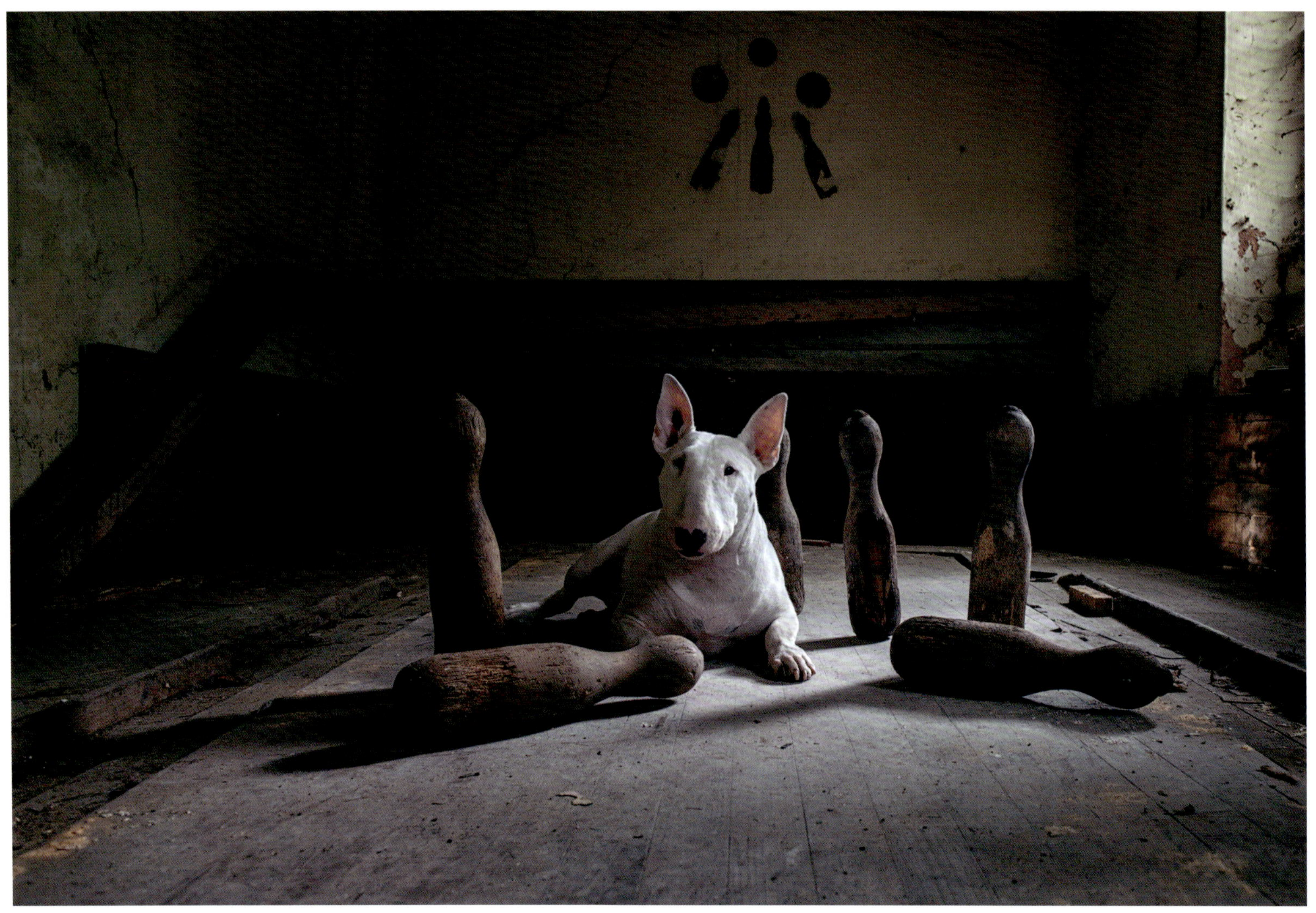

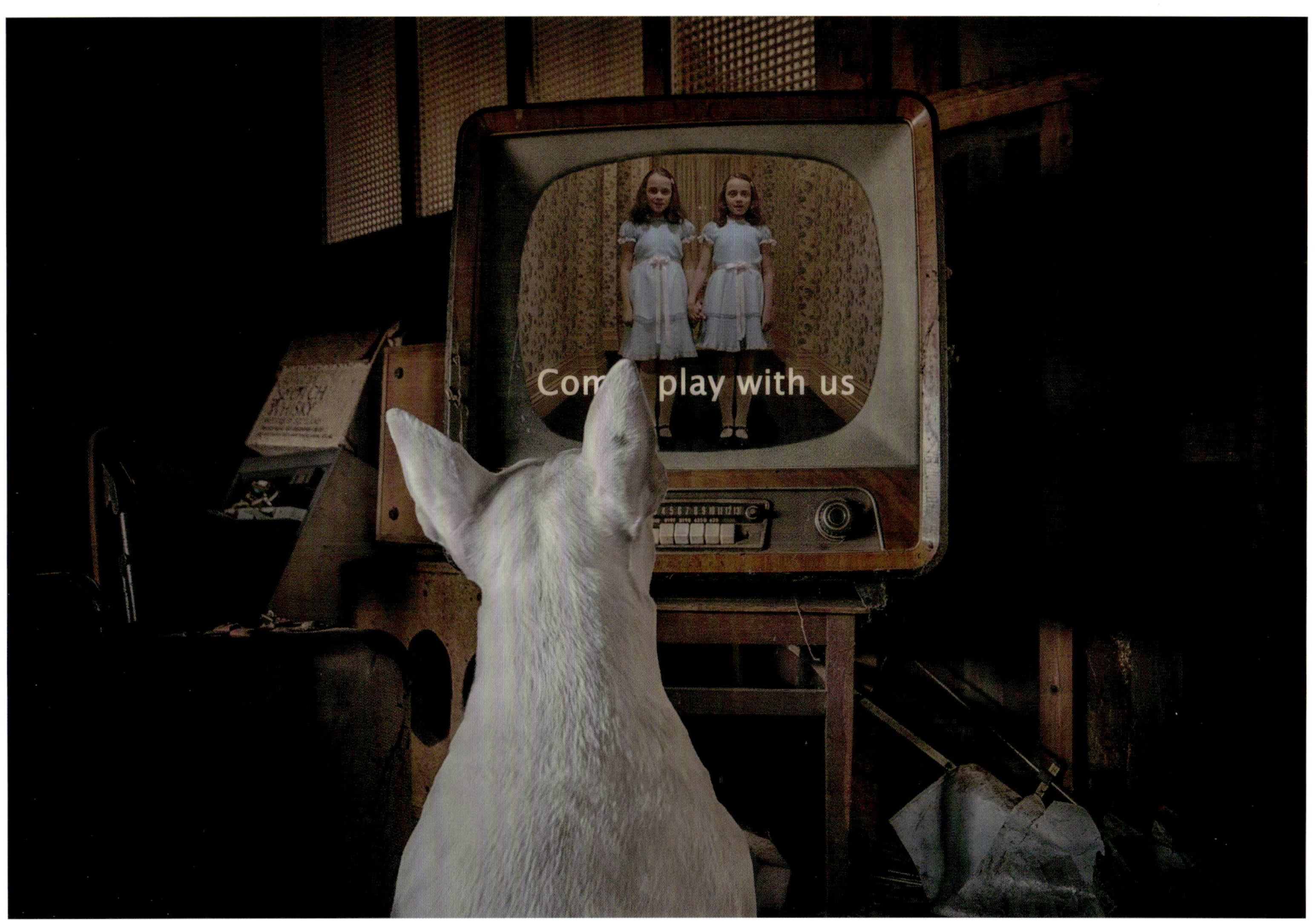

Come play with us

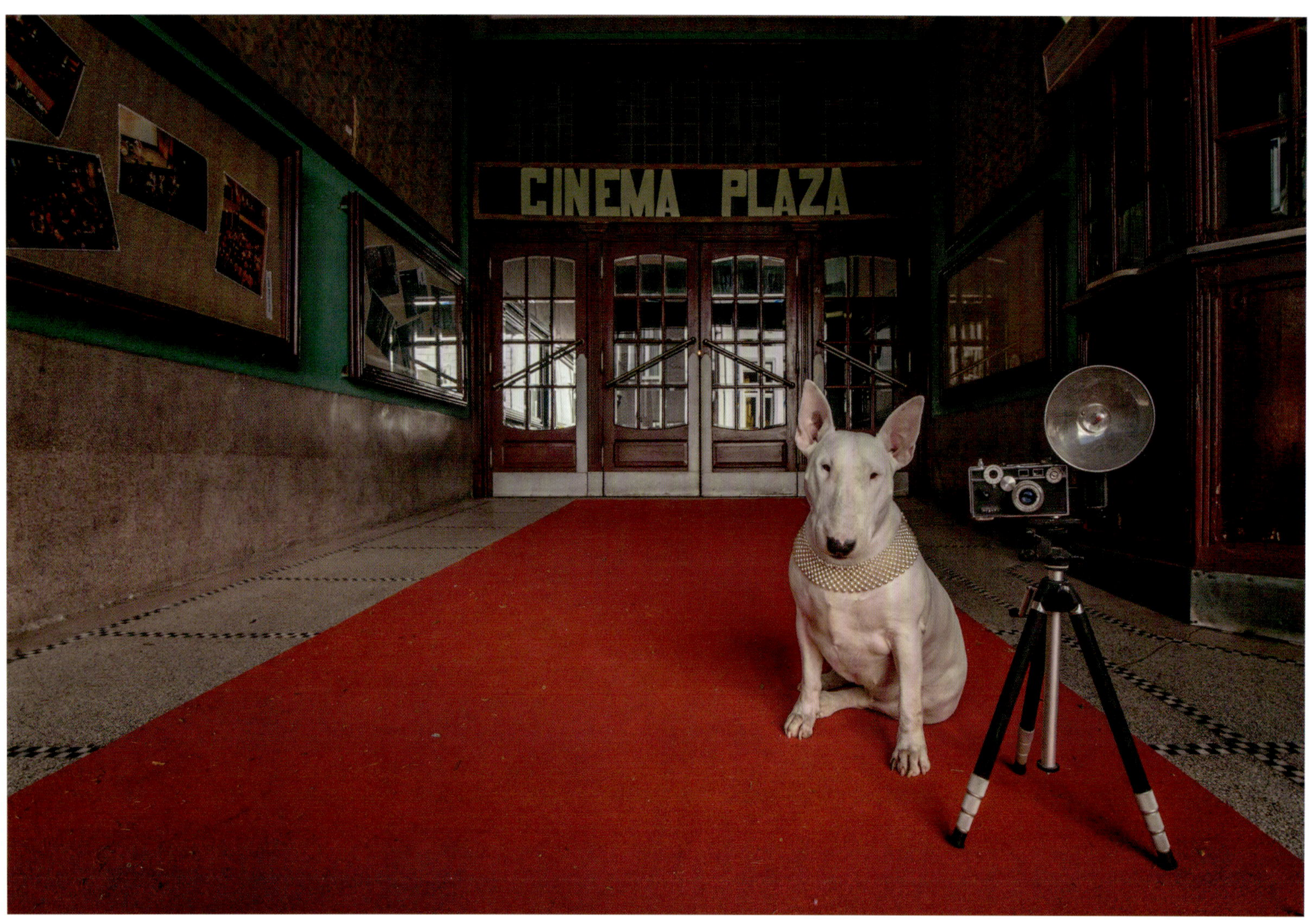

CINEMA PLAZA

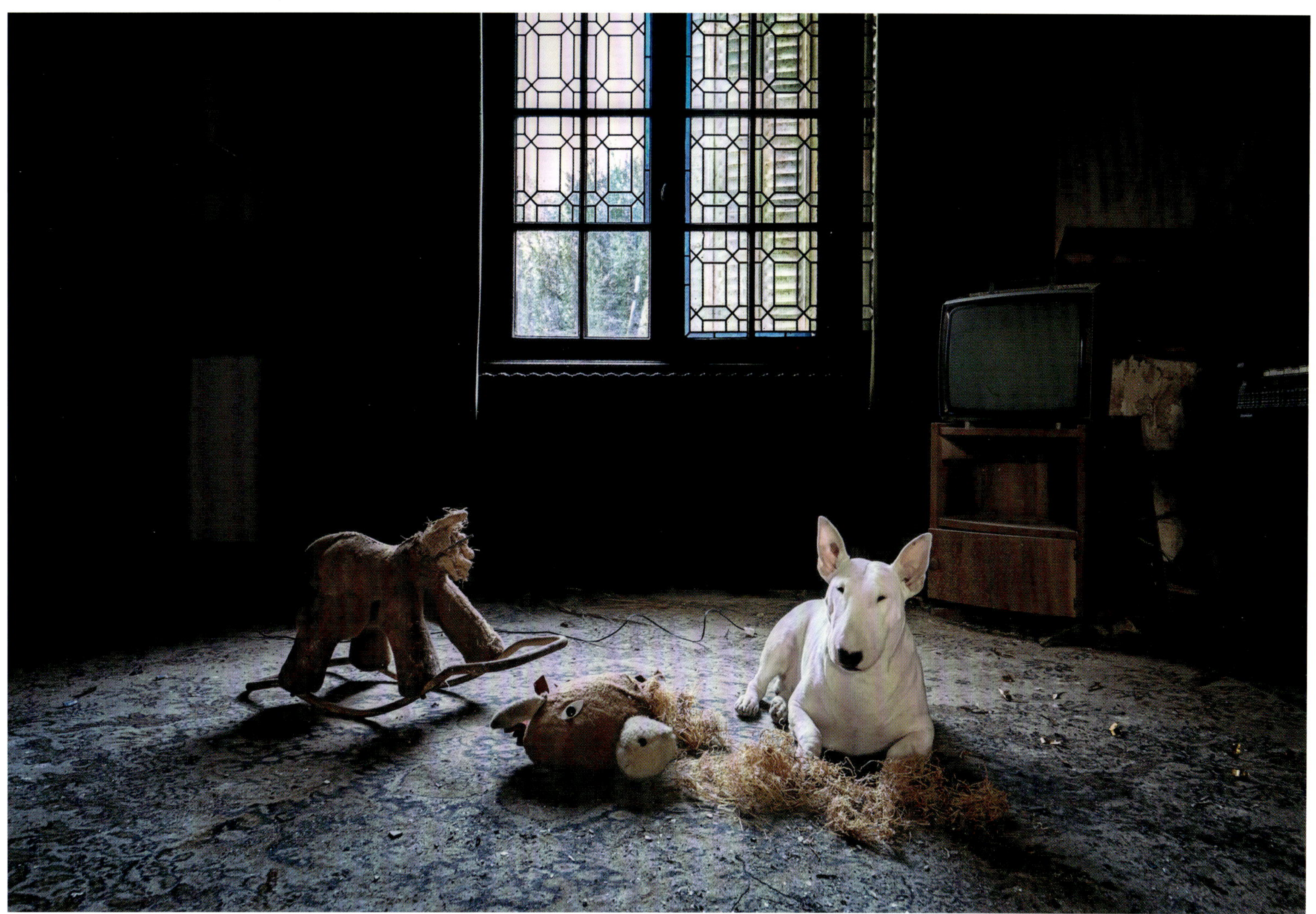

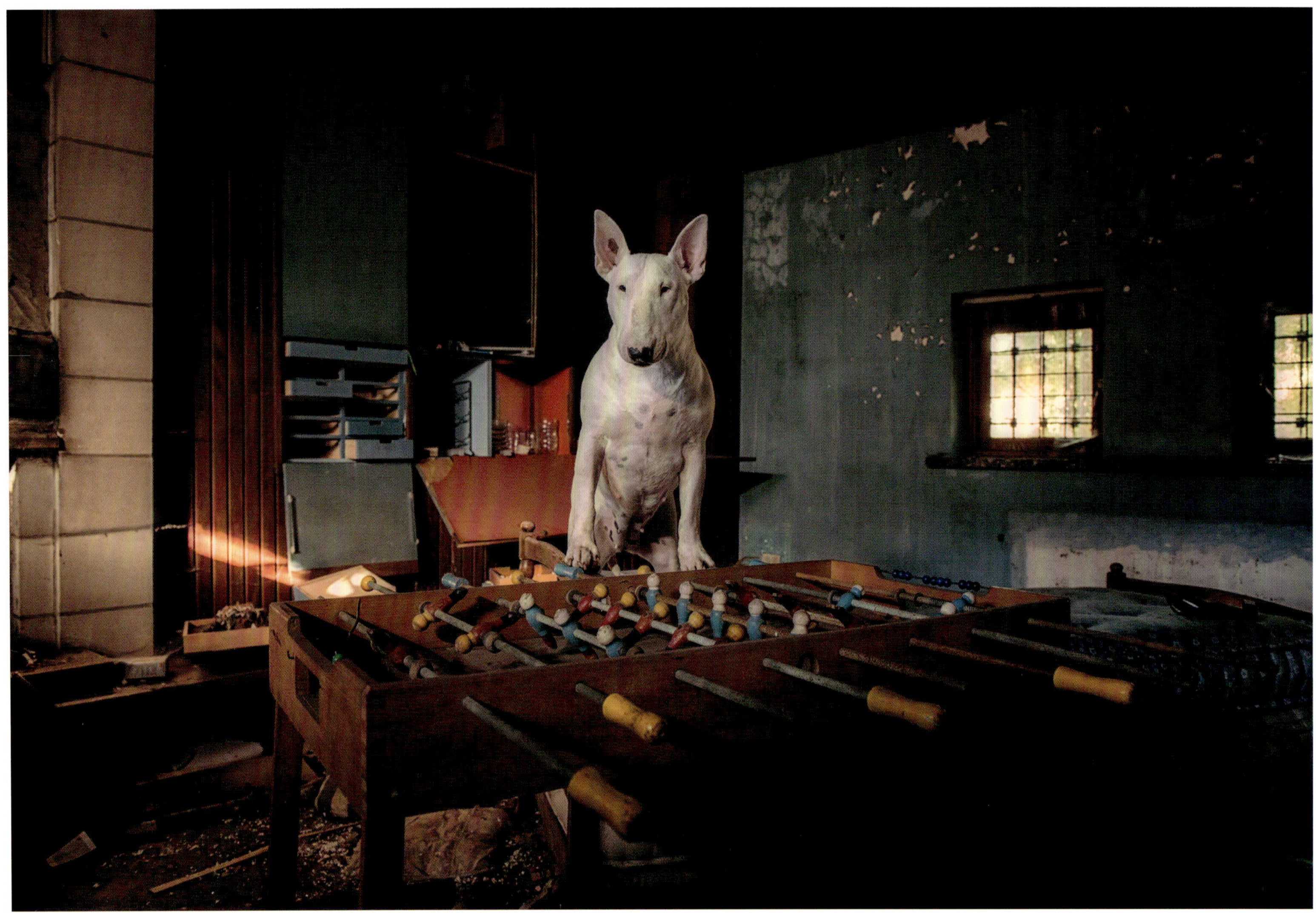

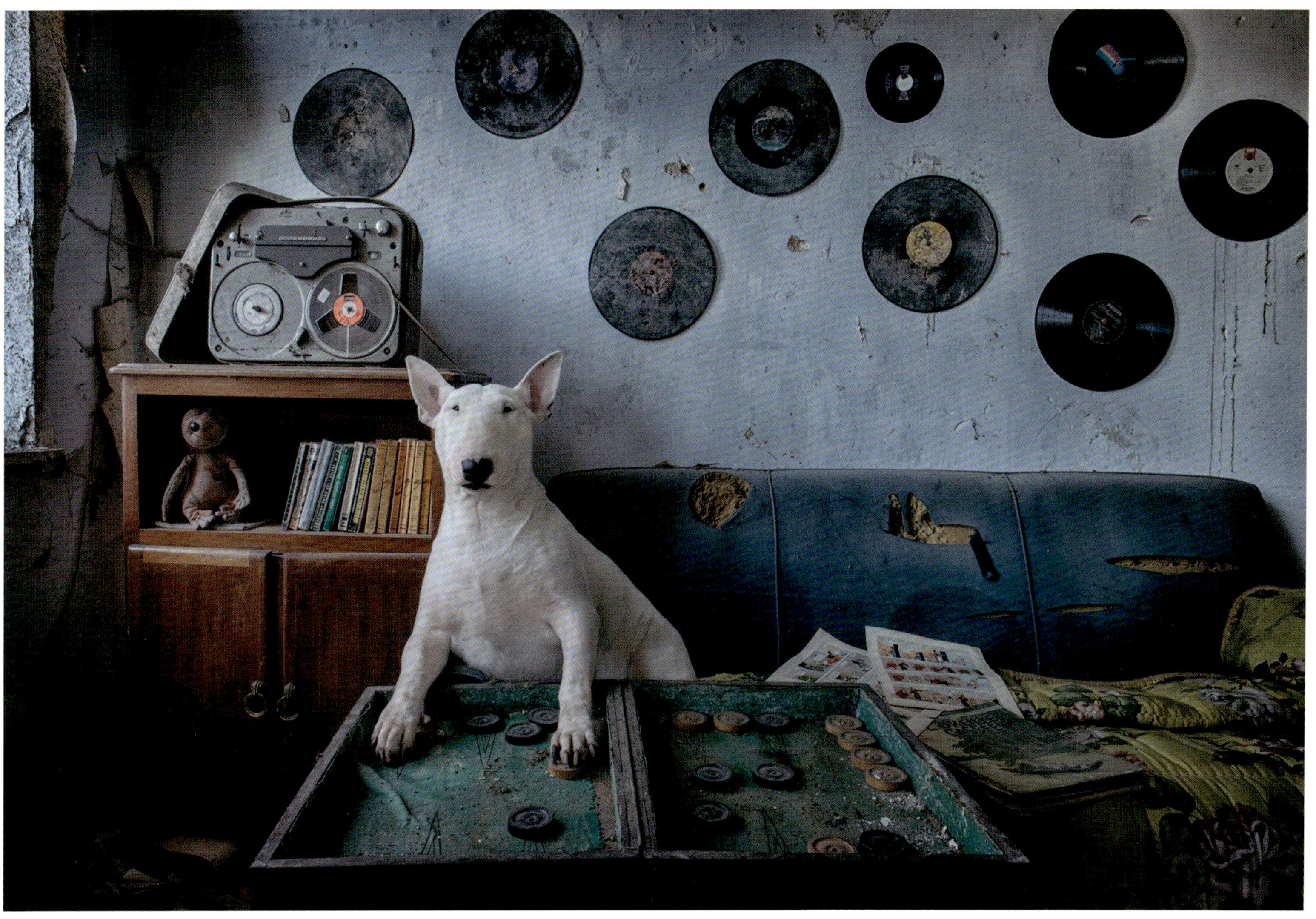

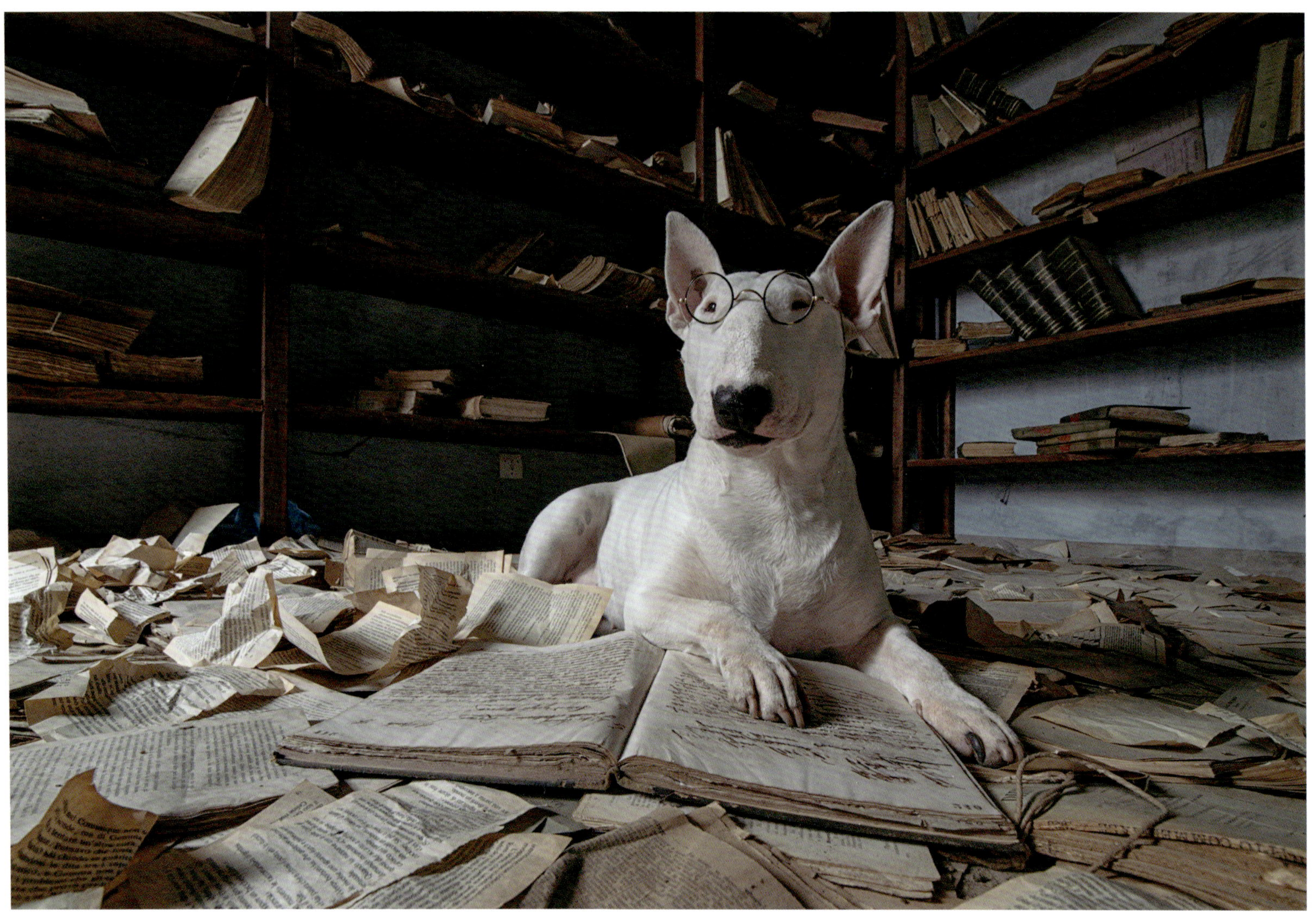

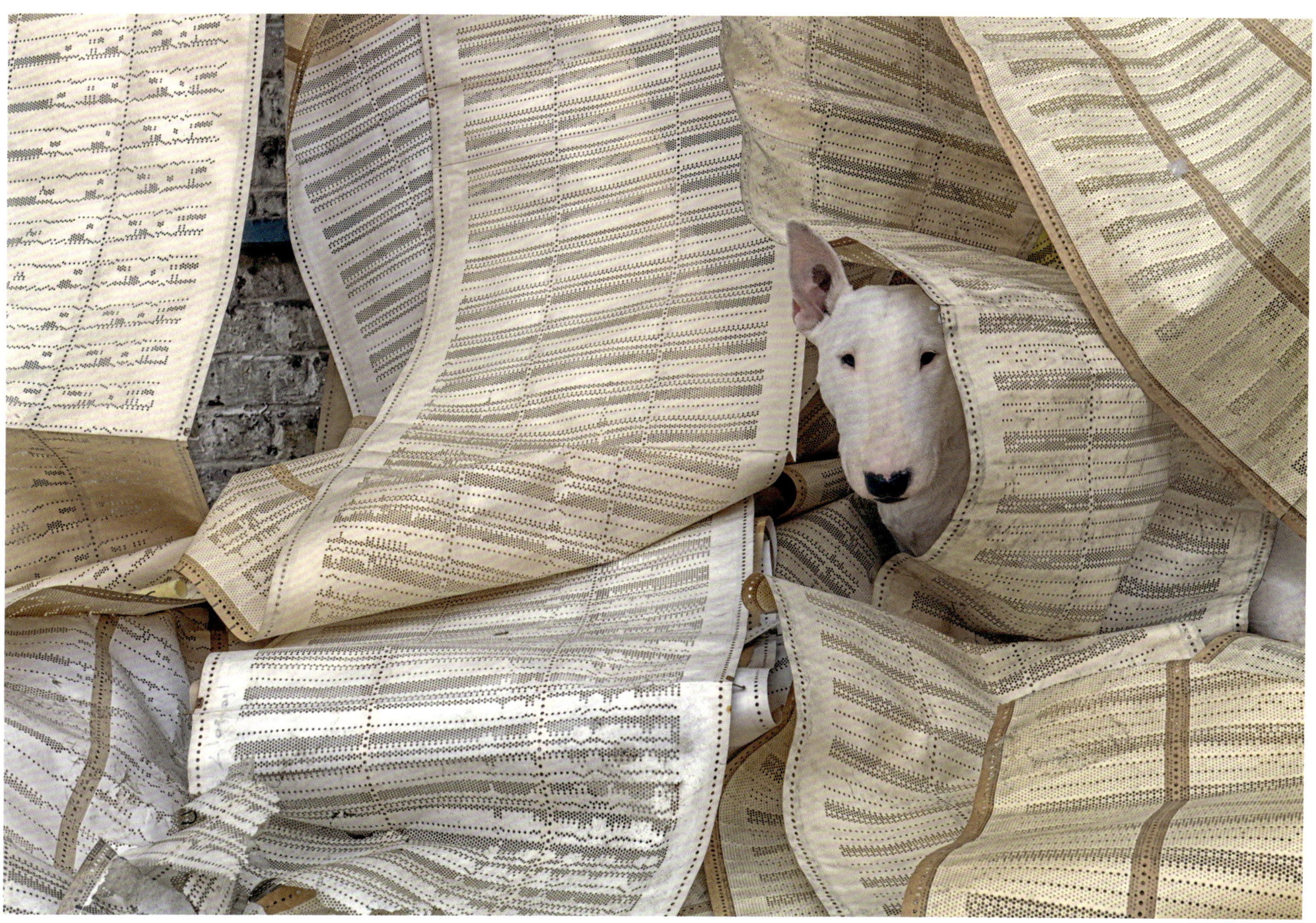

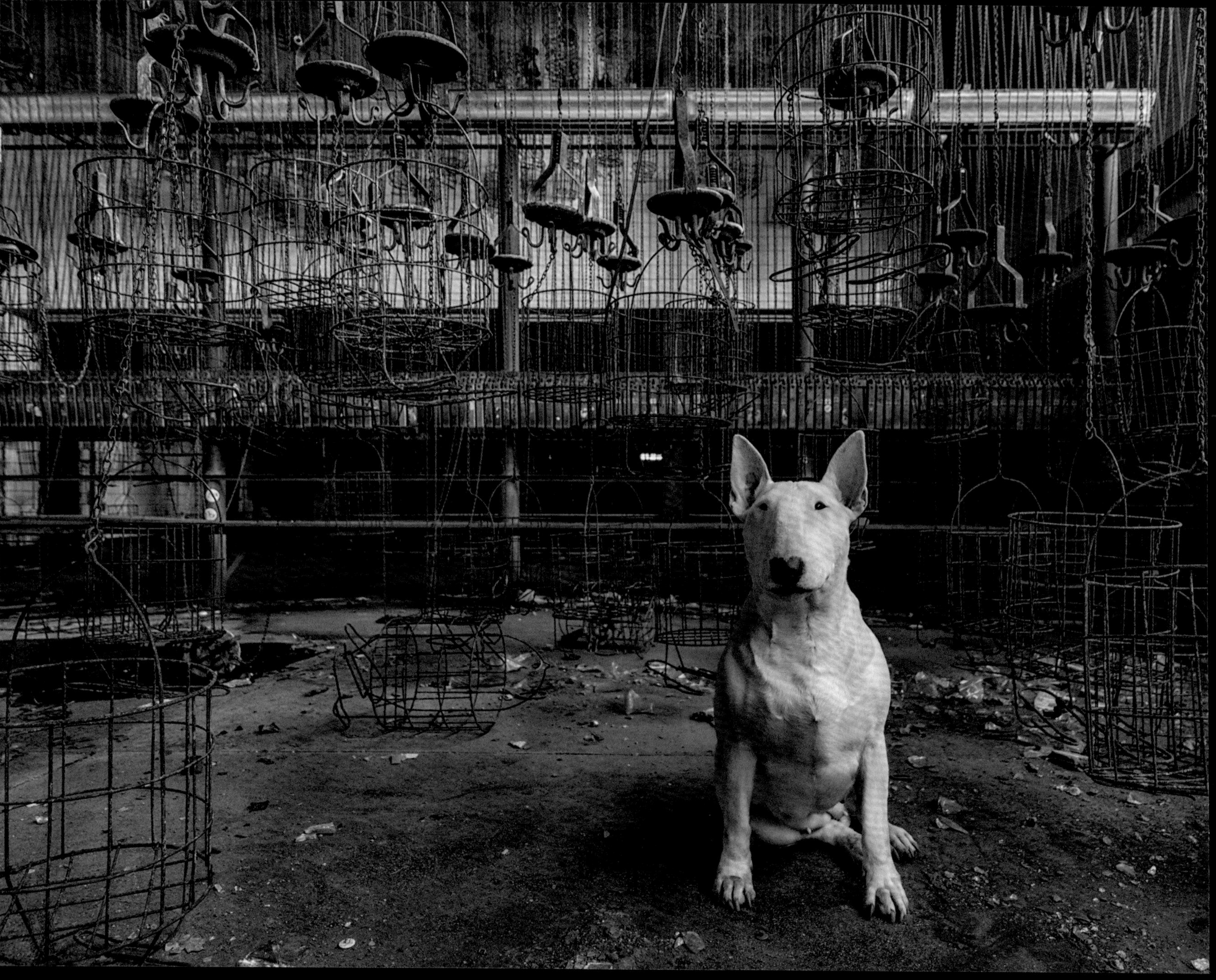

Coal Mine DT
Germany

Left Attached to the ceiling are the steel baskets where the workers would store their clean clothes. Each worker was allocated a basket and would attach the chain by padlock to steel eyelets on the wall.

For centuries, the coal industry played an important role in the supply of the world's energy. The demand for coal increased dramatically around 1850, due primarily to emerging industries with an increased need to produce iron and steel, the expansion of the rail network and the use of steam engines. All over Europe soil was examined for the presence of layers of coal, resulting in numerous coal mines opening in the regions around Liège, in Belgium, Rhineland and the Ruhr regions in Germany.

However, since the 1960s, more and more mines have been closed across Europe, not because their coal reserves had been exhausted, but because they were no longer profitable. For years, the Ruhr region had been one of Europe's largest coal-producing regions; in 1969 Ruhrkohle AG (RAG) owned 52 mines, 29 coke plants and had 183,000 employees. Now, only two working mines remain. Many mining buildings were demolished after the closures, but others were simply abandoned and still stand as if they are waiting for the miners to one day return.

During a conversation with a friend, Mark, I mention that I would love to go to Germany to photograph the so-called "hanging baskets" at an abandoned coal mine. By sheer coincidence he has just arranged to visit one known as Coal Mine DT, to meet two guys who want to interview and film him for a school project. He says we can join him if we want to, so a couple of days later myself and Claire are driving with Mark to Germany.

We park close to the location where we are meant to meet the guys who want to interview Mark and wait for them to arrive. Suddenly, a white bus with "RAG" emblazoned on the side drives past and stops at the gate up ahead of us. The driver gets out, opens the gate to the site and drives in. We decide to follow him and take a closer look to see what he's doing there.

Pretending to walk Claire, we take a slow stroll along the fence line, scanning the terrain out of the corners of our eyes. The bus is parked up, but we can't see anyone in or around it. Not sure what's

> *"Pretending to walk Claire, we take a slow stroll along the fence line, scanning the terrain out of the corners of our eyes."*

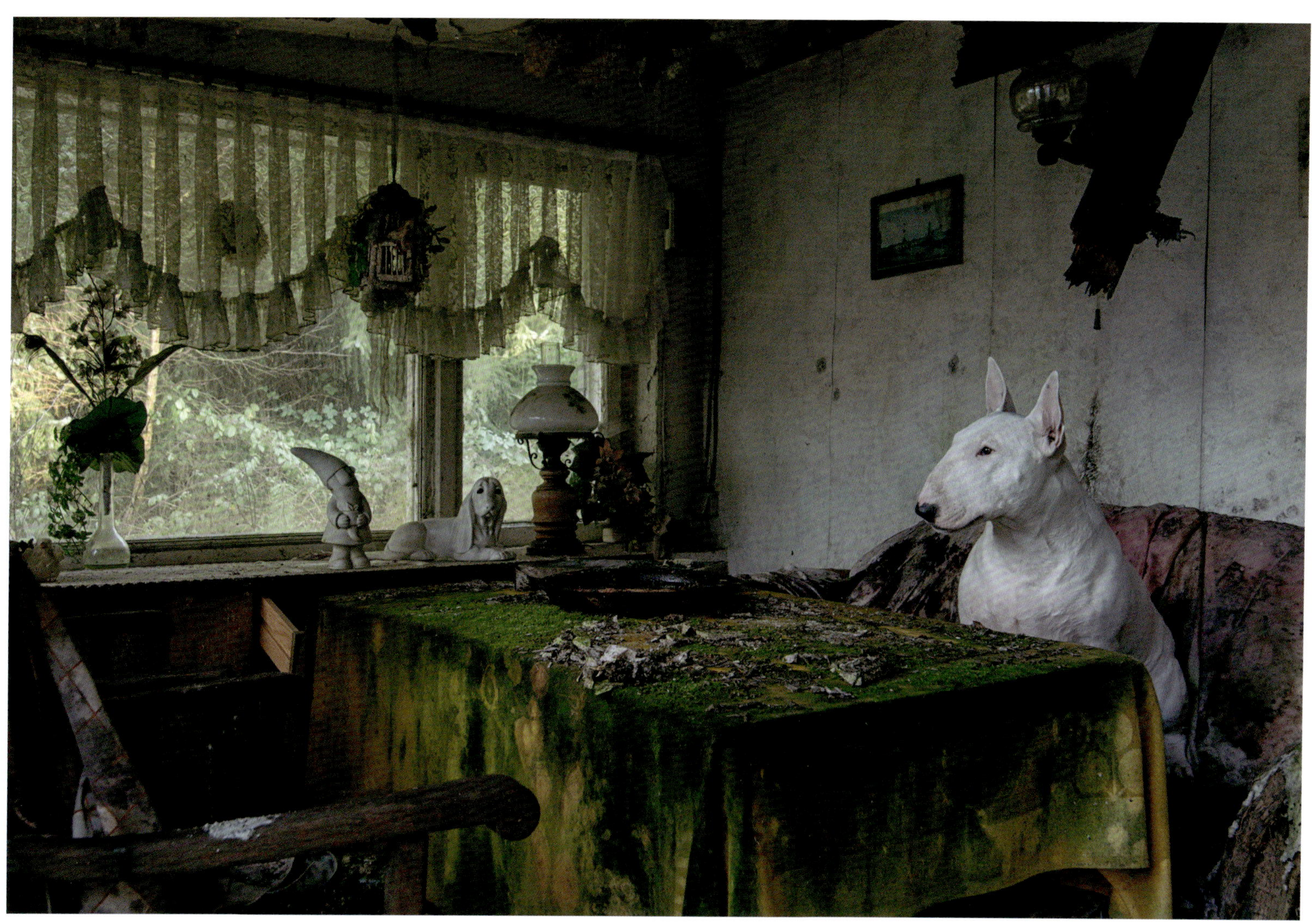

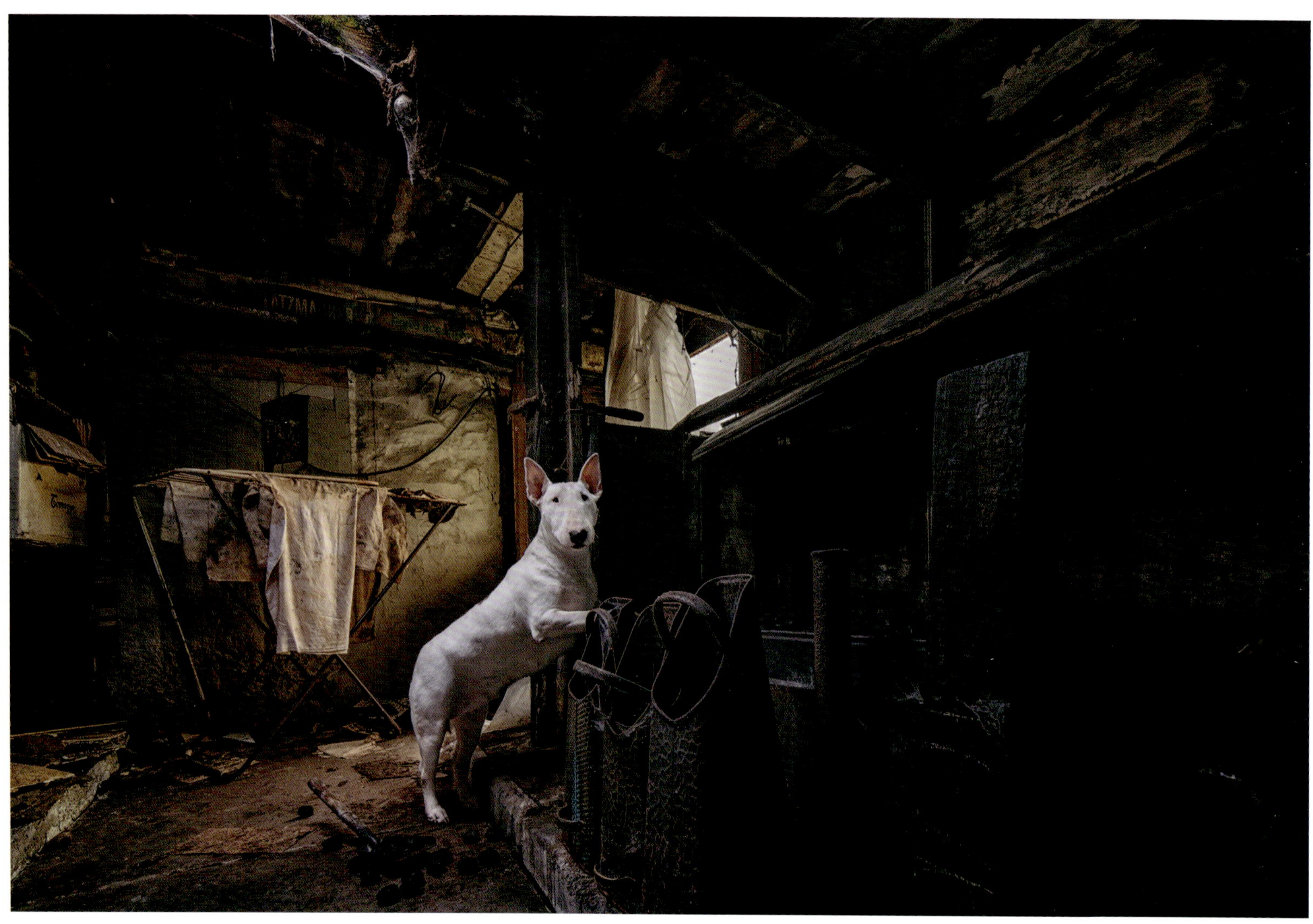

going on, we walk back to the car, just as the two guys we're meeting arrive. We wait out of sight and after half an hour we check the site again: the bus is still there.

Rather than waste any more time we elect to visit another location in the neighbourhood: an abandoned holiday cottage in the middle of the woods. It takes us a while to find it, but after walking a mile and a half through the woods, we spot "our" house between the trees. While it looks promising from the outside, it surpasses our wildest dreams once we're inside: there's fungi and moss everywhere, with mushrooms growing out of the walls. It's small inside, so we're not there for long, and when we step outside we meet a German explorer who has been waiting for us to finish; he loves the idea of using Claire as a model.

We are soon on our way back for a second attempt to visit the hanging baskets in the coal mine. When we arrive, the bus has gone, but all the gates have been closed and locked. Fortunately, Mark has been here before and knows where the holes in the mesh fence are. At the back of the mine building there should be an open window, but we soon discover it has recently been closed up – perhaps that's what the driver of the bus was here for? To our surprise, though, the

door next to it is wide open. It's as if they knew we would be coming! Once inside the mine I can't help but think of all the men who, day after day, performed heavy, dusty and dangerous work deep underground. Every day they would put all their clothes and valuables in a steel basket – the "hanging baskets" I want to photograph – and raise it up with an iron chain to keep its contents safe and clean. As they returned from the mine, the workers would bring their basket down again, before returning home. Sometimes, though, one stayed raised and the clothes went unclaimed, meaning an accident had taken place somewhere underground; perhaps as deep as 4,000ft (1,200m) below where we are standing. In the cramped subterranean corridors, danger lurked everywhere.

Mining was – and still is – very dangerous and the miners would call each other "kumpel", which means something a bit like friend or buddy. It is time to photograph my "kumpel", but if I want to photograph Claire near the baskets we have to be very careful, as the slightest touch will set the metal baskets rocking back and forth for minutes and we don't want them blurred in the pictures. But my kumpel is an experienced professional. Without touching a single basket, she positions herself perfectly in between them, waiting for me to take my shots.

Villa Heil
Belgium

Right I often wonder why houses that have clearly been decorated with a huge amount of love are abandoned by their residents and why they leave behind their personal effects. This house is no exception.

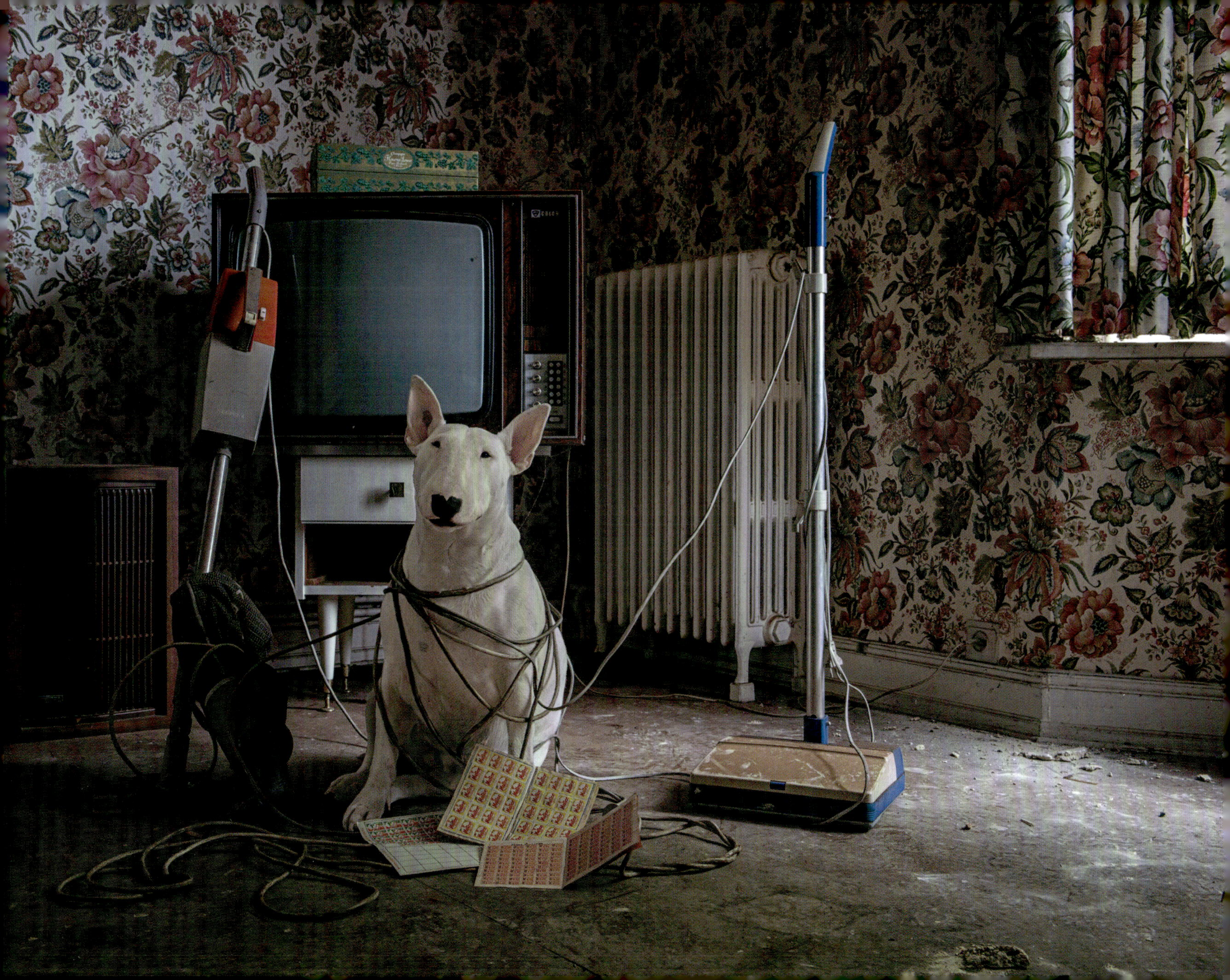

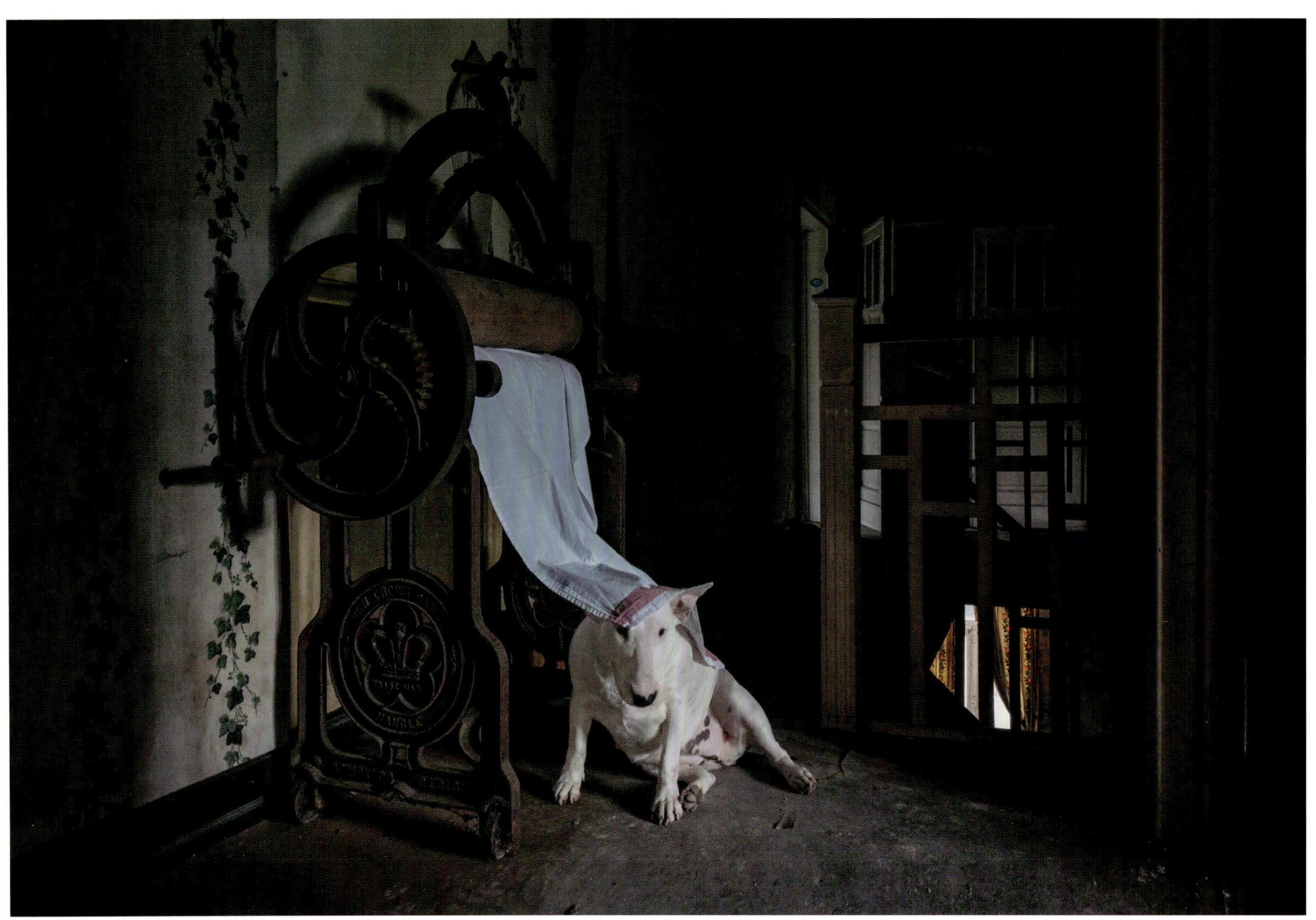

On Saturday 12 September 1914, fierce battles took place between Belgian and German troops in the small hamlet of Vijfhuizen, in the Belgian municipality of Erpe-Mere. The German troops were too strong, burning down the house of the notary and a few neighbouring buildings, before forcing the Belgian soldiers to withdraw.

The notarial office, also known as Villa Heil, was rebuilt on the same spot in 1923, which explains why the hundreds of legal papers, old files and records that can still be found in the basement don't date back further than the early 1920s. The archive is now completely permeated by moisture and mould, and the shelves bow under the weight: as soon as I saw it, I knew that I wanted to take some pictures of Claire in this basement.

The first challenge is to get into the property without being seen. The current notary's office sits beside the driveway to the original building and when the employees are at work they keep an eye on the older property. This means it is better to try and enter at the right side of the house, where there's a 5ft (1½m) high concrete wall. With the help of my two buddies, Anita and Jacqueline, I lift Claire over the wall and we cross to the building. The back door is wide open and we sneak cautiously inside. We have heard stories about a caretaker who checks the premises regularly, so we are extra careful.

The left wing of the building has suffered severe damage after part of the roof was destroyed during a storm. Rainwater has caused the floors to rot and some are partially collapsed, so we decide to concentrate on the safer parts of the building instead. The decay is still to die for in these rooms.

Anita and Jacqueline are taking pictures in the basement so I decide to leave that to last. I am standing in the kitchen, thinking how I'm going to photograph Claire when a car drives around the corner of the house and parks right next to the door we came in through. It looks like we might be in trouble, but before the driver sees us I run through the hallway and down into the basement to warn my friends. We turn off our flashlights and stand in the pitch-black cellar, not knowing who is coming. We are dead silent.

When I ran into the basement I closed the door behind me, so it's difficult to hear anything. After about 15 minutes we sneak upstairs very carefully, opening the door to listen. We don't hear a thing so decide that it's now or never. Without making a sound, we tiptoe to the back door. The car is still parked right in front of the door, but hopefully its driver is somewhere upstairs, which will give us a chance to get away safely.

As soon as we're outside we run towards the bushes and get out of sight as soon as possible. Back at our car we burst out laughing, imagining what would have happened if the car's driver had walked down to the basement and discovered three women and a bull terrier standing there in complete darkness.

Palacio de Comenda
Portugal

Right The Palacio de Comenda is situated at the top of a cliff overlooking the Sado River as it flows into the Atlantic Ocean.

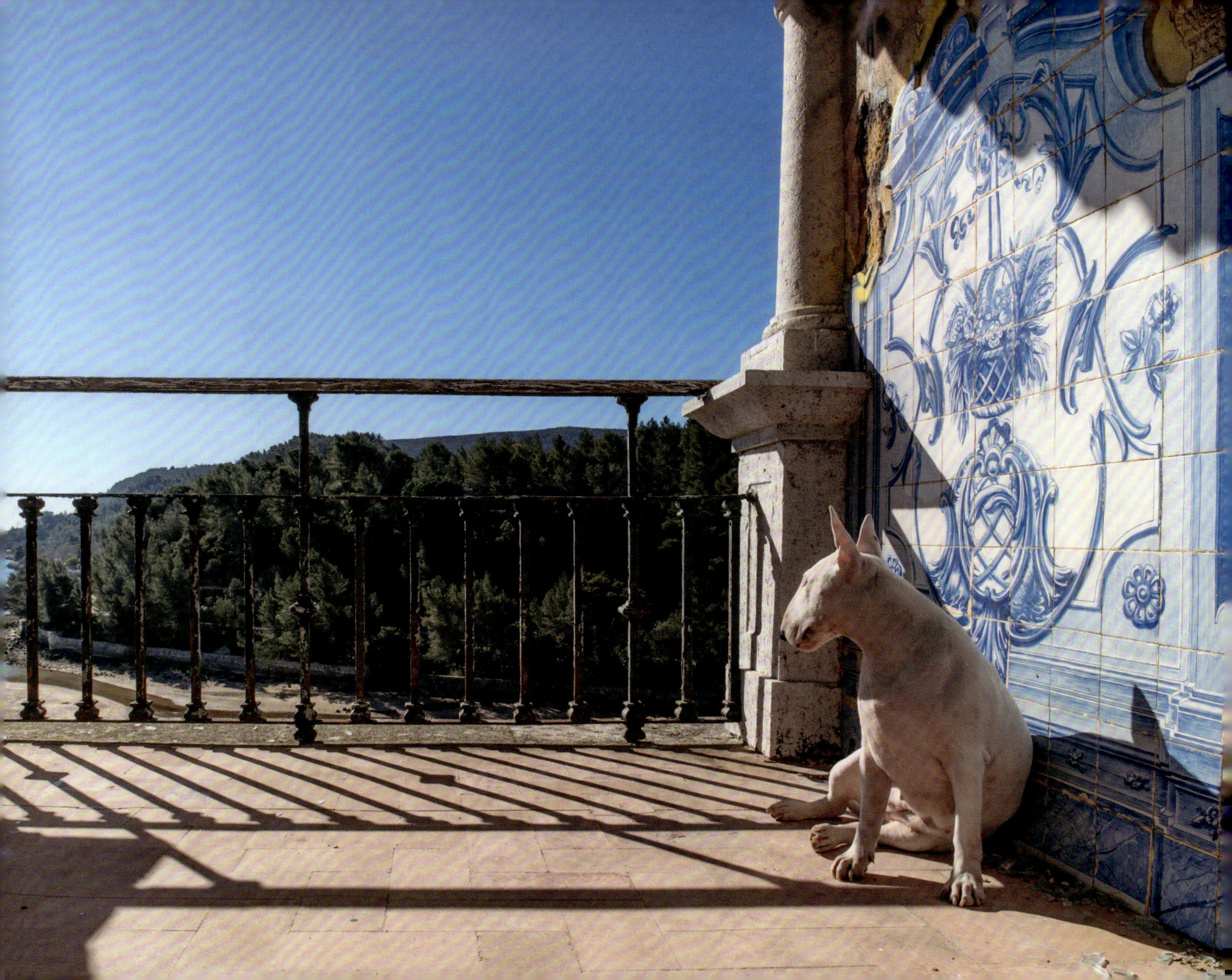

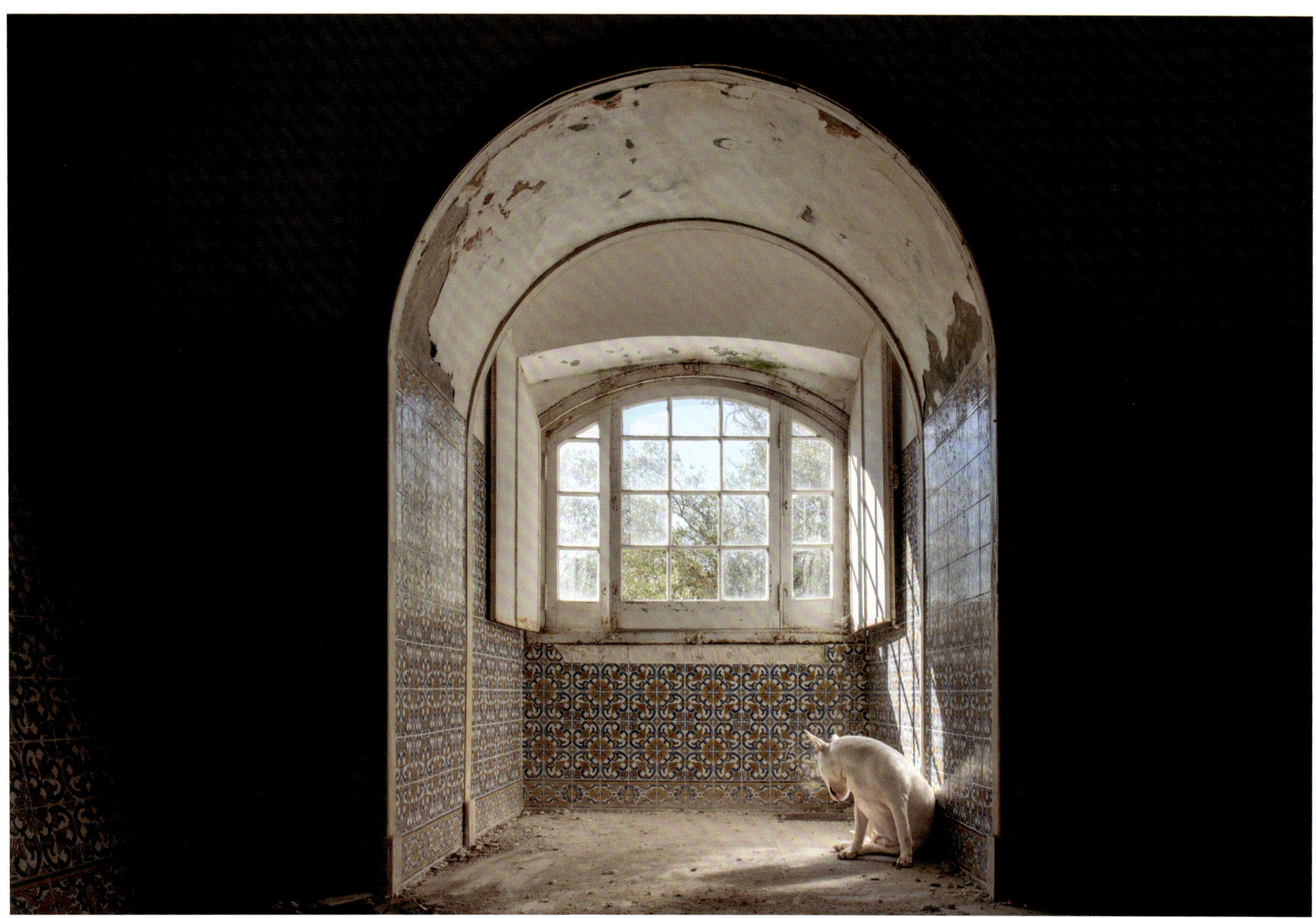

In downtown Dallas on Friday 22 November 1963, the weather was sunny and warm. When the 1961 Lincoln Continental turned on to Elm Street the crowd was cheering and both Jacqueline Kennedy Onassis and her husband were smiling back at the massed spectators. They were enjoying their trip until, seconds later, John Fitzgerald Kennedy, the 35th president of the United States of America, was shot. He would later die of his injuries.

In the period that followed, Jackie Kennedy was a symbol of strength, with much of her grieving done in private. Yet, inside she was struggling immensely with her grief and memories of the assassination. So, after the funeral she withdrew from public view with her two children.

In her book, *Jacqueline Bouvier Kennedy Onassis*, Barbara Leaming writes that Jackie "was a frail, bereaved woman who arrived at Palacio de Comenda in the Serra da Arrábida in Setubal shortly after her husband's murder in 1963." How long she stayed at the palace that she used as a kind of refuge isn't mentioned, but Palacio de Comenda is the ideal place for someone who wants to withdraw from public life for a while. It has five floors, 26 rooms, numerous bathrooms, a wine cellar, two swimming pools and private access to a remote beach.

It is through the private entrance on the beach that Claire and I access the property – it's not often that we can combine a stroll at the beach with an explore. Claire almost runs up the stairs – it's clear she's enjoying this – while I follow slightly more slowly. I reach the top of the stairs and have a good look at the palace; although, today "palace" is something of an overstatement. All of the windows have been smashed, the walls are sprayed with graffiti, most of the old Portuguese wall tiles have been stolen and a beautiful tile tableau at the entrance has been vandalized with spray paint. We walk upstairs and it's the same story: broken windows, graffiti, stolen tiles.

The only things unchanged are the balconies and the view across the Sado Estuary, which is just as beautiful as it would have been all those years ago. I stand on a balcony and look out, imagining Jackie's children, Caroline and John Jr., playing on the beach, too young to understand the full horror of what had happened, while their mother relives that fateful day over and over again.

It might sound strange – and perhaps it is my imagination – but sometimes it is as though Claire somehow senses a person who once lived in an abandoned house and starts taking on their character. While I am admiring the beautiful view, Claire sits down with a pensive, almost sad look on her face. She stares for minutes without seeming to focus on anything. If only she could talk...

Left "Azulejo" is a Portuguese word that refers to beautiful, glazed tiles. Azulejos have often been used since the 13th century to decorate walls. The ones in this cellar are well preserved.

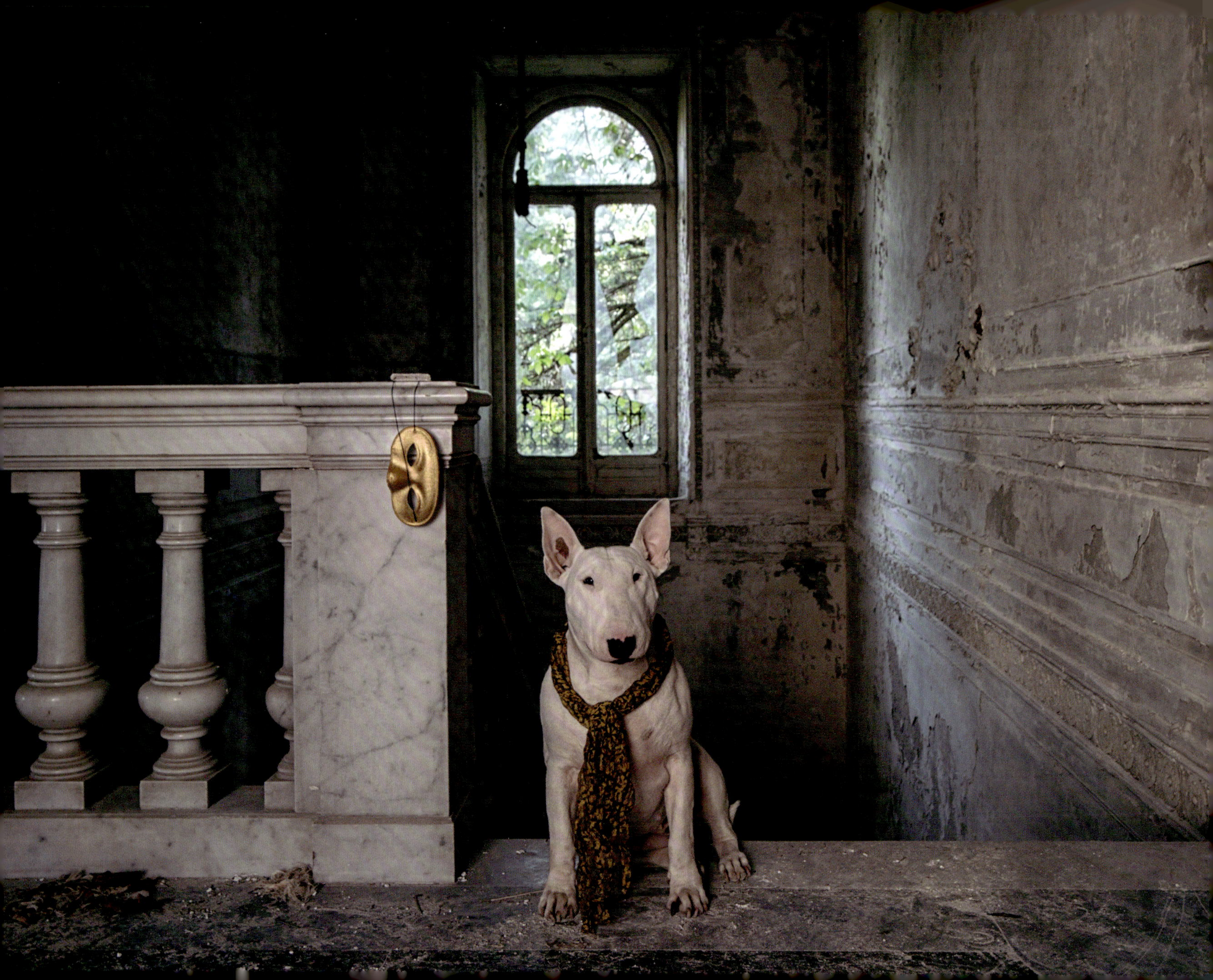

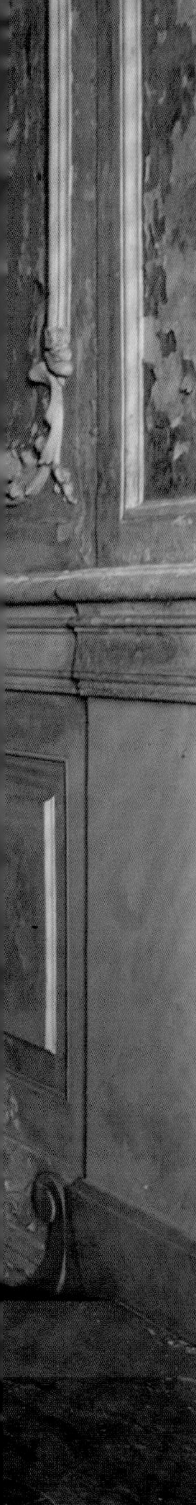

Villa Minetta

Left The marble staircase of the Villa Minetta is as beautiful as ever, and if I close my eyes I can almost hear the footsteps of the former residents.

We start our walk by following a narrow country road, leaping over a creek and pushing through the woods that will lead us to the former residence of a Count. If there is a path I cannot see it, so we stay close to our Italian friend who effortlessly finds his way. Suddenly, the outline of the mansion appears in front of us and we're back in the second half of the 19th century, standing in front of a villa that saw the rise and fall of the Italian monarchy.

The Villa Minetta was home to the son of the owner of one of the largest shipping companies. He lived with his wife and four children in this beautiful residence; a five-storey building surrounded by a 15-acre (six hectare) park full of trees that were hundreds of years old. The entrance hall was so beautiful that it swept guests off their feet thanks to its Ionic-style marble columns, painted ceiling and intricate mosaic floor. The impressive lounges and other elegant rooms were all decorated with stucco, relief, frescos, columns and statues.

The exceptionally wealthy resident was the richest man in Italy in his time and a remarkable character. He was born in Genoa and after he graduated in law he joined his father's shipping company.

The company expanded fast, from a fleet of 571 vessels in 1865 to a little over 1,500 in 1869. They mainly shipped goods and passengers between Genoa and South America, but were also one of the largest importers of coal from England.

The rich and famous were often invited to the estate to attend exuberant parties, lavish balls and receptions. High-ranking guests included King Victor Emmanuel II and his son Prince Umberto di Savoia. Victor Emmanuel II was King of Sardinia from 1849 to 1861, and on 17 March 1861 he became the first king of a united Italy since the 6th century. The royals stayed at the villa with their entourage and a date plate was placed in one of the rooms to commemorate the event. The Count died in October 1906 and his family left the estate in the 1930s, but the building's history didn't end there.

In 1939, the Italian dictator Benito Mussolini formed an alliance with Adolf Hitler and signed a military covenant. On 10 June 1940 the Italians declared war on England and France, and the villa became the headquarters for the German Schutzstaffel, or "SS" as they were more commonly known.

> *"The royals stayed at the villa… and a date plate was placed in one of the rooms to commemorate the event."*

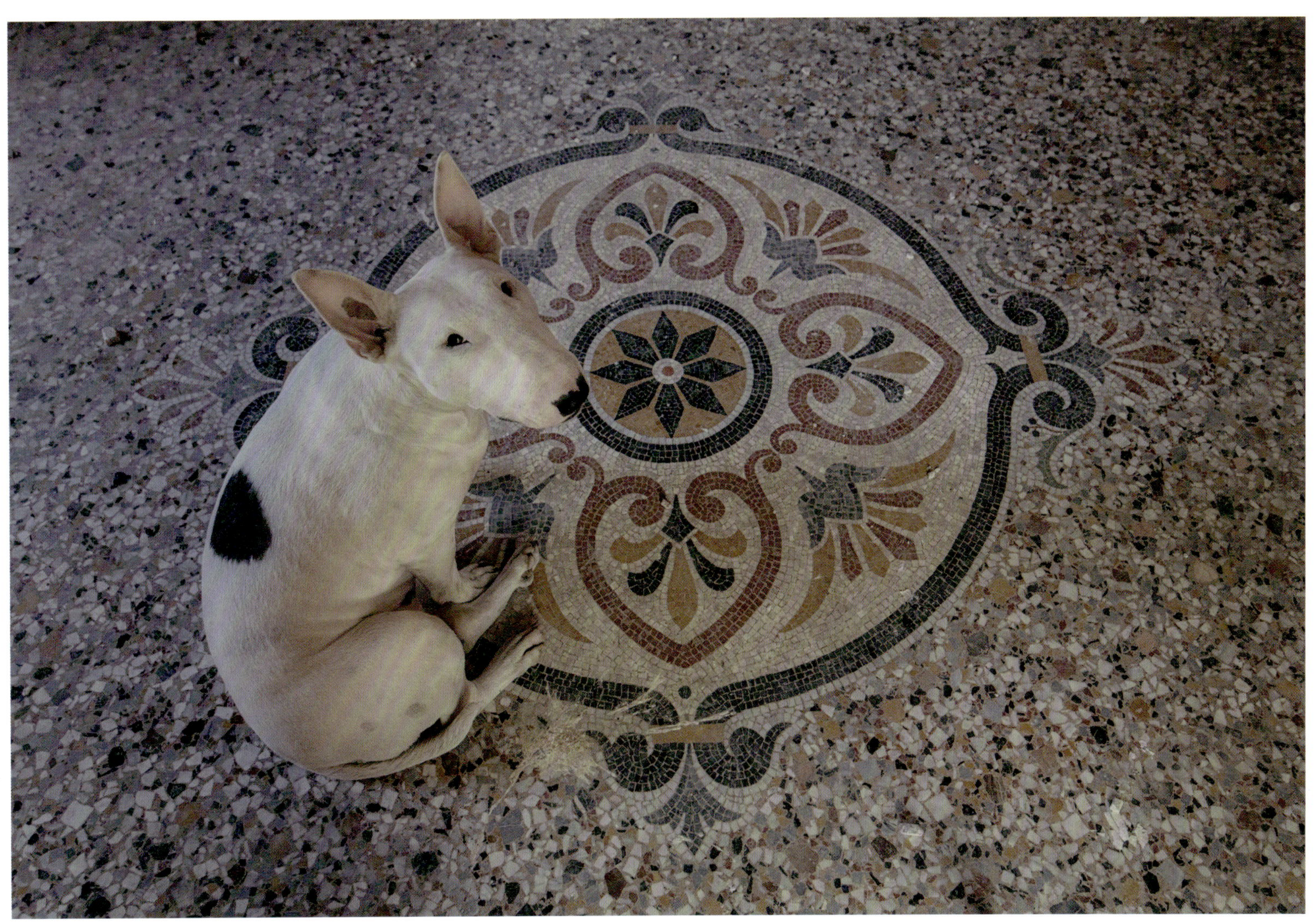

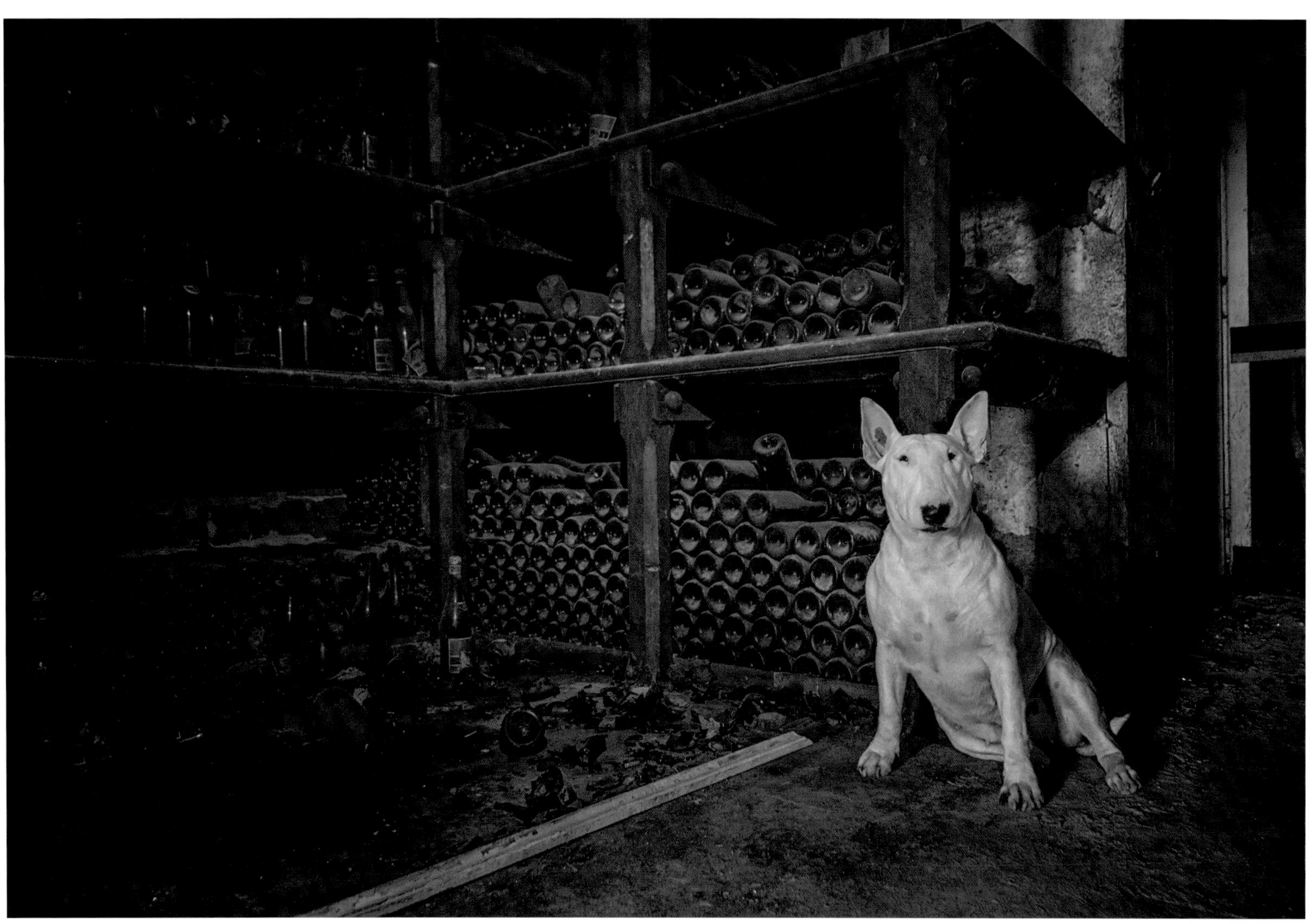

Four years later, Mussolini created Repubblica Sociale Italiana (the Italian Social Republic) in the north of Italy. After the liberation of Rome by the Allies in June 1944, there was a fear that the northern part of Italy would be lost as well, so the RSI army, which included both German and Italian units, was reorganized to defend the Ligurian coast. The commander of the army was Mussolini's newly appointed Minister of Defense, Marshal Rodolfo Graziani, better known as "The Butcher of Ethiopia". Graziani's headquarters would be "our" villa and it was here, on 29 April 1945, that he surrendered to the U.S. Army. On 2 May, American Jeeps were parked side by side on the lawn next to the villa and the Stars and Stripes was raised; the war had ended.

Shortly after, the villa came under the ownership of the Palmiri family. They were a well-known circus family, headed by Giovanni Palmiri or "Red Devil" as he was known in the circus ring. However, on 30 June 1949 disaster struck when, while he was performing an act that involved riding a motorbike along a high wire, Giovanni slipped and fell 65 feet (20m) to his death. Although the Palmiri family continued performing in the years that followed, Giovanni's widow and her family never returned to the villa.

After the circus family left, the villa was bought by the Spinoglio family, who built a swimming pool, tennis court, sauna and dressing rooms in the park. The property was soon up for auction, though, with the prestigious auction house Il Ponte Casa D'Aste charged with organizing the sale. Rumour has it that Dodi al Fayed was interested in buying the villa for himself and Diana, Princess of Wales, but sadly both their lives ended in the Pont de l'Alma tunnel in Paris.

Today, the door to the villa hangs wide open, inviting us in. We enter the house that once was loved by so many people, but all that is left is an empty shell with dust that lies on the floor like a thick carpet. The interior has been vandalized and plundered: all of the fireplaces – which were once present in every room – have been stolen; old decorations and tiles have been taken; part of the roof has collapsed; the once sturdy wooden stairs are too weak to bear weight; and, while walking upstairs, you can sometimes see through holes to the room below. Some parts of the house have been well preserved, though, and in one of the upstairs rooms the beautiful mosaic floor is still undamaged, while the marble staircase is as beautiful as ever. Smaller stairs take us down to the basement, where we find the wine cellar. If only walls could talk.

Left Villa Minetta is more commonly known as Villa del Vinaio because of the thousands of bottles of wine stacked in the cellars.

Villa del Medico

Italy

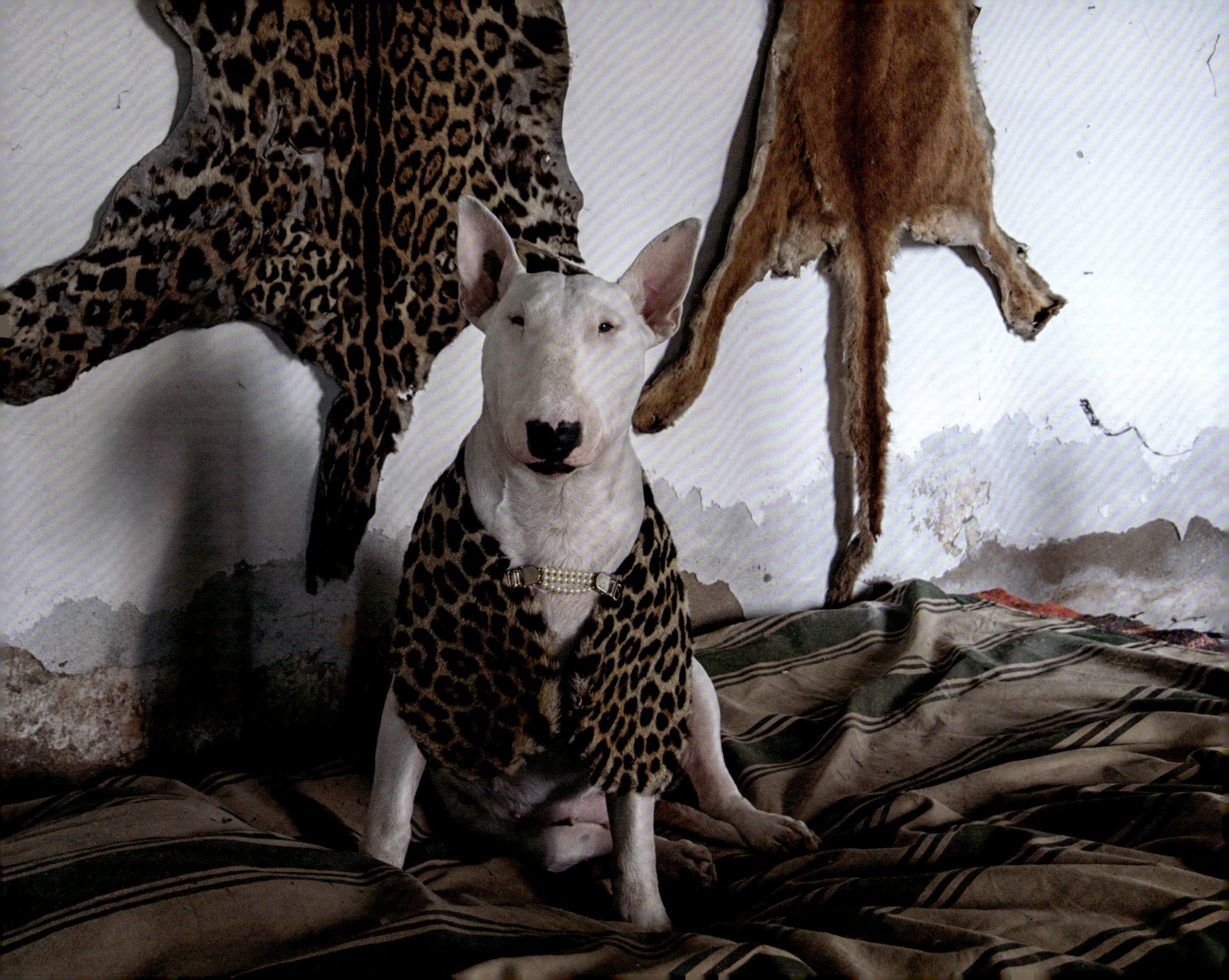

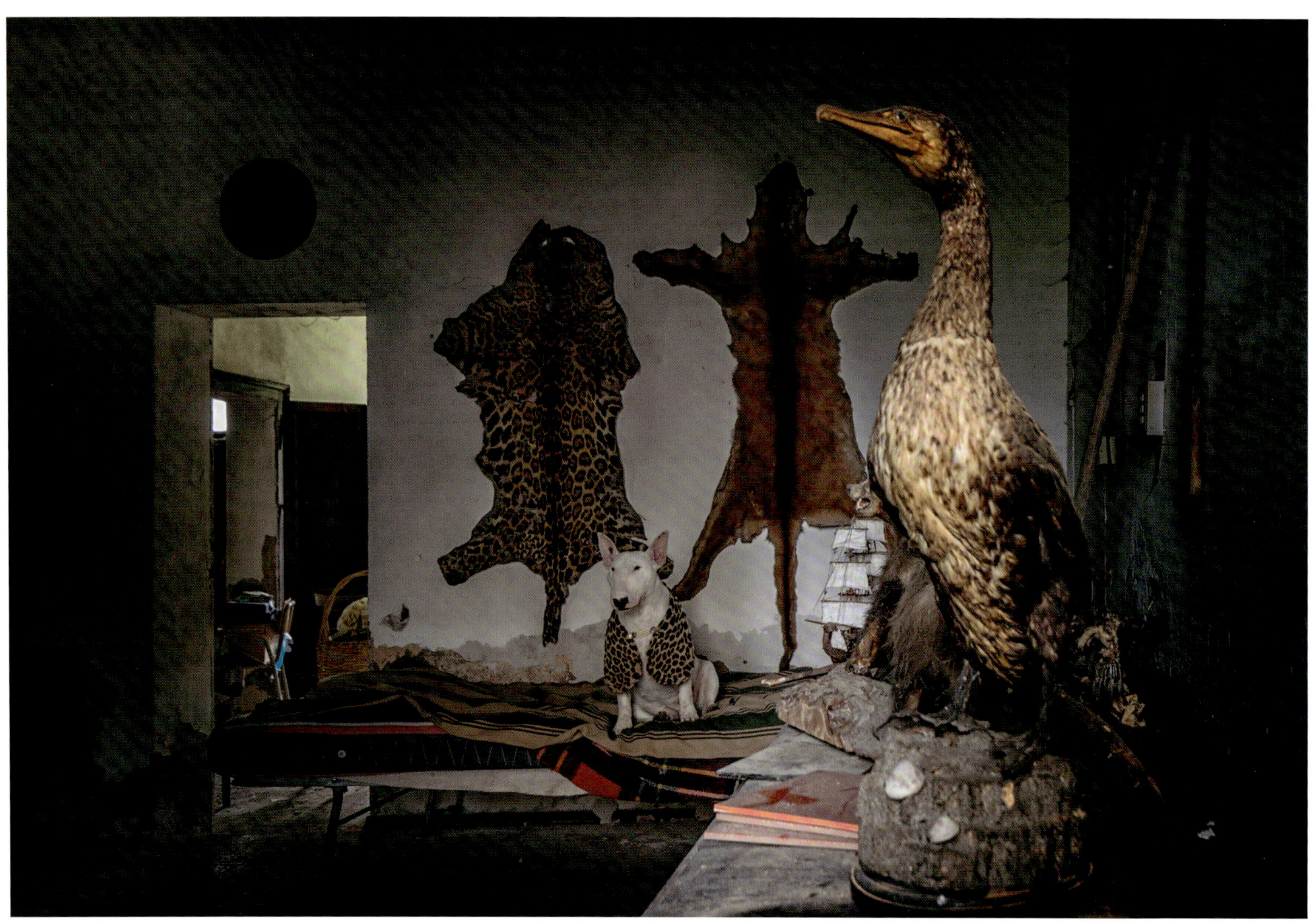

The landscape we're driving through is rather dull and reminds me a bit of home. We're heading to a villa that once belonged to a doctor, although in reality it's more like a large farm. There's a large parking area next to the property and we're fairly certain that nobody will suspect us of anything; with our camper van we look like tourists. Even so, having parked the van, Anita and I wander through an adjacent orchard with Claire, rather than taking a more direct route to the farm.

Out of sight of the road we start searching for the entrance and find the front door is open. We walk along a corridor and into the first room on our right. We are greeted by dust-covered taxidermy and on the wall are two animal skins; a tawny coloured skin that looks like a cougar to me, and one that definitely belonged to a jaguar.

Claire jumps on to the bed that sits beneath the skins and I put on the leopard-fur collar I've brought for her to wear. Personally, I would never wear exotic fur – even if it were vintage – and most people know about my wildlife photography and love of animals. However, one of my favourite thrift stores had a number of fur items that they couldn't sell, including the collar, and the saleswoman felt it was better to try and find a use for them than just throwing them away; she had immediately thought of my photographs of Claire.

I haven't even taken my first picture when I hear someone outside. Peeking through the window I watch as a man opens the gate to the farm and starts driving up the track towards the building we're in. I call out to Anita, who is busy photographing somewhere upstairs, but get no reply, so I grab my stuff, put my camera strap around my neck, and walk outside with Claire as fast as I can.

I decide not to hide, as this guy has probably been warned by someone that there are people trespassing, so I tell Claire to sit while I pretend to study and photograph the building, just like a tourist would do. As the car approaches I wave to the driver and give him my biggest smile. He stops and opens the window: "Attenzione! Attenzione!" he shouts, before pointing at the roof and adding "Pericoloso! Pericoloso!" I nod my head to show him I understand the Italian for "dangerous" and tell him I'm only taking photographs of the outside of the building. He believes me and my "dumb tourist" routine, waves, drives off and closes the barrier behind him.

After he's gone I go back inside and continue to photograph. Anita later tells me she didn't hear a thing.

Work Gallery
Working like a dog…

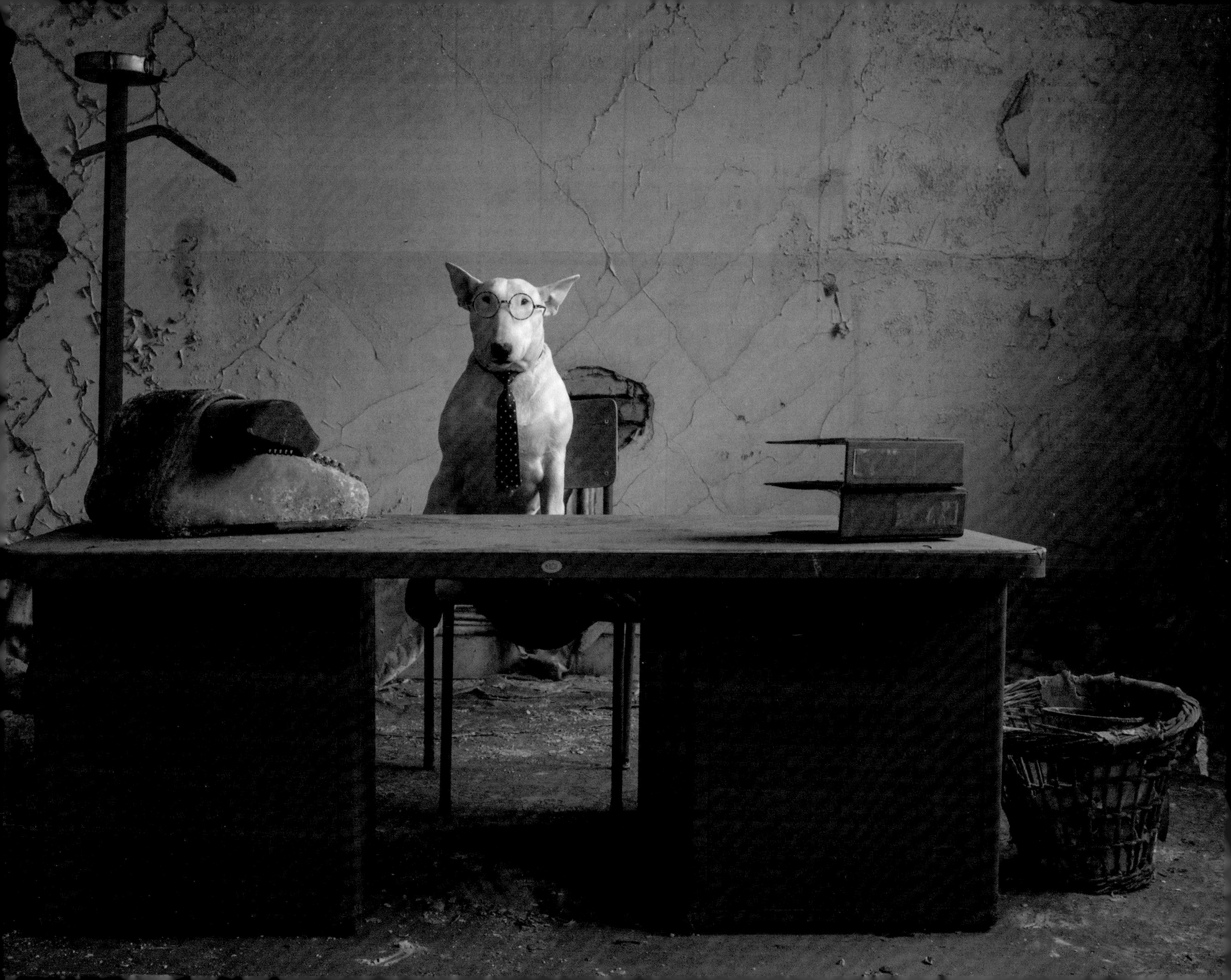

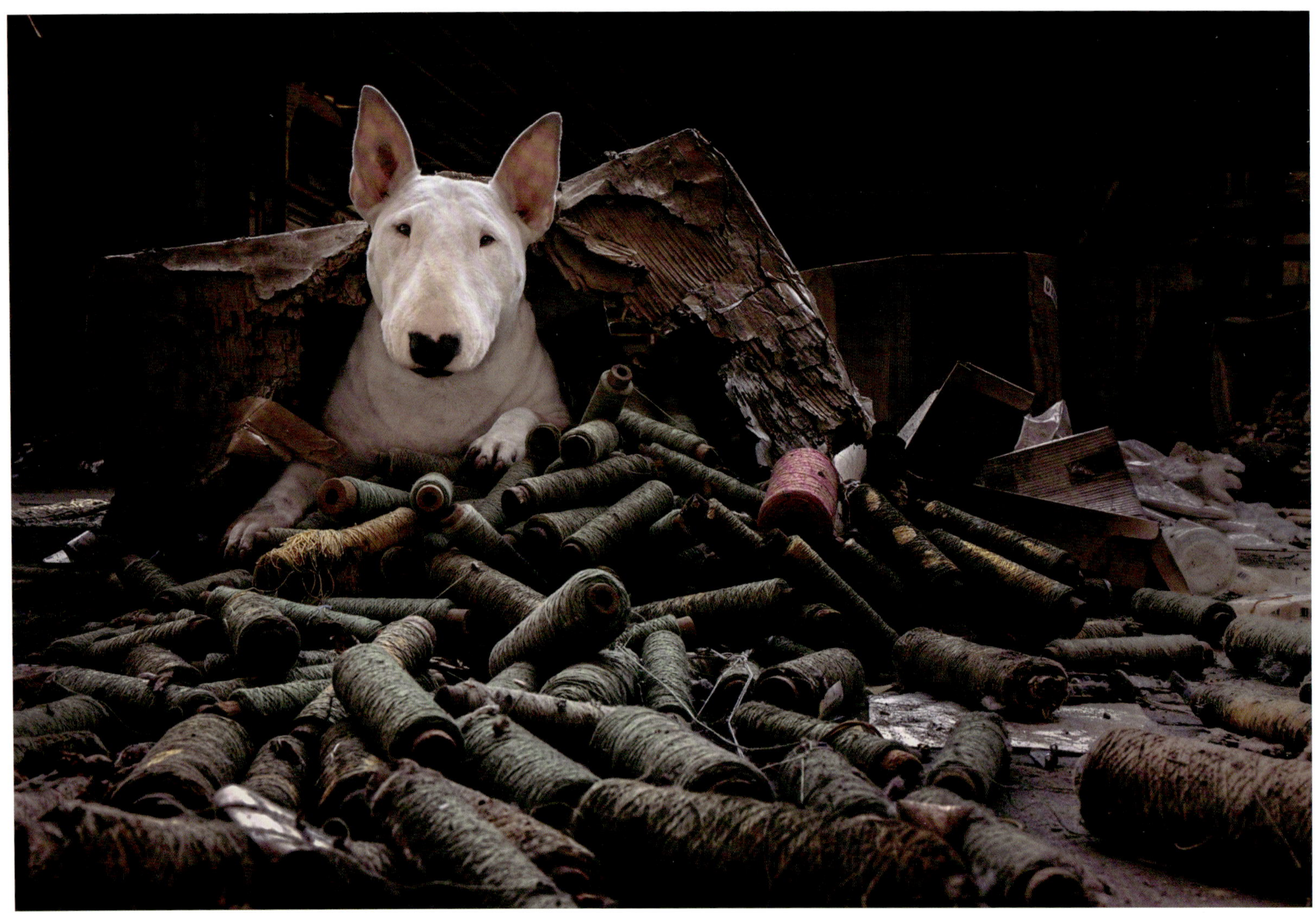

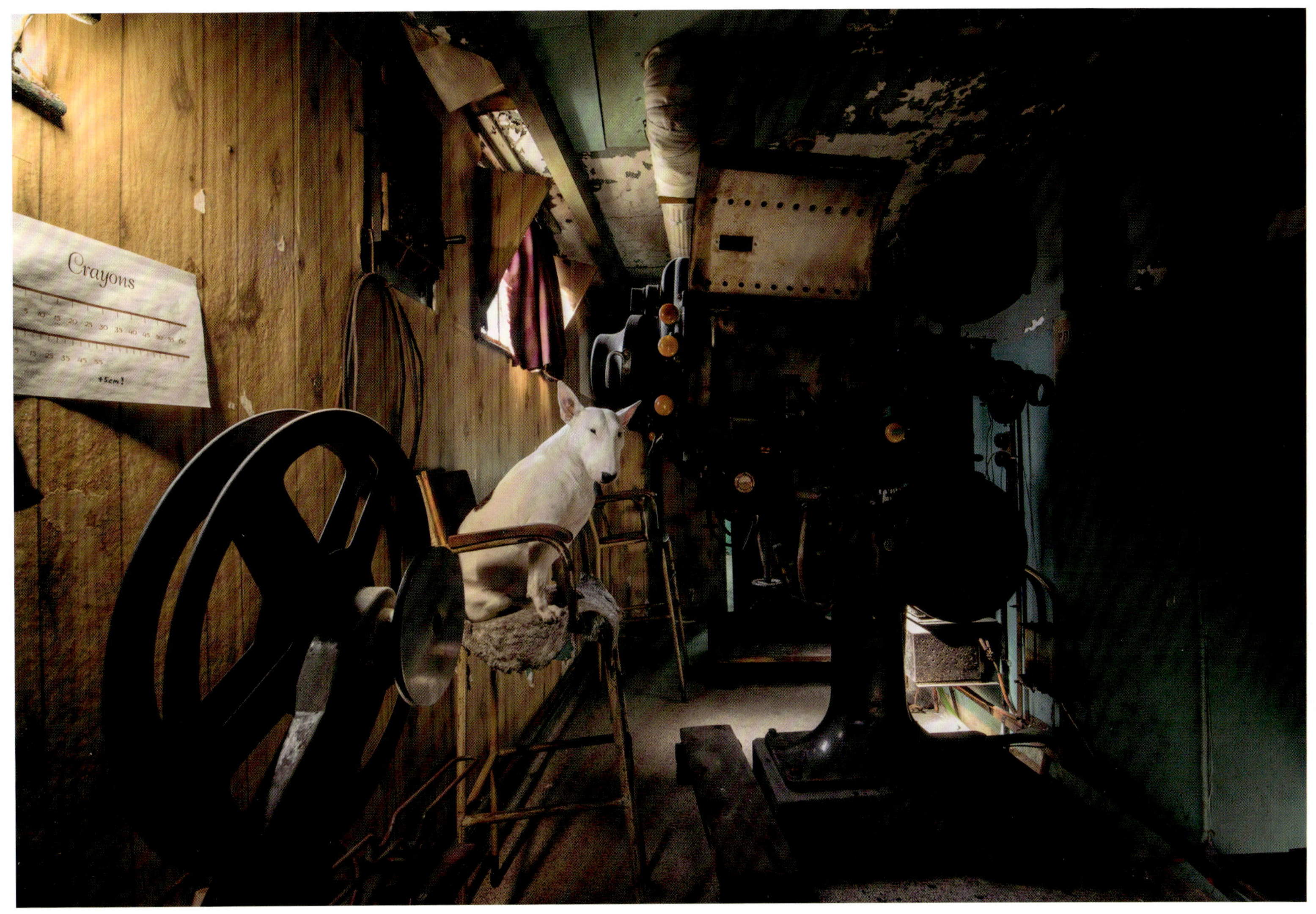
Crayons

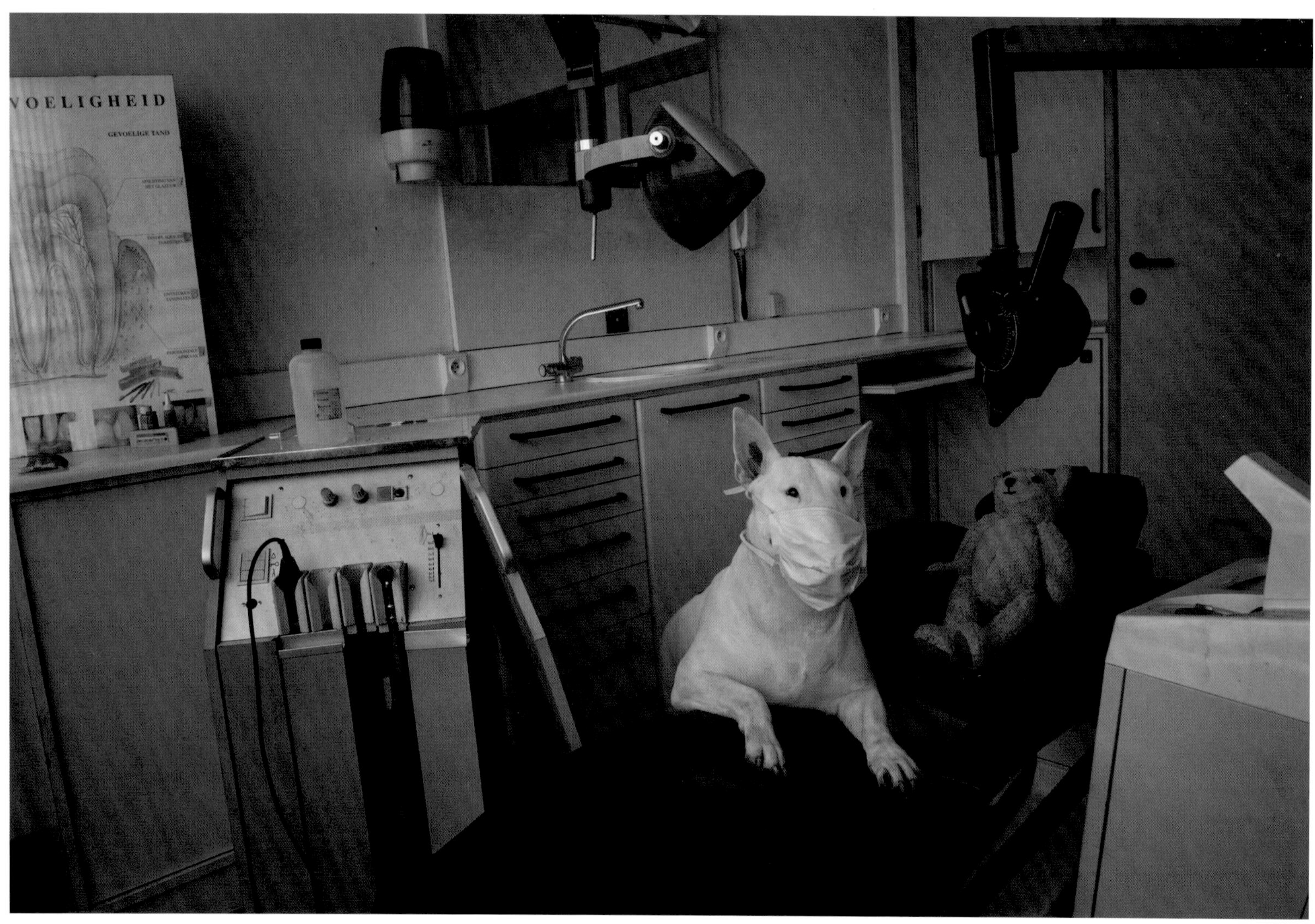

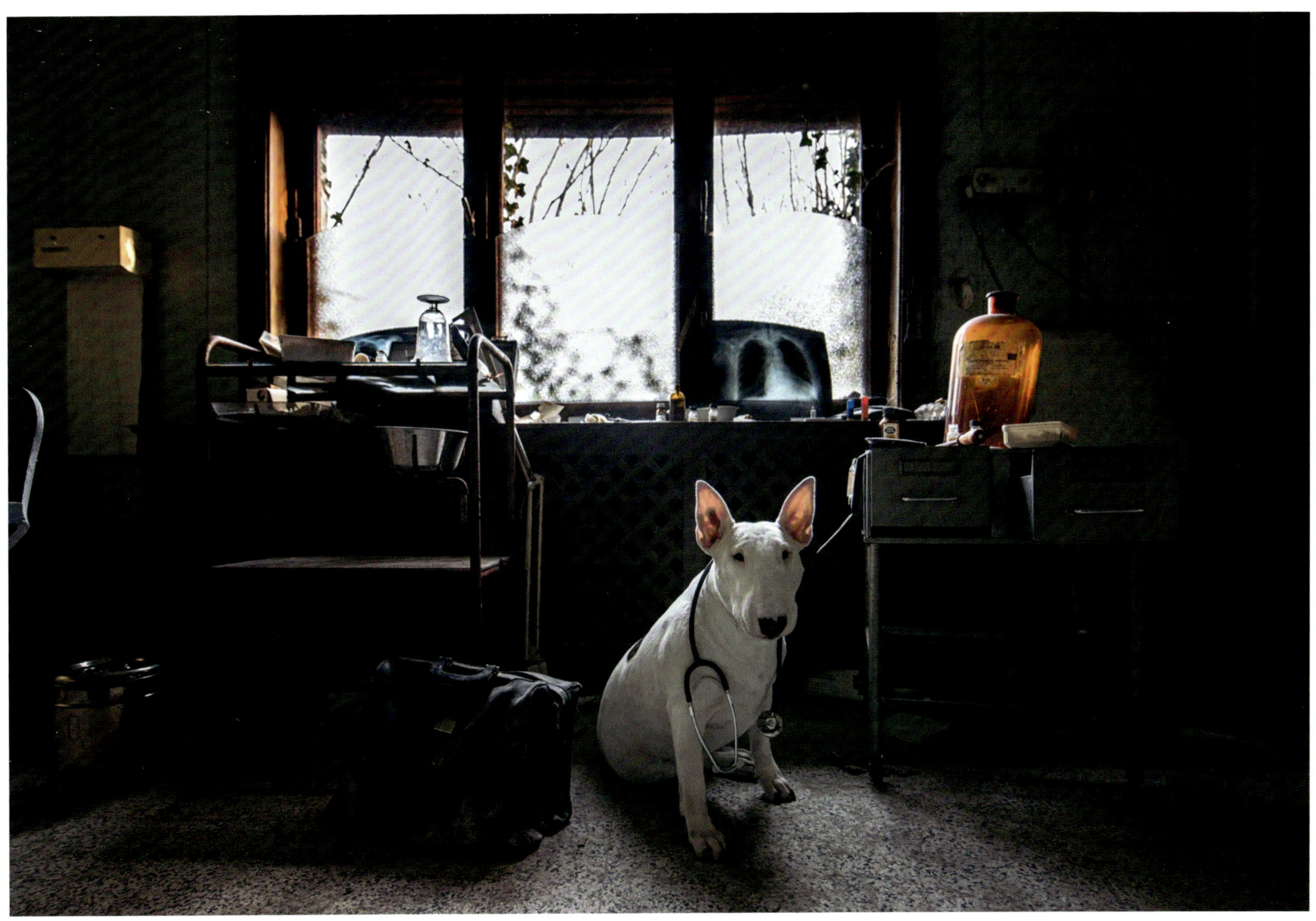

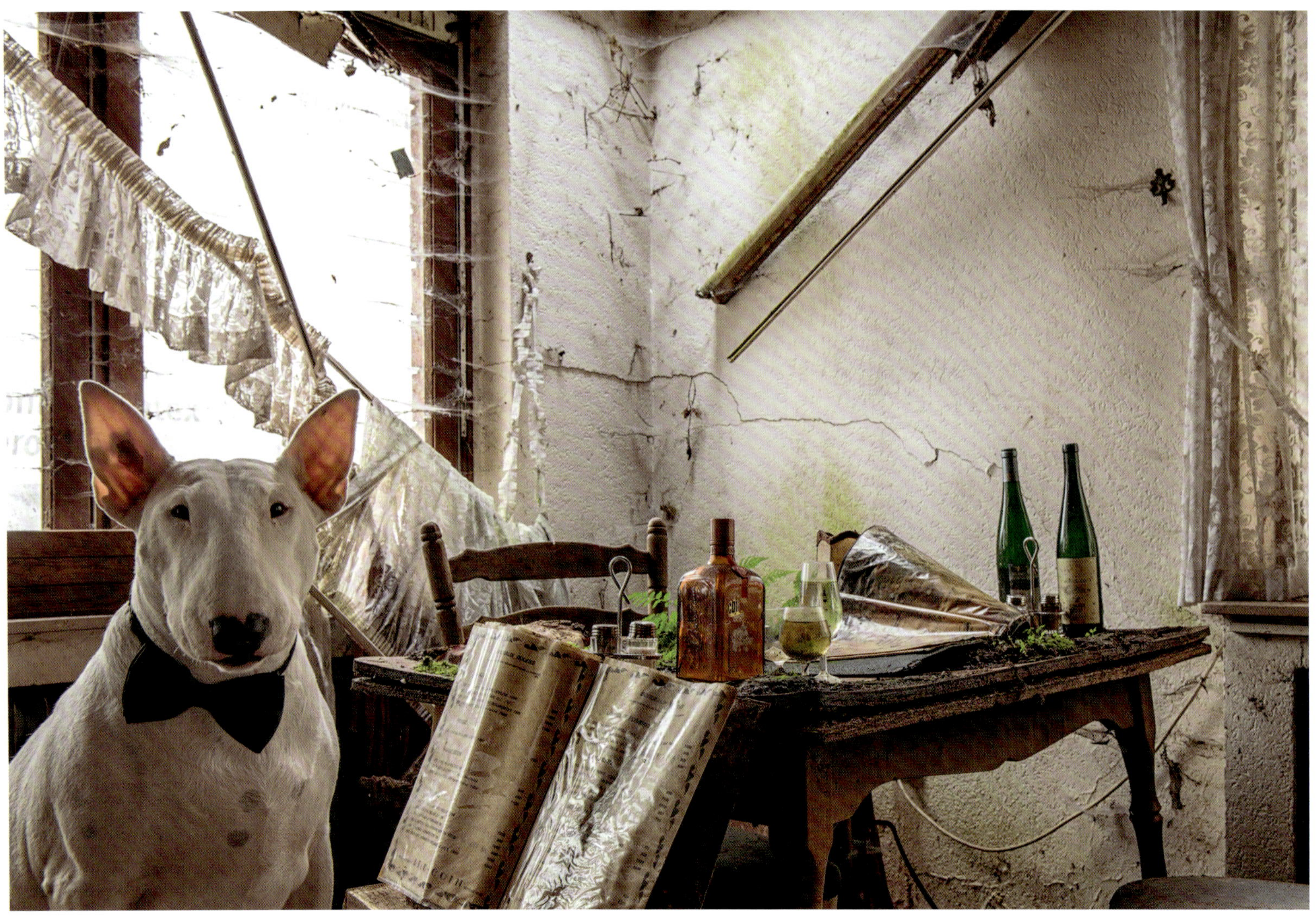

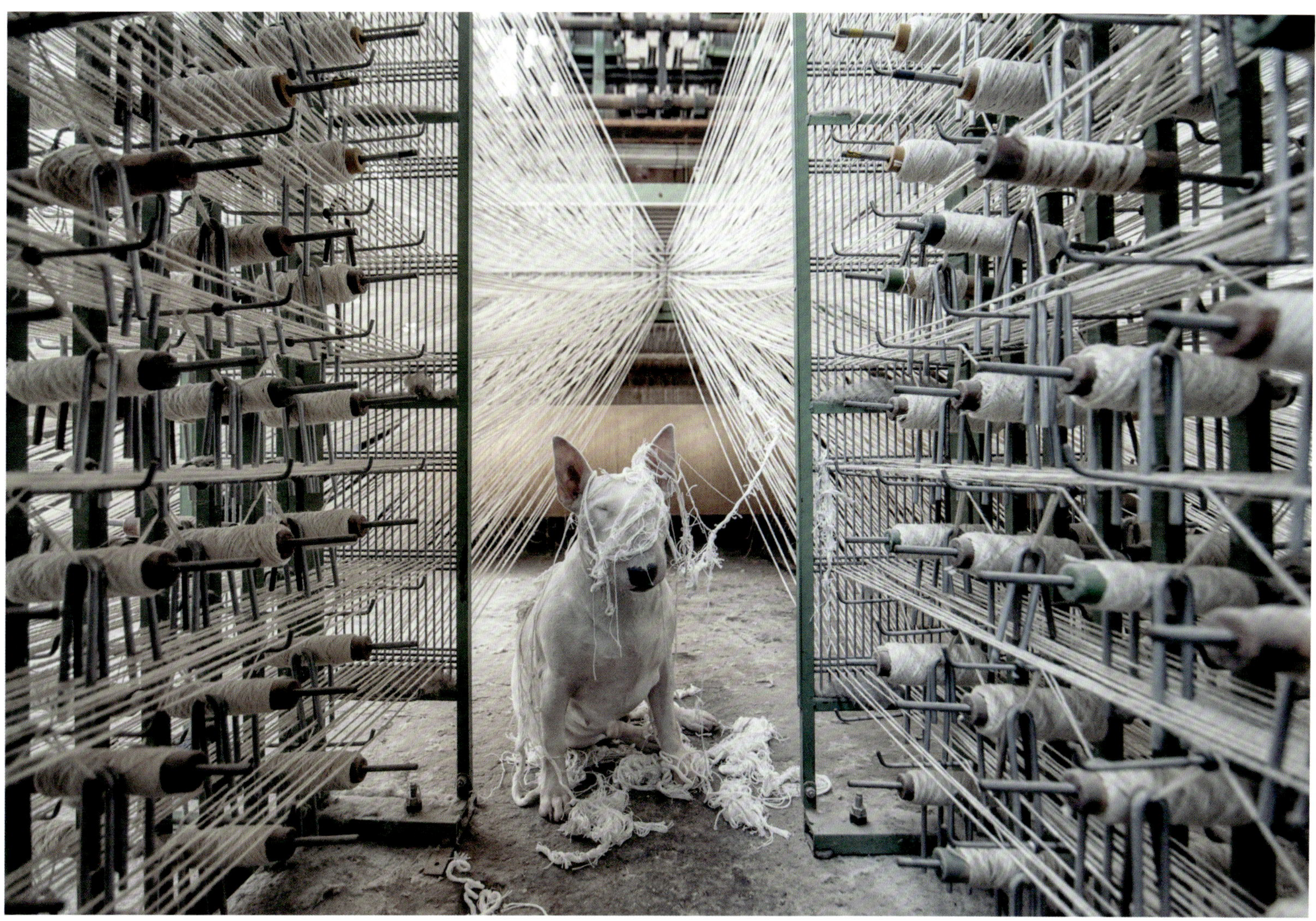

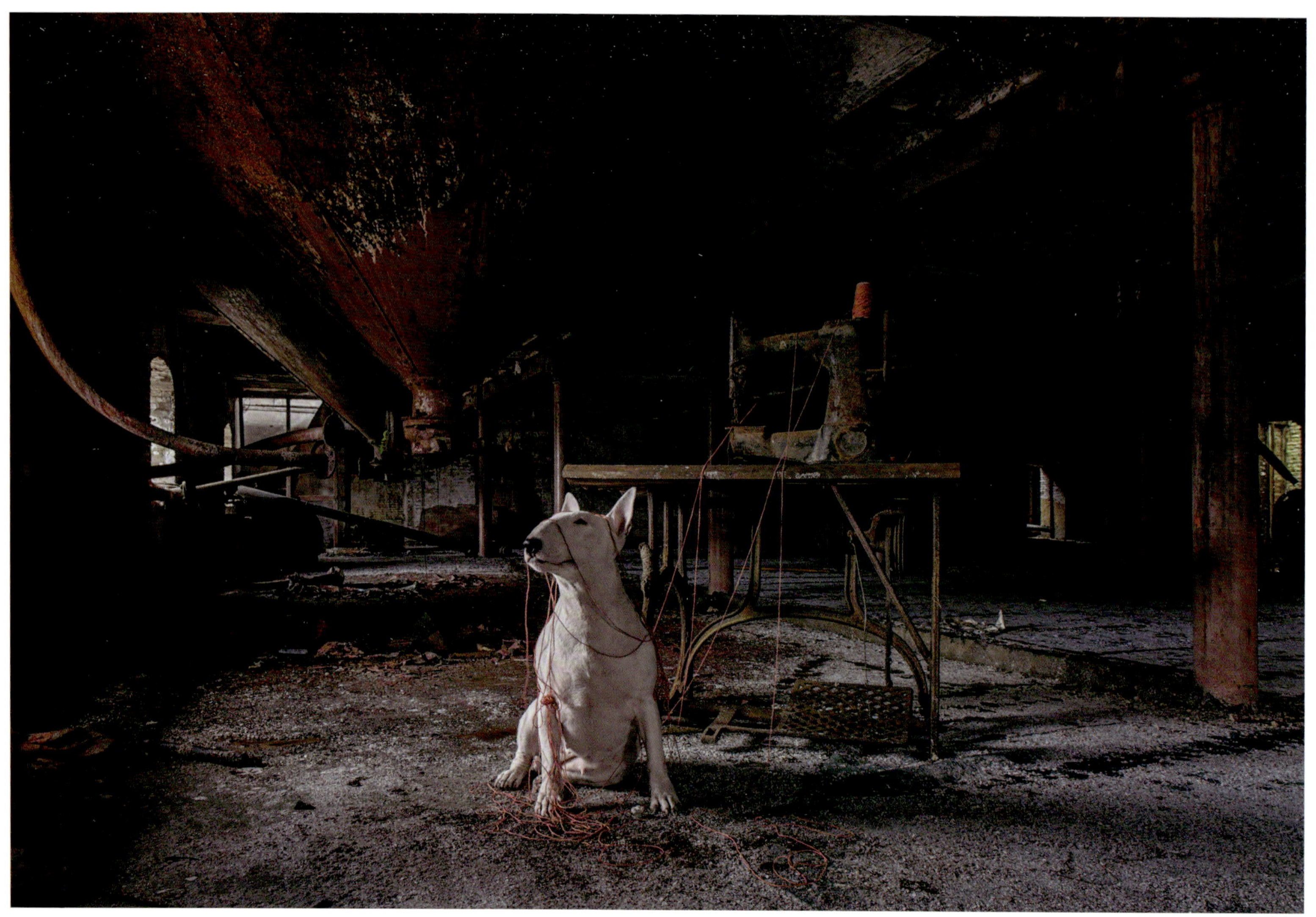

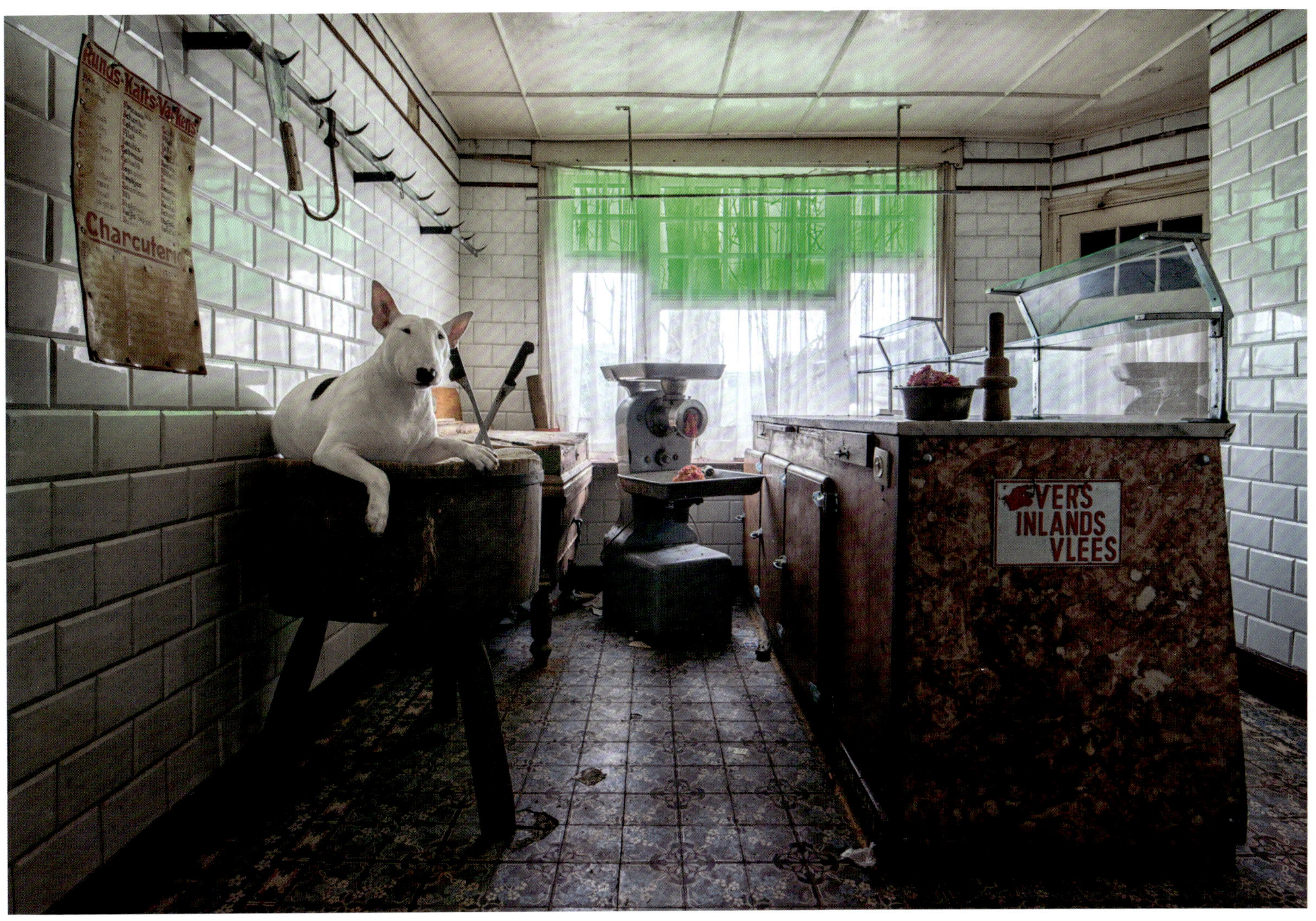
Runds·Kalfs·Varkens
Charcuterie
VERS
INLANDS
VLEES

Castello dell'Artista
Italy

Right This is an image I have had in mind for almost two years, but it is hard to get good shots in the sparse light.

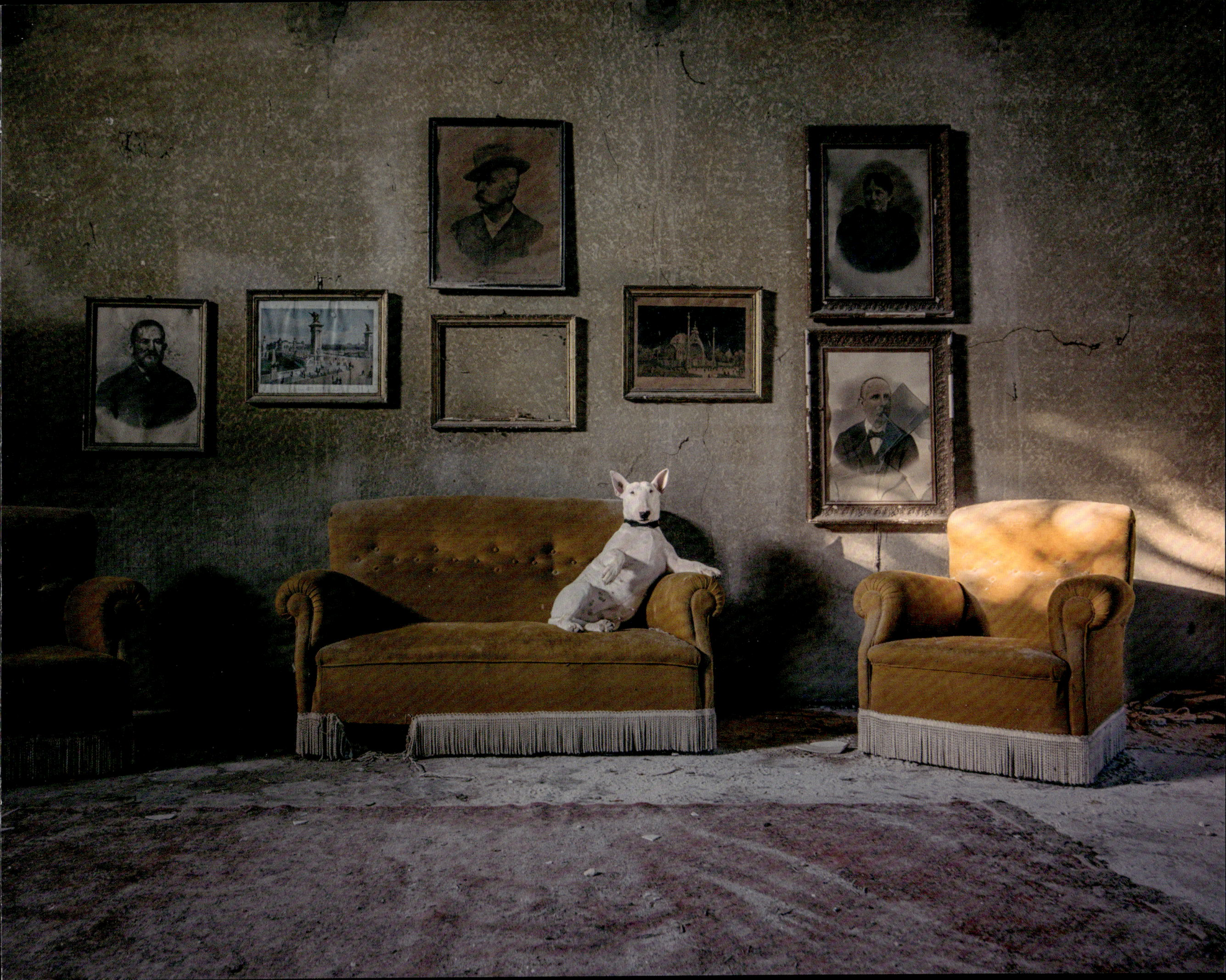

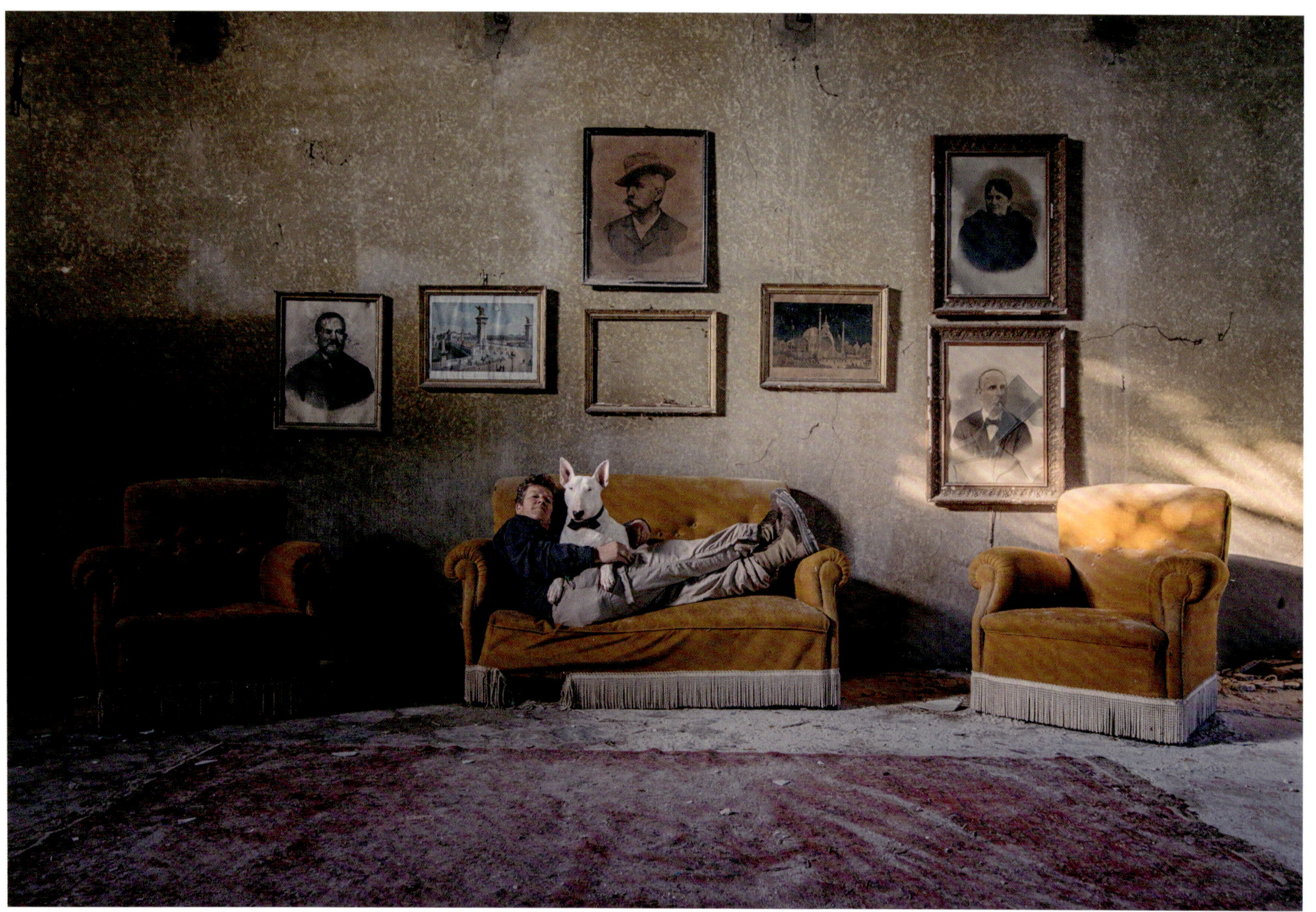

Our camper van cruises down a twisting road, through countryside dotted with small lakes, vineyards and a huge patchwork of square paddy fields growing Italian risotto rice. The sun is setting and Claire is dozing in the back of the van, having raided my friend's bag when we weren't looking and eaten almost all of her food. As planned, we will arrive at the small village where our destination lies under the cover of darkness. This tiny village has been untouched by urban development and the present population is pretty much the same as it was centuries ago; it's a place where everyone knows each other and they will call the carabinieri immediately if they suspect you are heading for the abandoned castle.

I park our van by the cemetery just outside the village and the next morning, a few hours before dawn, we set out towards the Castello Dell'Artista. We cross a large field in darkness and push our way through thick bushes to the castle walls, in search of an open door. When we find it, it is pitch black inside, so I grab my flashlight and start looking for the "famous" room that has drawn us here.

Two minutes later we are in the room and for a moment I am speechless. It is much bigger than I'd expected and so very dark. It will be at least two hours before the sun rises, so the long wait begins.

I begin to imagine what has happened within these walls over the centuries. The oldest part of the castle – the tower – dates right back to the 5th century, but between the 14th and 15th centuries it was extended into a complex that served as a house-fortress. This building witnessed the fall of the Western Roman Empire and had been under the reign of a landowning royal family who ruled the area for centuries. I look at the huge walls and imagine paintings by Renaissance painters such as Mantegna, Titian and Rubens hanging there. Perhaps the troubadour Sordello da Goito entertained the residents and their guests with his didactic poems, love songs and satirical pieces – maybe even in the same room where Claire and I finally see the first rays of light.

It's time to get started and I decide to concentrate on the couch image first. After two hours of photography we leave this magnificent castle without being noticed, although by now the village has woken up; an old woman sweeps the porch of a small bar opposite the castle, people are chatting and a group of old men settle around a table. The regular customers of the bar have assigned themselves the task of keeping an eye on the abandoned castle and we are now the subject of their conversations. They are watching us with suspicion, but we couldn't care less – our mission is already accomplished.

Acknowledgments

There is a trend to thank everyone and everything possible in the acknowledgements. With this is mind, I wish to thank: James Hinks for developing the bull terrier as a breed back in the 1860s; all the open doors and windows so we could visit the most fantastic locations; and all the "blind" and "deaf" neighbours that didn't see or hear us entering a location. On second thoughts, maybe I won't follow this trend, but there are some people I do wish to thank.

My initial thanks are to Jason Hook, Jamie Pumfrey and Robin Shields at Ammonite Press for not only commissioning the book, but also for their continued assistance in editing and overseeing its production.

Thanks also go to my friends in the urbex community, especially those with whom Claire and I have had amazing and sometimes thrilling adventures. Thank you for wonderful journeys filled with humour and hilarity. A big shout out to the urbexers who spontaneously offered us help when we had to change plans unexpectedly and unintentionally. I couldn't have taken some of the photos in this book without you.

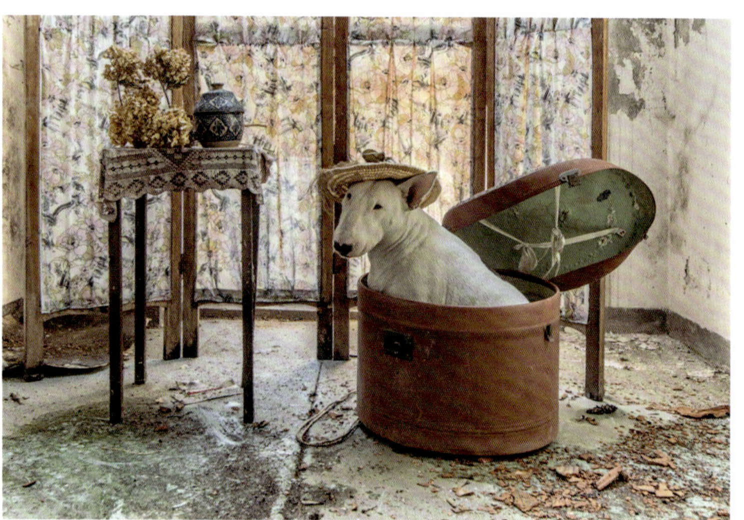

I'd also love to thank everyone who interacts with me and my posts on social media – my friends, followers and fans. #ThankYou for your loyalty and engagement #YoureTheBest. #Obrigado @RafaelMantesso, you are a great inspiration.

I am grateful to my husband Cees, who never complains when I want to check out locations during our holidays and then sometimes stay away for a couple of hours.

And last but not least, my loyal companion and super model, Claire. I certainly consider myself incredibly lucky for having such a great dog like her in my life.

Alice van Kempen